Cloud rEvolution

Laying the Foundation *Volume 1*

The Art of Abstraction *Volume 2*

The Cloud Effect *Volume 3*

CSC Leading Edge Forum

Yale Esrock
Richard Muñoz
Douglas Neal

CSC
Falls Church, Virginia, USA

CSC
3170 Fairview Park Drive
Falls Church, Virginia, 22042
United States

First publication September 2009 (Volume 1), October 2009 (Volume 2), December 2009 (Volume 3), January 2010 (Volume 4) online at CSC.

Published by Computer Sciences Corporation (www.csc.com), printed and distributed by Lulu (www.lulu.com).

ISBN 978-0-578-05116-1

Cloud rEvolution

CONTENTS

ABOUT THE *CLOUD rEVOLUTION* SERIES

Cloud rEvolution is a four-volume research series that examines the cloud continuum, from its foundational technologies to abstracted technologies to the ultimate abstraction, the cloud itself, and what it means for business.

The volumes, originally published separately, have been compiled here for easy reading. Read Volumes 1-3 on the pages that follow. Volume 4, a workbook, can be downloaded at the link below.

Volume 1: Laying the Foundation

Fundamental changes to core IT building blocks pave the way for cloud.

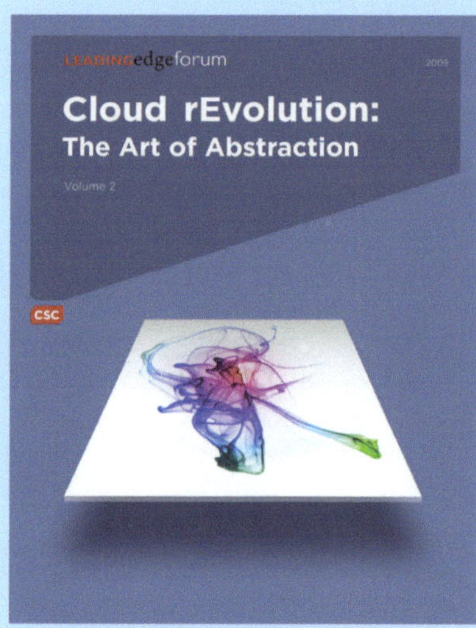

Volume 2: The Art of Abstraction

Abstraction loosens the IT stack, providing flexibility and efficiency.

Volume 3: The Cloud Effect

The rise of cloud operating and economic models has transformational impacts on business and IT alike.

Volume 4: A Workbook for Cloud Computing in the Enterprise

Cloud is a matter of when and how, not if; this workbook offers practical guidance for transitioning to the cloud.

Get the workbook at www.csc.com/lefreports

You can get the entire *Cloud rEvolution* series at www.csc.com/lefreports or by subscribing to the LEF RSS feed: www.csc.com/lefpodcast

LEADINGedgeforum

2009

Cloud rEvolution:
Laying the Foundation

Volume 1

CSC

As part of CSC's Office of Innovation, the Leading Edge Forum (LEF) is a global community whose programs help participants realize business benefits from the use of advanced IT more rapidly.

LEF members work to spot key emerging business and technology trends before others, and identify specific practices for exploiting these trends for business advantage. Members enjoy access to a global network of thought leaders and leading practitioners, and to a powerful body of research and field practices.

LEF programs give CTOs and senior technologists the opportunity to explore the most pressing technology issues, examine state-of-the-art practices, and leverage CSC's technology experts, alliance programs and events. LEF programs and reports are intended to provoke conversations in the marketplace about the potential for innovation when applying technology to advance organizational performance. For more information about LEF programs, visit www.csc.com/lef.

The LEF Executive Programme is a premium, fee-based program that helps CIOs and senior business executives develop into next-generation leaders by using technology for competitive advantage in wholly new ways. Members direct the research agenda, interact with a network of world-class experts, and access topical conferences, study tours, information exchanges and advisory services. For more information about the LEF Executive Programme, visit lef.csc.com.

LEF LEADERSHIP

WILLIAM KOFF (left)

Vice President and Chief Technology Officer, Office of Innovation

A leader in CSC's technology community, Bill Koff provides vision and direction to CSC and its clients on critical information technology trends, technology innovation and strategic investments in leading edge technology. Bill plays a key role in guiding CSC research, innovation, technology thought leadership and alliance partner activities, and in certifying CSC's Centers of Excellence and Innovation Centers.
wkoff@csc.com

PAUL GUSTAFSON (above right)

Director,
Leading Edge Forum

Paul Gustafson is an accomplished technologist and proven leader in emerging technologies, applied research and strategy. Paul brings vision and leadership to a portfolio of LEF programs and directs the technology research agenda. Astute at recognizing how technology trends inter-relate and impact business, Paul applies his insights to client strategy, CSC research, leadership development and innovation strategy.
pgustafs@csc.com

RICHARD DAVIES (left)

Vice President and Managing Director, LEF Executive Programme

Richard Davies directs a global, strategic research and advisory program aimed at helping CIOs and other enterprise IT leaders understand and exploit the ever-expanding intersection between business and information technology. Richard has over 20 years of experience in the IT market and has held a variety of sales and marketing positions both nationally and internationally.
rdavies5@csc.com

DAVID MOSCHELLA (above right)

Global Research Director,
LEF Executive Programme

David Moschella guides a series of strategic research initiatives aimed at helping CIOs and other enterprise IT leaders benefit from the growing intersection between business and information technology. David's key areas of expertise include globalization, industry restructuring, disruptive technologies, environmental strategies, and the co-evolution of business and IT. He is an author and former columnist on IT industry trends.
dmoschella@csc.com

In this ongoing series of reports about technology directions, the LEF looks at the role of innovation in the marketplace both now and in the years to come. By studying technology's current realities and anticipating its future shape, these reports provide organizations with the necessary balance between tactical decision making and strategic planning.

The Cloud rEvolution *report series examines the technology and business aspects of cloud computing. Although each volume is valuable on its own, the full scope of the* Cloud rEvolution *is best obtained by reading all the volumes. To receive the entire* Cloud rEvolution *series, visit www.csc.com/lefreports or subscribe to the LEF RSS feed: www.csc.com/lefpodcast*

Cloud rEvolution:
Laying the Foundation

Volume 1

CONTENTS

Get all LEF reports by subscribing to the LEF RSS feed: www.csc.com/lefpodcast

Preface

Supercomputers assembled from game stations. Data storage for a few cents per gigabyte. A mobile phone that runs full-scale applications like a computer. A network that spans the globe and extends into space. A server that fragments into multiple virtual machines, each of which can do its own thing and be turned on and off like a light switch. Processor, memory and I/O resources that are liberated from the confines of a single server and shared dynamically across the data center. An entire portable, disposable infrastructure that is comprised of software instead of hardware.

Welcome to the new world of information technology (IT). In this new world, a marketing manager who wants to do a detailed data analysis of national sales can fire up a few virtual machines for half an hour and do it on the spot. No more waiting months for a free server in the data center and being at the mercy of IT to carry out the request. Order up your computing, pay for it with a credit card and run the analysis yourself — all for the cost of lunch.

Sweeping changes underway in IT — namely, cloud computing and its underlying building blocks — are yielding unprecedented speed and agility, the ability to do more with less, and new levels of cost savings. Since the business can only change as fast as IT, these changes are having an enormous impact on the business's ability to unleash innovation and address changing markets and customers ahead of the competition.

The Cloud rEvolution *report tackles these sweeping changes in a four-volume series. Volume 1,* **Laying the Foundation**, *introduces the Cloud rEvolution and explores the digital foundations — the core building block technologies — that lay the groundwork for cloud computing. Volume 2,* **The Art of Abstraction**, *explores how abstraction loosens the IT stack, providing flexibility and efficiency as a precursor to the ultimate abstraction: the cloud. Volume 3 focuses on* **The Cloud Effect**, *describing the impact the cloud is having on IT and business tactically and strategically. Volume 4,* **A Workbook for Cloud Computing in the Enterprise**, *provides practical guidance for transitioning to the cloud, which is rapidly becoming a question of when and how, not if.*

THE PERFECT STORM

Although cloud computing can be viewed as an evolution in technology, the cloud computing phenomenon has arisen seemingly overnight. The overwhelming driver has been consumerization, which has compelled the likes of Google and Amazon to leverage their operational excellence with relentless fury. This was imperative in order to support their millions of customers — a full order of magnitude more than the largest single enterprise supports — under very different business models. The impact of IT consumerization has been nothing short of breathtaking.

And disruptive. The IT service delivery model unveiled by these companies, termed "cloud computing," is triggering a new marketplace with new characteristics: highly scalable IT services, obtainable on demand, paid for as used, and available globally.

Although the rush to embrace the cloud is being fueled first and foremost by IT consumerization, three related forces are also bearing down. The result is a "perfect storm" of conditions that are unleashing the cloud computing phenomenon. (See Figure 1.)

Figure 1 THE PERFECT STORM

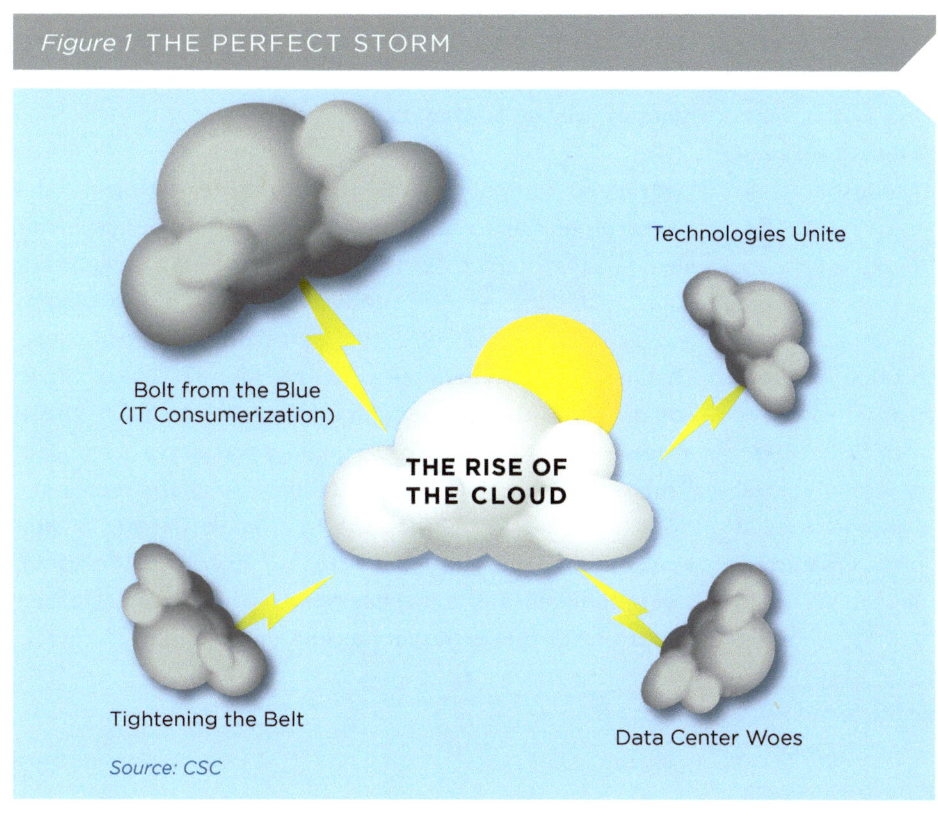

Source: CSC

- intelligent mobile devices make cloud access convenient

- services, borrowed from Service Oriented Architecture (SOA), are the basis of the cloud delivery mechanism

- abstraction, ranging from all manner of virtualization to new abstractions like multitenancy, help cloud providers manage their massive infrastructure and deliver services cost-effectively, and help wean enterprises from physical products located on site

Thus cloud computing reflects new combinations of existing technologies and techniques. This "combinatorial evolution," discussed on page 10, is the source of limitless technology invention and business innovation.

A BOLT FROM THE BLUE

As already mentioned, the lead force in the storm is IT consumerization, which has shaken up the IT industry by introducing serious competition from unexpected sources. In this case, the sources of competition were three companies — Amazon, Google and Salesforce.com — driven by the massive scale of consumer (or consumer-like) IT. Two of these companies (we thought) were not even in the IT industry. As a result of their primary (we think) lines of business, these companies burst upon the scene offering IT services from world class data centers of unheard-of size, unique models of IT delivery, value propositions that are difficult to match, and the promise of bountiful, inexpensive IT capabilities delivered from afar. The IT industry was at the same time stunned, skeptical and fearful that the ball game might have just changed.

TECHNOLOGIES UNITE

The second force of the storm is the confluence of several key technologies and architectural concepts that have enabled cloud and made it practical. Key among these:

- grid computing provides flexible, massive computing power using inexpensive hardware

- gbiquitous, high-capacity bandwidth makes cloud access practical

DATA CENTER WOES

The third force of the storm is the plight of the enterprise data center. Many data centers find themselves out of computing capacity or even out of physical space to expand. Complexity of data centers has grown to the point where they are often difficult to effectively manage. Cooling, electric and other utility costs are skyrocketing. And government and community pressures for green computing add to the woes of the beleaguered IT manager. With cloud computing, the need for green computing doesn't go away but essentially shifts to the cloud provider (though overall, everyone in the IT ecosystem is responsible).

TIGHTENING THE BELT

The fourth force of the storm is the economic environment. In this tight economy, IT budget cuts are common, and the ability to make new capital expenditures to fund needed resources may be nonexistent. By providing an attractive economic value proposition devoid of the need for capital expenditure, cloud may provide IT organizations with a way to survive the economy. As *BusinessWeek* declared, ". . . with the economy of its currently parlous condition, businesses have never needed cloud computing more."[1]

So, while the unique business models of some unexpected competitors seem to have precipitated the cloud phenomenon, it is the perfect storm of IT consumerization, new combinations of enabling technologies, data center management issues, and tight economic conditions all converging in the same approximate time frame that has caused the rapid uptake of cloud mania that is currently sweeping the IT industry.

COMBINATORIAL EVOLUTION

This perfect storm of events fits neatly with economist Brian Arthur's notion that technology innovation is about combining and recombining existing technologies in new ways, rather than being an invention that comes out of nowhere. This "combinatorial evolution," the subject of Arthur's latest book, *The Nature of Technology: What It Is and How It Evolves*,[2] disrupts the current order and is often created by players outside the current order (e.g., Google and Amazon) who view the world differently.

And it is not so much the technology but how the technology is used (Arthur's "arrangements") that is crucial. Google's real innovation in its data centers is not the technology per se but how Google uses the technology to achieve operational excellence, driven by the enormous scalability the company needs. Hardware is cheap and disposable, not a precious fixed asset. This is a shift in thinking that translates to, among other things, high reliability and much lower labor costs to manage the data center (fewer people per machine required). The cloud is about novel approaches using existing and evolving technologies.

As such, cloud is also about faster innovation. Cloud computing carries with it an expectation that technologies can be combined and recombined quickly to create innovation. Apple's iPhone — an excellent example of combinatorial evolution — and its wealth of rapid innovations illustrates this well. Combinatorial evolution, then, facilitates a stream of innovation — which can come as a jolt to enterprise IT, long comfortable with annual assessments that now need to be monthly, weekly or even daily.

Cloud computing carries with it an expectation that technologies can be combined and recombined quickly to create innovation.

With cloud computing, the key existing technology — the central organizing function or backbone of the cloud phenomenon — is the Internet. According to Arthur, as the backbone of a new technology evolves supported by related technologies and techniques ("arrangements"), it presents new opportunities. That is why the maturation of the Internet (a.k.a. cloud computing) is so important. Cloud has the potential to shape a new era in the life of computing and serve as a core structure — and style — that defines our global economy. No one would argue that the Internet is already a vital structure and because of it life will never be the same; cloud computing is a manifestation of new Internet-based opportunities that is triggering profound business change.

Cloud has the potential to shape a new era in the life of computing and serve as a core structure — and style — that defines our global economy.

CLOUD: A MORPHING OF THE DIGITAL DOMAIN

Cloud computing is too broad — involving people, technology and the economy at large — to be labeled a single technology. Rather, cloud computing fits Arthur's description of a technology *domain:* "A domain will be any cluster of components drawn from in order to form devices or methods, along with its collection of practices and knowledge, its rules of combination, and its associated way of thinking."[3] More precisely, according to Arthur, cloud computing represents a morphing of the digital domain, which "emerged in the 1940s and is still building out."[4] For example, cloud computing harnesses existing technologies in wholly new ways, drawing from grid computing, utility computing, SaaS, Web2.0 and the ubiquitous Internet. In addition to its technology components (e.g., computers, networks, software), cloud computing consists of several practices (e.g., services, virtualization) and newly applied approaches to computing (e.g., multitenancy, pay per use, on-demand provisioning). Technologist James Urquhart supports this notion, calling cloud computing "an operations model, not a technology."[5]

The resulting economic or social changes brought about by new combinations in a technology domain can take decades. Evolutionary technology change can trigger revolutionary effects in the world, which in turn can drive further technology change. As Arthur puts it:

> A new version of the economy slowly comes into being. The domain and the economy mutually co-adapt and mutually create the new.
>
> It is this process of mutual change and mutual creation that we call a revolution. Each era in the economy is a pattern, a more or less self-consistent set of structures in business and industry and society set in place by the dominant domains of the day. When new bodies of technology — railroads, electrification, mass production, information technology — spread through an economy, old structures fall apart and new ones take their place. Industries that once were taken for granted become obsolete, and new ones come into being.[6]

With cloud computing, the focus is not just on reducing costs but, more importantly, being able to do entirely new things. "The very existence of cloud will not just make activities cheaper; cloud will make new activities possible that were not possible before," Arthur says. "All physical business processes suddenly have access to cloud computing and a very different set of economics, triggering new processes and products. This reaches across all businesses and affects the global economy. This is a revolution."

A rEVOLUTION IN THE MAKING

Thus we are witnessing a rEvolution in the making: Cloud represents an evolution in technology and a revolution in business. Although cloud is on an evolutionary technology path, cloud's impact on business is potentially revolutionary, for it represents an epic shift from products to services. IT goes from being monolithic, fixed, expensive and slow to modular, flexible, cheap and fast. Cloud completely changes the complexion of IT and those who use it, impacting not only the business of IT but the business overall.

For example, cloud computing triggers:

- *Massive cost shifts* — The new reality is cost reductions of over 90 percent in some cases, such as storage and bandwidth. Hence we see entirely new business models that offer free multi-gigabyte e-mail accounts and similarly unprecedented pricing discounts.
- *Provisioning on demand* — No more waiting. Cloud delivers servers in minutes, not months, which completely changes the business's ability to experiment and innovate.
- *Disposable infrastructure* — The notion of IT as a disposable commodity, not a luxury good, is a major mindset change for the IT department. IT processing capacity is increasingly built on cheap and easily replaced ("throwaway") hardware.
- *New levels of collaboration* — The future of business is collaboration, and the future of collaboration is in the cloud, where there are no corporate or geographic boundaries. Watch for new partnerships, cross-functional teams, personal networks and company-customer co-creation initiatives.
- *A new playing field* — IT vendors are scrambling to respond to the perceived cloud threat. At the same time, enterprises are scrambling to figure out how to gain competitive advantage from the new cloud opportunities. The result will be new business models previously not possible.

These are just some of the revolutionary changes underway. Although their impact is being felt today, it will take years if not decades to fully realize cloud's revolutionary power, once all the supporting technologies and techniques are available and mainstream.

Meanwhile, organizations need to start understanding how the cloud might impact them in terms of IT and the business. That is, how cloud computing is being used today to make enterprise operations more scalable, virtual and collaborative, while simultaneously shifting to on-demand and variable cost models. To this end, the *Cloud rEvolution* report probes

Cloud represents an evolution in technology and a revolution in business.

Figure 2 THE CLOUD REVOLUTION SERIES

Volume 1:
Laying the Foundation

Fundamental changes to core IT building blocks pave the way for the cloud.

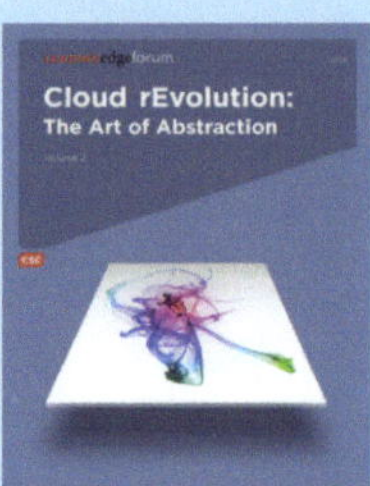

Volume 2:
The Art of Abstraction

Abstraction loosens the IT stack, providing flexibility and efficiency.

Volume 3:
The Cloud Effect

The rise of cloud operating and economic models has transformational impacts on business and IT alike.

Volume 4:
A Workbook for Cloud Computing in the Enterprise

Cloud is a matter of when and how, not if; this workbook offers practical guidance for transitioning to the cloud.

Source: CSC

four areas critical to the enterprise and its journey into the cloud (see Figure 2):

- **Volume 1: *Laying the Foundation* —** Fundamental changes to core IT building blocks pave the way for the cloud. These digital foundations fall into three categories: universal power (e.g., multicore processors and virtual machines), universal information (e.g., storage and database advances) and universal access (e.g., unified high-speed networks and new "edge" devices). These technologies lay the foundation for cloud and are strong building blocks in their own right, providing significant capabilities and levels of performance.

- **Volume 2: *The Art of Abstraction* —** Abstraction is causing the once rigid IT stack to flex and slowly break apart. Long used in IT, abstraction has assumed new importance, primarily in the form of virtualization. Properly implemented, abstraction is the key to enhancing flexibility, improving IT resource utilization, simplifying resource management, improving reliability, reducing IT costs, "greening" the data center and reducing vendor lock-in. Abstraction affects all layers of the stack and lays the groundwork for the ultimate abstraction: the cloud.

- **Volume 3: *The Cloud Effect* —** If the enterprise stack was already breaking apart due to abstraction, it begins to disappear altogether as product-based hardware and software in the enterprise data center morph into network-based services in the cloud. We explore the "cloud effect" — the cloud's influence — on IT and the business. IT shifts from on-premise products to network-based services; shared IT resources, scalability and automated management are essential. Providers face new competitors and adapt to new business models. "Cloudonomics" changes cost structures from fixed to variable for users and from "fine china" to "paper plates" for providers. Enterprises seek cloud benefits through private clouds.

  Cloud offers enterprises many opportunities for faster innovation and improved agility. Cloud levels the playing field for large and small organizations, offers new ways to collaborate, and provides better business intelligence due to lower barriers to entry for compute-intensive data analyses. It will take years if not decades for cloud's full business impact to play out.

- **Volume 4: *A Workbook for Cloud Computing in the Enterprise* —** The cloud is an engine of transformation across the business, not a substitute location for current data center processing. The on-demand, pay-by-the-drink character of cloud computing matches well with the growing needs of firms for innovation and the rise of "double-deep" business employees who are business- *and* IT-savvy. The role of IT shifts from doing things to or for employees, to providing cloud platforms for employees to do IT themselves. For existing applications, the first question should be: Can we use the transition to the cloud as an opportunity to move non-core applications up the stack in the cloud in a way that frees up management attention? For example, instead of re-hosting my existing e-mail system in the cloud, could I switch to a SaaS e-mail provider such as Google? Initial applications in the cloud will center on those that use non-sensitive data, such as development and test applications. Over time, as familiarity and security in the cloud grow, disaster recovery will move to the cloud. Ultimately the cloud and the data center will switch roles, with the local data center being the disaster recovery site and the cloud becoming the production site.

Let's get started with the foundation.

DIGITAL FOUNDATIONS OF THE CLOUD rEVOLUTION

The technical underpinnings of cloud computing are many and generally not new. What cloud computing represents is a new set of IT capabilities enabled by the next stage of digital foundations. These digital foundations involve existing and evolving information technologies, combined in new ways to enhance how we find, acquire and access information. Once again, the information age is creating innovation in how we work and live through advances in, and new applications of, core foundational technologies. This volume will explore these digital foundations and what they bring to the emerging model of cloud computing.

A HISTORIC PERSPECTIVE

As cloud computing is explored and adopted, its digital foundations — the individual technologies underlying cloud computing — follow a common pattern of how technology has driven economic, social and cultural change in the past. History, and now Brian Arthur, show that change driven by technology is seldom the result of a single technology but rather new combinations of a wide set of technologies, evolved and applied in manners not previously possible or imagined.

Within the digital domain, there are several examples of this as the domain has continued its steady build-out and morphing over nearly 70 years. (See Figure 3.) For each of the digital domain's technology waves, many of the underlying technologies were actually invented many years prior to the wave; then, maturation, adoption, cost, integration and new applications evolved together into a critical mass driving change.

Each wave builds upon the technology, capabilities and use of the previous waves. Unlike previous waves, where new technology largely emerged from business and government environments, cloud computing has emerged amidst the consumerization technology wave. Given that this wave is driven by consumer-led technology innovation, the enterprise has a learning curve to climb as it is now following, rather than leading, the wave.

Figure 3 MAJOR CHANGES IN THE DIGITAL DOMAIN STEM FROM COMBINATIONS OF TECHNOLOGIES

TECHNOLOGY WAVE	SUPPORTING TECHNOLOGIES*
EARLY DIGITAL COMPUTERS (1941-1965)	vacuum tubes, electronics, binary mathematics, punch cards, logic design, magnetic tape, electric typewriters, radar, electrical engineering, transistors, analog computers
THE INFORMATION AGE (1966-1992)	mainframes, minicomputers, PCs, microprocessors (Intel 8080), high-level programming languages, timesharing and multi-tasking operating systems, Ethernet and TCP/IP, hypertext, Arpanet and early Internet, GPS satellites
INTERNET/DOT-COM ERA (1993-2001)	graphical user interfaces, browsers, HTML, search engines, asymmetric key encryption, multi-tiered architectures, relational databases, the Internet, Web applications, sensors
CONSUMERIZATION ERA (2002-TODAY)	multicore processors, Web 2.0, virtual machines and appliances, autonomic systems, social Web sites, instant messaging, mobile computers, smart phones, voice over IP, high density storage, very large database systems, consumer broadband networking

Source: CSC

** Many were invented before the actual wave took place.*

CLOUD STARTS WITH A FIRM FOUNDATION

Just as a good building architect understands the possibilities and limitations of the construction materials used, IT leaders wanting to benefit from cloud computing need to explore its digital foundations first. Through a deeper understanding of the digital foundations enabling cloud computing, organizations will be better equipped to take advantage of advances in cloud computing, address its current limitations, and cut through the hype and doubt that currently surround cloud.

> **IT leaders wanting to benefit from cloud computing need to explore its digital foundations first.**

The technologies making up the digital foundations for cloud computing cover a wide spectrum. To navigate this spectrum, this volume examines the digital foundations from the same perspective as the LEF's original *Digital Foundations* report:[7] universal power, universal information and universal access. Figure 4 summarizes the key technologies that make up the digital foundations for cloud computing. The next three sections describe a select set of these technologies.

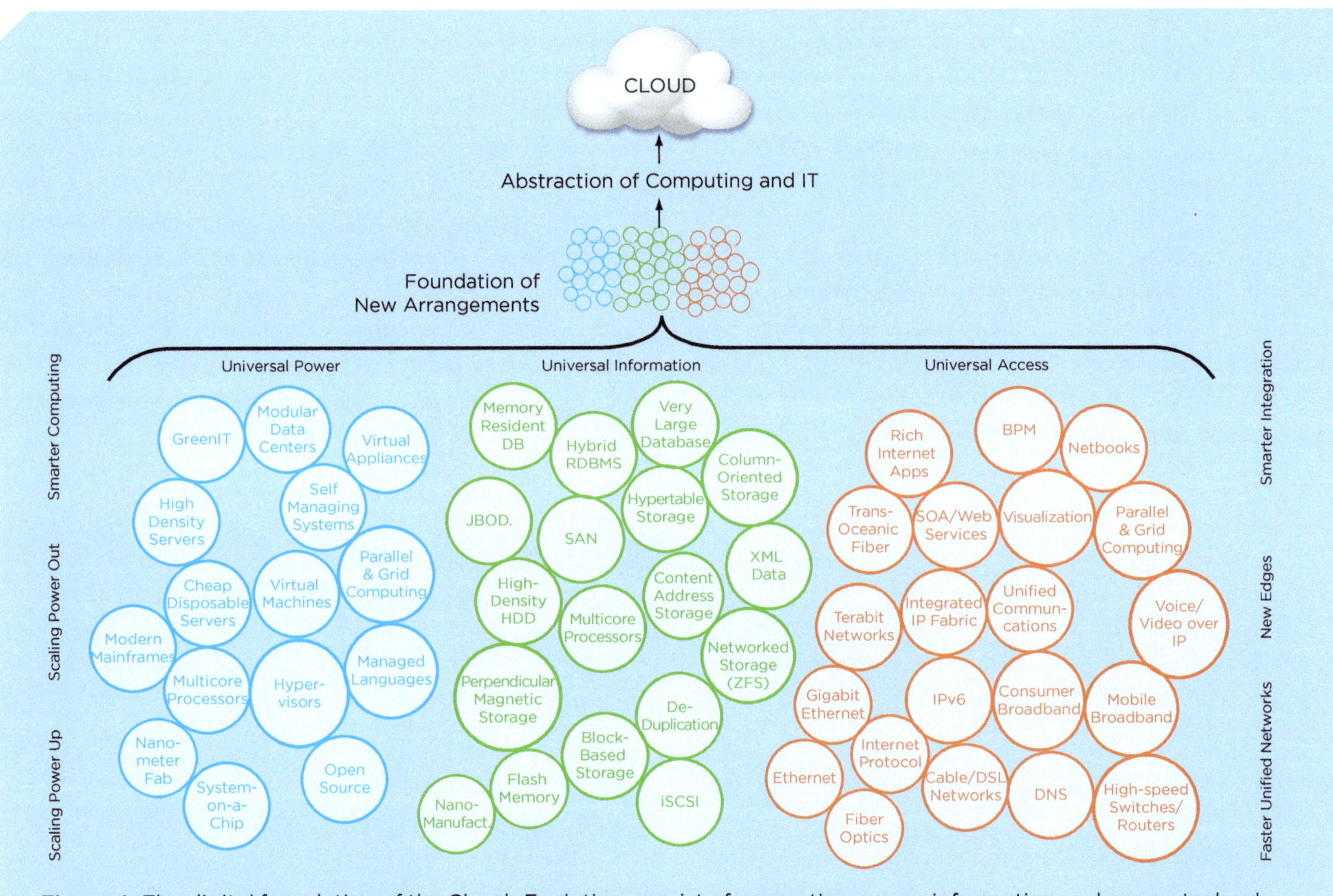

Figure 4. The digital foundation of the Cloud rEvolution consist of computing power, information and access technologies.* The combinatorial evolution of these technologies creates new technologies and techniques (arrangements) that yield unprecedented efficiency and innovation, ultimately delivered via the cloud. These combinations are many and varied, driven by consumerization, globalization and new demands on IT.

* *The technologies shown are representative, not exhaustive.*

Source: CSC

UNIVERSAL POWER

Computing power continues its transformational change that started over 60 years ago with the invention of the semiconductor transistor. Moore's Law has repeatedly been challenged but has withstood the test of time. The universal power of computing systems today takes some highly evolved forms, with new twists amplifying and accelerating how much computing power can be applied.

While computing power has traditionally grown through faster processors, new computing systems are now more often based on new arrangements of existing technologies, not radical new technologies. These new arrangements, described further below, increase the density of computing power while reducing its need for increasingly expensive electrical and cooling sources — to the point where data centers can be built to support extremely large audiences. The computing power needed for delivering cloud services is made possible by the amplification effect of many technologies stacked on top of one another, from multicore processors to self-managing data centers. Any single technology boosting computing power would be insufficient to support cloud computing; it is the combination — the integrated arrangement — of these technologies, coupled with advances in telecommunications, that enables the cloud.

Any single technology boosting computing power would be insufficient to support cloud computing; it is the combination — the integrated arrangement — of these technologies, coupled with advances in telecommunications, that enables the cloud.

FROM MULTICORE TO HIGH-DENSITY RACKS OF TRAYS — LAYERS OF INCREASING POWER IN HARDWARE

The heart of all computers, the CPU chip or central processing unit, has continued its exponential rate of change but has taken on a new dimension: multiple cores.[8] Although individual computer processing units have continually increased in speed — both by design and by clock rate — the concept of putting multiple processors (cores) together on a single chip has moved symmetric multiprocessing, or parallel computing capabilities, into the mainstream. Intel and AMD continue to add more processing cores to their main chips, creating microscopic high performance parallel processing computing systems.

By adding an increasing number of cores to each processor chip, Intel and AMD have instantaneously doubled or quadrupled[9] the processing capacity of new servers. Even Sun Microsystems has evolved its SPARC chip architecture so a new Sun SPARC server can replace entire racks of older servers. Although the effect of multicore processors is more amplified in servers, a growing number of new PCs are now multicore systems. And even mobile devices such as the iPhone will soon embed chips with many processor cores.[10]

To satisfy the thirst of these new multicore systems, systems have begun the move to 64-bit computing, supporting massive amounts of memory (up to several terabytes of RAM per server). Intel's latest production processor designs, Nehalem and Lynnfield, are designed to make sure the flow of program and data between memory and core processors is as fast as possible. Intel's QuickPath Interconnect approach disposes with the traditional "front-side-bus" way of connecting to memory, instead combining embedded memory controllers, intelligent cache design and parallel memory access paths into a parallel microarchitecture that brings memory access speeds up to 32 gigabytes per second *per processor core.*

While increasing the density and power of each CPU, processor companies simultaneously began addressing two of the increasing problems in chip design: heat and power consumption. A combination of energy-efficient transistors (made possible, in part, through the use of high-density circuits in silicon) and power-aware processor control is enabling servers to become more powerful, but also use less energy.

These new processors are packed with increasing density into data center racks, increasing processing power per server, per rack unit, and hence per rack in the data center. Blade servers started the trend towards increasing the density of computing power in the data center; since their introduction they have evolved to become an easy way to expand data center capacity with a small energy and space footprint. By increasing the overall density of computing power while keeping power and cooling requirements down, computer manufacturing continues to meet the exponential computing capacity requirements necessary for the cloud. But this is just the first of many elements in amplifying computing power to cloud levels.

PARALLEL COMPUTING EVERYWHERE

Parallel computing multiplies the available computing power available by running applications or software in parallel across multiple processors. Through "parallelization" of computing systems, businesses and government have been able to scale computers to handle extremely large workloads.

However, parallel computing has traditionally been the purview of expensive supercomputers. Over the past decade, parallelization became more accessible through the rise of grid computing, where hundreds to thousands of commodity servers or even PCs could be linked together to handle larger workloads. The scalability needs of large Web sites have also driven new parallelization technology that combines network and computers to form a single large computing environment.

Now parallelization of computing power is within reach of everyone. The combination of parallelisms at the micro level — multicore processors — and at the extremely large level — global distributed computing networks — brings computing resources even closer together to support the capacity needs for the cloud.

Although parallel computing techniques have been applied since the first general-purpose computer (ENIAC), the rise of grid and large-scale Web computing systems has led to a growing repertoire of tools to tap the power of thousands of servers very quickly. These tools are becoming key ingredients in the new technology assemblies for cloud.

Now parallelization of computing power is within reach of everyone.

VIRTUAL MACHINES AND PORTABLE CODE — STACKING UP APPLICATIONS

Many applications and operating systems, particularly legacy systems, do not and often cannot take advantage of the new advances in processor and server technologies. Today's single server is often too powerful to be fully utilized by a single application or even operating system. Rather than dedicate a single operating system or application to an underutilized server, several technologies have emerged that enable multiple operating systems (and thus many applications) to run simultaneously on a single server. With this "virtual machine" approach, a single server's processor and other resources can be shared by multiple operating systems.

Although virtual machines have been around for over 40 years in mainframe environments, the use of virtual machines — running multiple operating environments on a single computer — has grown significantly over the past decade. Besides being driven by the vast increases in processing power and memory capacity, virtual machines have hit mainstream use because of:

- Widespread use of machine and device emulation technology such as VMware, Virtual PC and Xen.
- Incorporation of special hypervisor support in microprocessors to enable faster switching between different running operating systems.
- Widespread adoption of software platforms that isolate the application code from the underlying hardware, Java being the primary example.

As the adoption of virtual machines has risen, so has the sophistication of the technology used to support virtual machines. Intel has extended its virtual machine support beyond the microprocessor and into its supporting chipsets, such as its VT-d and VT-c technology. AMD has also introduced virtualization support in its chip designs, including its AMD-V nested paging.[11] As shown in Figure 5, with virtualization support built directly in the chips, virtual machines (VMs) can directly access I/O devices, gain better network performance, and off-load the work typically done by the hypervisor software, thereby reducing the overhead involved in running multiple operating systems on the same hardware.

application virtual machines, the concept of running software code in a "virtual" execution space dates back to the use of LISP and APL in the 1960s.

The most successful of all application environments using virtual machines for execution is Java, which introduced the JVM, or Java Virtual Machine. JVM compiled and executed code partially compiled into a machine independent, interme-

Figure 5 HARDWARE SUPPORT FOR VIRTUALIZATION BUILT DIRECTLY INTO PROCESSORS AND SUPPORTING CHIPSETS

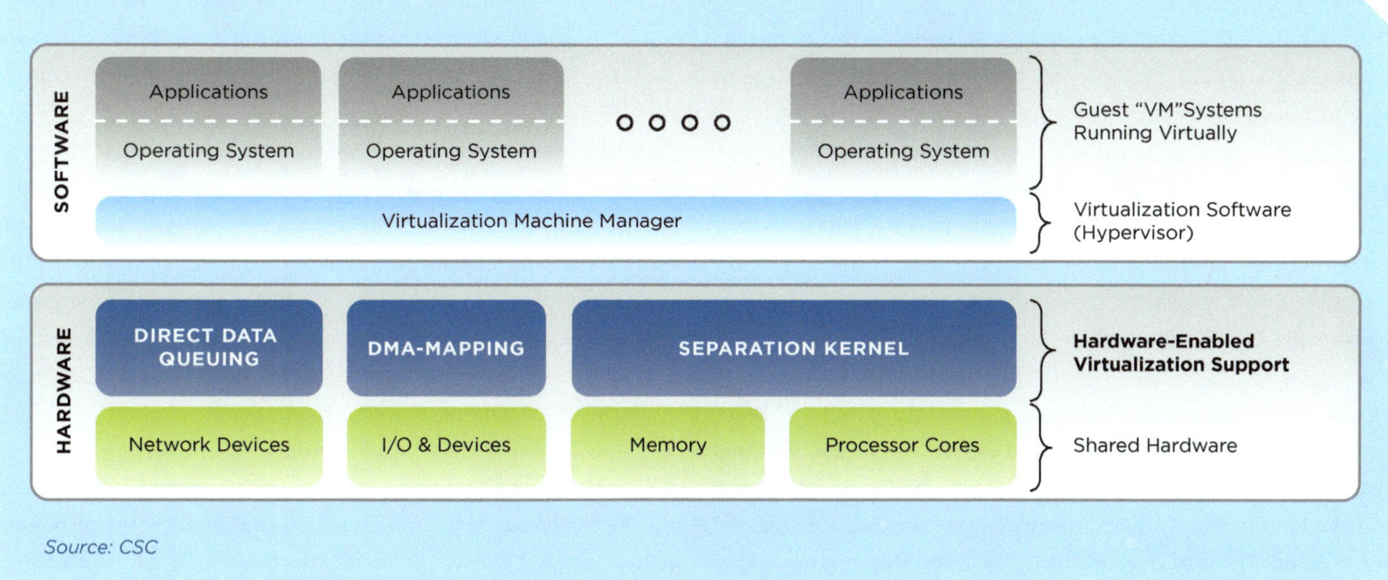

Source: CSC

Virtual machines make the data center more flexible. As described in detail in Volume 2, *The Art of Abstraction*, VMs can be instantly migrated to other physical servers as needed, especially helpful if power sources have reached their limits, hardware maintenance must be performed, or applications need to be moved to new hardware. The hardware itself can adopt different roles over its lifetime, being used for production purposes early on and then development, test or otherwise lower-availability roles later. This morphing, aided by virtual machine techniques that liquefy the server's role in the data center, extends the useful life of the machine, spreads capital costs over a longer period, and delivers additional green benefits.

Virtual machines also have been realized in software alone, where application code is written and executed in a managed software environment that separates the code from the underlying hardware and even operating system. Often called

diate programming language called Java bytecode. The result is that Java is an application programming language that is mostly independent of the specific hardware it can be run on. Instead, JVMs are created for different computing platforms; each JVM can then execute (with few constraints) the same Java code. "Write once, run everywhere" is the motto that helped drive Java to wide acceptance across the industry.

The use of virtual machines for application code, such as for Java and as introduced by Microsoft in 2000 with .NET (dot-net), enables a level of application portability. This portability is not just across different hardware and operating system platforms; it also enables application code to be moved dynamically, allowing code to be executed in different systems based on available processing capacity and relative location to users or data. Further, the use of application software virtual machines has simplified application design and implementation, where many aspects of traditional coding — such as memory management, dynamic linking and device management — are largely managed by the virtual machine.

From Virtual Machine to Virtual Appliance. Taking the virtual machine approach a step further are companies who are developing modular components that combine application services, platforms and hardware into virtual appliances. VMware already has a library of 900 such appliances, each a pre-packaged, pre-installed, pre-configured virtual machine that runs on systems using the VMware Player software. Examples of such virtual appliances include spam filters, security gateways and continuous database backup systems.

The virtual appliance approach has evolved from earlier attempts to create lightweight application platforms, such as Sun's JavaOS. What has driven the move to appliances is the wide availability of virtualization platforms and the rise of flexible open source operating systems. For example, JeOS (Just Enough Operating System) is an open source operating system customized to provide just the parts of the operating system a virtual appliance needs (in contrast to a full operating system like Linux, on which JeOS is based).

Virtual machines and appliances are a good example of Brian Arthur's "subassemblies" of existing technologies, in this case to create a lightweight application platform delivering specific functionality. An increasing number of cloud applications are built using these pre-fabricated systems that are no longer tightly bound to the hardware platform they are running on. Volume 2, *The Art of Abstraction*, discusses how the concept of virtual machines expands to the broader use of system virtualization, where abstractions make servers into easily transformable and dynamic resources in the cloud.

Redefining the Physical Server. As a result of being able to run many applications and operating systems on a single server, the nature of the physical server has also evolved into a system tuned to do more than one thing. Combining many servers, applications and related system components (recall Arthur's "arrangements") is one of the driving forces behind Cisco's entry into the server market. Seeking to address problems its customers face in the data center, Cisco announced its Cisco Unified Computing System in March 2009. The system brings together network, compute and virtual machine resources — typically siloed — and optimizes them holistically. With Unified Computing System (UCS), Cisco is combining all elements in a modern data center architecture into a single integrated platform, creating a fabric of server, storage networking, 10 gigabit networks, and virtual switches connecting hundreds of server blades.[12]

Expanding from its network roots, Cisco's vision is to virtualize the data center and bring efficiency and agility to the enterprise, which can deploy IT infrastructure more precisely according to need, with more automation and less manual intervention. Cisco represents a new player in the server market and will compete head on with partners like IBM and HP. "As Cisco shakes up the market, it is also shaking up what we mean by a server," notes Bill Koff, chief technology officer in CSC's Office of Innovation. With UCS, Cisco is working to reduce the physical complexity of servers by virtualizing more than just the processor. Now network cards, network switches, storage, and even memory are virtualized.

In addition to creating a computing and networking powerhouse, Cisco's UCS is built to reduce the environmental footprint of each server. Through its "Catalina ASIC" (application specific integrated circuit), UCS enables a single two-processor server to contain up to 384 gigabytes of memory.[13] This eliminates the need for additional servers that would normally have been necessary for memory intensive applications, such as running many virtual machines.

Looking ahead, Cisco cloud evangelist Christofer Hoff sees the formation of the "intercloud," a global network of clouds delivering a cohesive, elastic, flexible mesh of on-demand processing power (for example, delivered from the lowest-cost cloud service at a given point in time).[14] Here's how Hoff sees the intercloud playing out: "In the short term we'll need the innovators to push with their own APIs; then the service brokers will abstract them on behalf of consumers in the mid-stream, and ultimately we will arrive at a common, open and standardized way of solving the problem in the long term with a semantic capability that allows fluidity and agility in a consumer being able to take advantage of the model that works best for their particular needs."[15] The intercloud shifts the balance of IT power from centralized to distributed architectures because it gives enterprises a wider range of IT delivery options. Overall, the intercloud advances the concept of computing power being rendered in the cloud.

Today's advanced computing servers and tomorrow's possibilities will redefine competition and enable new levels of performance and efficiency in the enterprise. Traditional server manufacturers like HP and Sun are largely taking a path to increase computing power and density through sophisticated

Today's advanced computing servers and tomorrow's possibilities will redefine competition and enable new levels of performance and efficiency in the enterprise.

and complex technology design, packing multiple microprocessors and systems-on-a-chip into powerful machines contained within a typical data center rack. Cisco's more holistic approach with UCS, however, requires knowing multiple administrative disciplines: server, operating system, network switching and storage management. In UCS and most high-density blade systems, the processor, storage and network all have to play nice together, but most IT organizations don't have a lot of people who know all those specialties.

These new advanced server products are only one potential way to increase data center capacity to support cloud services. Another way is a more low-end approach. Rather than buy very powerful high-end servers, Google has chosen to buy low-cost components like multicore processors, and then assemble and deploy very cheap, disposable computers in its data centers. Even though not every company will mimic Google and move to a "Dell-like" assembly for its own IT operations, Google's approach shows how the company has been able to reshape its IT economics by disintermediating (removing assembly from the supply chain and doing it in-house). Google's servers are treated like cheap commodities held together with Velcro that are easily replaced when they fail.

It remains to be seen if cloud is best served by high-end, highly reliable advanced servers or many cheap throwaway servers. Either way, cloud has an enormous appetite for computing power, which will be satisfied by the many new arrangements of power described below.

BACK TO THE FUTURE WITH MODERN MAINFRAMES AND NEW RISC SYSTEMS

Much of the increase in computing power has revolved around the x86 processor. Although now evolved into 64-bit technology, the commodity computer processor is still based on the original Intel microprocessors from the 1980s and compatibility with the early Intel instruction set, the defined built-in operations of the processor. The focus on the x86 processor is largely due to its commoditization by the PC and low-cost server industries. Intel and AMD produce millions of these processors, lowering their costs significantly while keeping up with Moore's Law. Given its ready availability and low acquisition costs, a significant amount of the server infrastructure being used for cloud is based on x86 processors.

However, many businesses use non-x86 systems today, including mainframes and high-powered RISC processor systems. In some cases, businesses have been using mainframes for decades; IBM in particular has evolved its mainframe technology not only to support old but critical applications, but also to meet the scalability needs of business. Many RISC processors remain in use to support high-performance computing needs and were adopted because, unlike the typical x86-based systems, they enable highly scalable ("scale up") server environments. Even as Intel and AMD provide high computing performance at low cost, the mainframe and RISC processor vendors — primarily IBM, Sun and Fujitsu — have continually kept their technologies a step ahead of the commodity processors.

The result is that mainframes and RISC-based servers still make up the high end of enterprise IT systems, reaching levels of combined performance, reliability and compatibility with mission-critical software that has seldom been equaled by their x86 relatives. Here are some examples of how these enterprise-class systems have evolved over the past few years to maintain their edge:

- IBM's latest zSeries mainframe, the z10, is built to support hundreds to thousands of virtual machines running on the same physical system, far beyond the typical 100 or fewer on a high-end x86/x64 server. Furthermore, by incorporating specialized processing capabilities, mainframes can reach very high levels of I/O performance.[16]

- Although under threat of cancelation, Sun's UltraSPARC RK ("Rock") project is developing a SPARC processor design that will enable far higher scalability than existing SPARC systems, as well as be one of the first mainstream processors to support transactional memory.[17]

- IBM's Power processor servers will soon benefit from the new Power7 processor, which will support up to 1,000 logical partitions — areas to run separate operating systems.[18] Also, the Power processors enable even finer granularity resource allocation for virtual machines using micro-partitioning.[19]

So unlike large distributed arrays of commodity x86 servers, mainframes and RISC servers concentrate massive amounts of computing power into a smaller set of boxes. Not only do these systems provide compatibility with a still significant number of legacy enterprise applications, but they are also able to run larger numbers of operating systems on the same platform. In addition, they are built for multitenancy from the start, include ways of metering use, support more centralized system administration, and often incorporate capabilities not found on x86 systems, such as integrated hardware support for cryptographic processing and high-performance network communications.[20]

In early 2009, IBM and SAP demonstrated the ability to run SAP in a cloud configuration based on IBM's Power6 servers running the operating system AIX. The technology demonstration, which was completed in collaboration with the European Union's Reservoir project, showed how virtual SAP systems could be migrated between geographically separate data centers, an approach called intercloud workload mobility.[21]

Although they are individually much more expensive then x86-based systems, what makes the mainframe and RISC systems even more interesting, particularly for potential use in cloud computing environments, is that they no longer are tightly bound to proprietary, high-license-cost operating systems. Nearly all of these non-x86 enterprise servers and mainframes now support Linux and other low-cost open source software.

It is this ability to run open source software that makes these high-end systems even more relevant, particularly as application solutions built on open source software are increasingly decoupled from the specific hardware they can run on. PHP applications running on Apache don't really care what processor they are running on; this kind of portability makes the new mainframes a viable choice, especially for applications where vertical scalability ("scale up") is the best, if not only, option.

"To move to the cloud, many companies will still need to rely on their legacy applications, making access to these systems in the cloud a necessity," observes Bill Koff, chief technology officer in CSC's Office of Innovation. "So far the cloud has been primarily about x86 applications and infrastructure. However, with the broad adoption of open source and virtualization platforms, compatibility between non-x86 and cloud environments is no longer an obstacle."

UNLOCKING PROCESSING POWER THROUGH OPEN SOURCE SOFTWARE

Open source provides many new components, easily assembled, to create a rich computing environment for new applications. Compared to traditional enterprise software, these capabilities come with negligible or no license costs. At the center of open source systems (OSS) is the main open source operating system, Linux. Loosely similar to UNIX, Linux has been widely adopted to power data center systems and enterprise applications. With its ability to be deployed on cheap x86 boxes and IBM zSeries mainframes, Linux has arguably become the de facto workhorse operating system for the enterprise.

In addition to running on Linux, many enterprise applications today are built and run on a cornucopia of open source software platforms. Many OSS platforms like Apache and MySQL have matured over the years to provide more enterprise-level capabilities. Now, the open source community provides software previously limited to high-priced products, including parallel computing frameworks like Hadoop, business application packages like SugarCRM, and even platforms to run Microsoft .NET applications using the Mono runtime framework.

Further, open source has made itself a major player in supporting virtual machines. The Xen hypervisor is the most popular open source software that enables Linux to host other guest operating systems on the same platform. From hypervisors to ERP, open source provides a near limitless source of enterprise software that runs on almost any computing platform. The result is that open source software has become a first-class citizen in the data center.

Open source software has become a first-class citizen in the data center.

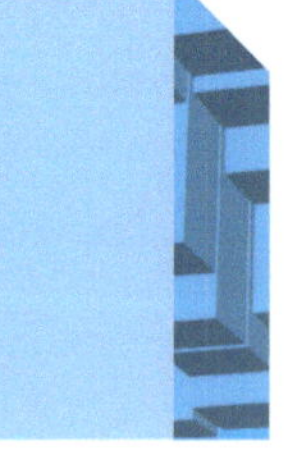

It's no surprise, then, that the cloud is largely based on open source software and systems (right now). Most users of Amazon's cloud computing services use Linux and the LAMP stack (Linux, Apache, MySQL and Perl, PHP or Python) to run their applications. As Amazon's cloud is itself built using open source software, Amazon's own cloud Application Programming Interface (API) has been replicated in Eucalyptus, an open source implementation of a cloud infrastructure platform. The role of Eucalyptus and other emerging cloud creation platforms is described in Volume 3, *The Cloud Effect*.

THE NEW DATA CENTER: DENSER, MODULAR AND GREENER

With the introduction of its Unified Computing System, Cisco has taken most of the common elements of a data center — servers, storage and networks — and created a new assembly of technology that enables a new kind of data center. Google is also developing a new kind of data center, using cheap computer components instead. Regardless of the specific technology used, the new data center emerging has three key characteristics:

- *Denser* — With the introduction of blade servers, data centers began increasing their computing capacity without increasing, and in many cases decreasing, the space needed. With the combination of new processors and innovative engineering, server vendors are packing more punch into every unit of rack space. SGI offers servers that reach a density of 21 processors (cores) and 11 terabytes of storage per one rack unit, or per 1.75 vertical inches in a standard data center rack.[22]

  In 2006, Sun introduced its "black box" concept, where data center equipment is housed in a single shipping container. Sun packed a large number of "skinless" servers (without their traditional cases) into this sealed environment, which allowed for a more efficient cooling method than the traditional raised-floor data center room. The result: even higher server density and computing power. In April 2009, Google gave the world a peek into its data centers, which pack 1,160 servers in a single shipping container.[23]

- *Modular* — Indeed, in contrast to the traditional data center rack, the sealed shipping container housing servers, storage and networking equipment is quickly becoming a common approach for increasing the amount of computing power per cubic foot of space. (See Figure 6.) This modular approach to deploying servers is also one of the keys for the creation of "mega" data centers. Rather than expand data and computing capacity server by server, Amazon, Google and other companies add massive capacity one shipping container at a time. Data centers have begun the transformation from white, windowless rooms into stacks of modular components with thousands of servers each, all pre-integrated and ready to be connected to — just plugged into — a network backbone, a cooling system and power.

  The result is the creation of an unforeseen scale of computing power reachable through the Internet. Now all major enterprise computer manufacturers offer container-based data center modules, but only a few companies right now are actively building or planning such mega data centers.

  New challenges emerge with these mega data centers, the primary one being availability. In June and July 2009, Google and other online service providers suffered outages affecting

Figure 6. The interior of SGI's ICE Cube container shows its extreme server and storage density. Such fully portable containers are the basis of the modern modular data center.

Source: SGI[24]

not just themselves but millions of users and companies. On July 2, 2009, Google App Engine, which hosts Web applications for many start-up companies, was taken down due to unforeseen data problems.[25] Earlier that same week, Rackspace users were faced with an outage triggered by a series of power problems.[26]

- *Greener* — Power consumption by data centers has increased significantly over the past decade, leading to rising costs to power systems and cool them to keep them running. The "greening" of IT, in addition to reducing IT's impact on earth's resources, has become an economic necessity for many companies trying to control their IT costs. From the processor chip to the computer design itself, server vendors now offer systems that operate not only faster but also with reduced power consumption and cooling requirements. Further, green data centers go beyond just using more energy-efficient computers to controlling how, where and when servers are used.

  Approaches to improving energy usage in data centers include powering servers with direct current (DC) rather than alternating current (AC) electricity, as well as using improved airflow designs. Google found that by putting an off-the-shelf 12-volt battery in each server, rather than using a central uninterruptible power supply (UPS), the company is able to reach 99.9 percent efficiency (over the typical 95 percent efficiency of using a large centralized UPS).[27] Providing even more control over power consumption, CA's Cassatt subsidiary introduced software that automatically shuts down and powers up servers based on usage patterns and activity levels.[28]

SMARTER SYSTEMS — SELF-MANAGING AND SELF-ORGANIZING COMPUTING CENTERS

With cloud data centers involving tens of thousands of servers, many traditional system management tools are no longer adequate to effectively manage such large computing environments. As the data center scales to massive size, associated processes and mechanisms also need to scale up. Taming and tethering the vast computing power of these new mega data centers is accomplished through smart software that automatically manages and organizes these systems.

New Approaches to System Administration — McKinsey & Company reported that in the average non-virtualized data center a single system administrator is needed to manage 30 to 40 servers.[29] Google, with more than 400,000 servers, has stated that its ratio is thousands of servers per single system administrator. In their paper "The Datacenter as a Computer," Luiz André Barroso and Urs Hölzle of Google describe data centers as "warehouse-scale computers," sometimes spanning multiple physical data centers.[30]

To manage applications and systems in these warehouse-scale computers, Google and Microsoft have developed their own system management tools to automate and offload many of the system administration and monitoring tasks typically left to humans. For its Windows Live data centers, Microsoft built Autopilot, which automates software provisioning and deployment, system monitoring and repair.[31] Upon failure of a component in a system, be it a computer or a network switch, Autopilot applies one or more recovery actions, including repairing, rebooting, reimaging and even replacing the component with other available resources. Every few weeks or so, people are dispatched to sweep through the data center (or containers) and physically replace dead servers with spares that are automatically discovered and set up for use.

However, automated management of large-scale data centers is needed only to make sure the applications can run. How do applications make effective use of the massive computing power? In short, applications no longer involve installation on a handful of machines; rather, applications are constructed and operated so they can be distributed dynamically across large clusters of homogeneous computing platforms. Distributed and parallel computing concepts, which evolved into grid computing in the 1990s, have evolved into a set of technologies and approaches that enable applications that support massive amounts of work for millions of concurrent users.

In the world of Google and Amazon, applications are partitioned into infinitely adjustable and fine-grained components that are glued together dynamically through standardized loose-coupling mechanisms such as REST-based Web services. These applications are often built on software platforms that incorporate the ability to dynamically assign application workload across many different servers, even expecting and dealing with the failure of any number of these systems.

New Approaches to Self-Organizing. There are limits, however, to how far humans can go to provide the distributed structure and explicitly manage very large-scale, complex systems. To tap the ever-growing availability of computing power, systems and applications must become self-organizing, with the ability to autonomously monitor, adjust, react to, protect and control their use of computing resources. Although it has been around for many decades, the field of autonomic computing is reaching a level of maturity and demand that is beginning to show how computing systems can be modeled after self-regulating biological systems. The initial focus of this field has been on autonomous management of systems, including the automatic detection of, and recovery from, failures in large systems.

As cloud environments grow to cover multiple data centers with hundreds of thousands of servers, it's this automatic detection and recovery — or self-healing — capability that becomes critical to ensure reliability of cloud services as servers, networks and even entire data centers are sure to fail. Even as current cloud providers face full outages today, they are all looking at monitoring and management to automatically adjust resources in case of inevitable failures.

The holy grail of autonomic computing and networking is the construction of self-organizing applications. Appistry's Enterprise Application Fabric software introduced many of the concepts of self-organizing systems, as EAF automatically determined how components of an application are distributed while avoiding any single point of failure. The open source ACE (Autonomic Communication Element) Toolkit, developed by the IST (Information Society Technologies) research project CASCADAS, aims to take this self-organizing ability even further by enabling lightweight software components that can interact and organize for larger capabilities. Using the basic architectural principles shown in Figure 7, CASCADAS prototyped and demonstrated an autonomic application called the Behavioral Pervasive Advertisement, which allowed advertising plasma screens to automatically adapt their content to the interests of nearby viewers.[32]

Cloud service providers are looking at smart technologies, like those being developed at CASCADAS, to not only reduce operational costs further but also to make clouds as self-servicing as possible. As we'll see next, smart storage and smart data are essential partners with smart systems. For these large and increasingly intelligent applications running on thousands of multicore servers, the information they consume and produce is taking new forms and being stored in new ways.

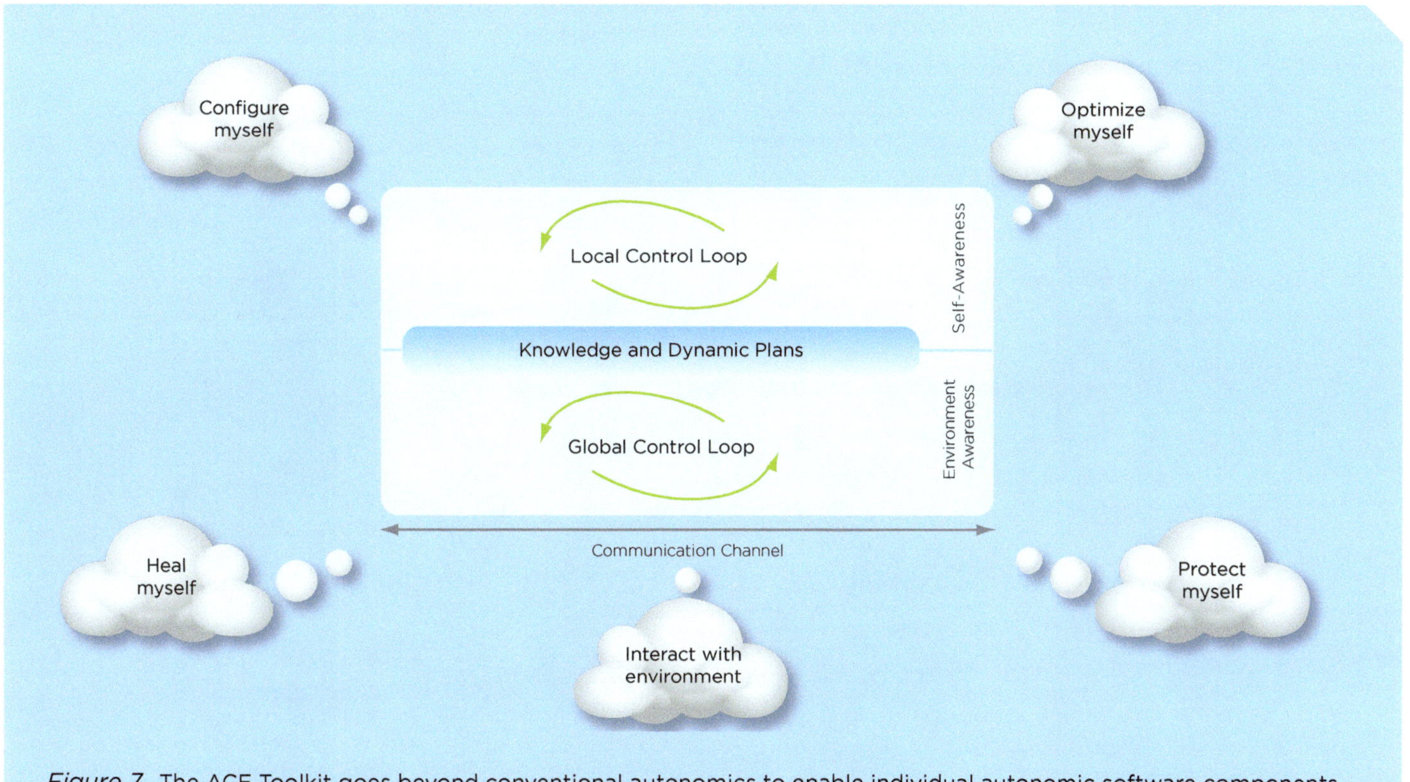

Figure 7. The ACE Toolkit goes beyond conventional autonomics to enable individual autonomic software components to interact and organize for unpredictable environments, dynamically self-adapting to evolving situations.

Source: CASCADAS

UNIVERSAL INFORMATION

The purpose of computing power is to process information. Whether simple data or more elaborate knowledge, information has reached a point where nearly all of it exists in digital form (in many cases, only in digital form.) The 2005 LEF Report, *Extreme Data: Rethinking the "I" in IT*, describes the new information environment:

> An information explosion is underway, giving rise to an era of extreme data and dramatic new applications. Extreme data is new types of data, generated by new devices, and being used in new ways — enabling new business processes, interpersonal connections and knowledge for business, government, communities and individuals. In this world, organizations need to understand and leverage their data opportunities, putting information to work for them like never before.[33]

As the world produces and stores data at an exponential pace, this data is expected to require over a yottabyte (a trillion terabytes) of new storage capacity every year by 2013.[34] Consumer content, both commercial and personal, is forecast to reach over 760 exabytes (760 million terabytes) of data by 2015.[35] This data will come from both traditional data sources, such as databases and documents, and new sources including cameras, sensors, mobile devices and any Internet-enabled device. Much of this data will reside on the device or in the cloud.

So what is enabling us to be able to handle and process all this data? Three areas of technology advancement are driving the creation, consumption and persistence of this data: unlimited data storage, smarter storage and smarter information.

UNLIMITED DATA STORAGE

Digital data needs to be put somewhere, even temporarily, in order to be processed. Digital data storage systems take a wide range of forms, but at the heart of most digital storage is the hard

Figure 8 DISAPPEARING ACT: SHRINKING STORAGE COSTS

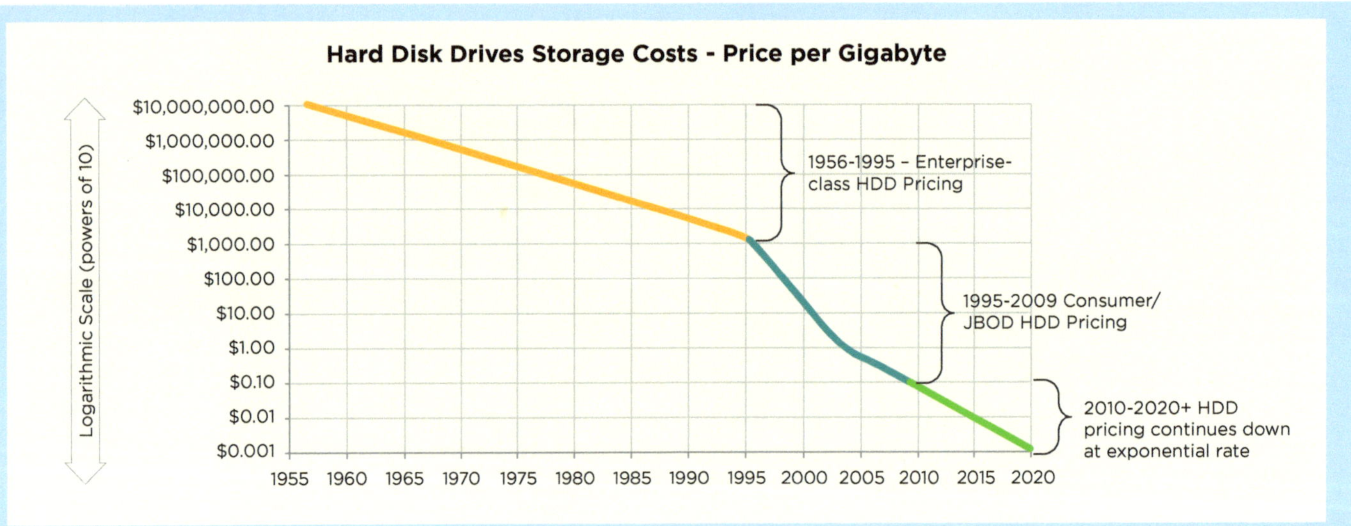

Chart created by CSC. Data for 1956-2007 from Ed Grochowski and PCWorld;[36] data for 2009 and beyond from Telephony Online[37] and CSC.

disk drive (HDD), where individual bits are stored on a spinning platter using magnetic fields. Although still fundamentally based on its original principles, hard drive technology has evolved at an increasing rate ever since the introduction of drives by IBM in 1956.

In the 1980s HDDs became a common form of data storage, where the average cost for storing a megabyte in data centers was around $10 (or around $10,000 per gigabyte, as shown in Figure 8). After 1995, the consumer market accelerated the price drop in HDDs. In 2009, the typical HDD on the consumer market offers 1 to 2 *terabytes* of storage at a typical cost of $100 for the entire drive (or around $0.05-$0.10 per gigabyte, as shown in Figure 8). For traditional enterprise IT needs, HDDs still tend to be more expensive, with manufacturers offering drives that spin at 15,000 RPMs (twice as fast as most standard drives) and are connected via high-speed fiber. However, increasingly, cloud service providers are relying more on cheap consumer drives using them in data centers as "just a bunch of disks" (JBOD). Industry analysts estimate that HDD shipments will grow in terms of actual disk capacity by 20-38 percent by 2011.[38] These estimates, however, may not account for additional breakthroughs in disk technology, including Dataslide's massively parallel disk drive "head arrays" that can simultaneously read and write on 64 points on a drive platter.[39]

Although not yet as cheap as traditional spinning platter HDDs, Solid-State Storage Devices (SDDs) based on flash memory technology have evolved to reach similar densities as HDDs while supporting much higher data transfer rates.[40] Sun recently introduced a set of modular SDDs for its servers, which can provide 100 times the read performance of traditional high-speed HDDs.[41]

With the cost of HDD storage continuing its accelerated drop since the 1980s, HDDs have become the workhorse for extremely large data storage needs, even reaching the point where traditional low-cost storage mechanisms like magnetic tape and optical storage have been relegated to niche positions in IT. Several companies, such as EMC and NetApp's Data Domain, provide backup and permanent storage solutions that use HDDs to store massive amounts of data cheaply and persistently. In fact, all drive and solid-state (flash) storage technologies are now seeing the same exponential drop in prices as these technologies evolve.[42]

To squeeze even more data onto disks, data de-duplication has become a popular technique to store data only once. A significant amount of data, such as documents or e-mail, is often duplicated by users across different servers. Storage systems, with initial focus on backup systems, are increasingly using de-duplication to store a set of data once and then refer to it using shorter indexes when that same data is referenced elsewhere. (See Figure 9.) The result is that storage systems — collection of many hard drives in the form of disk arrays — can show data capacities of greater than 100 percent compared

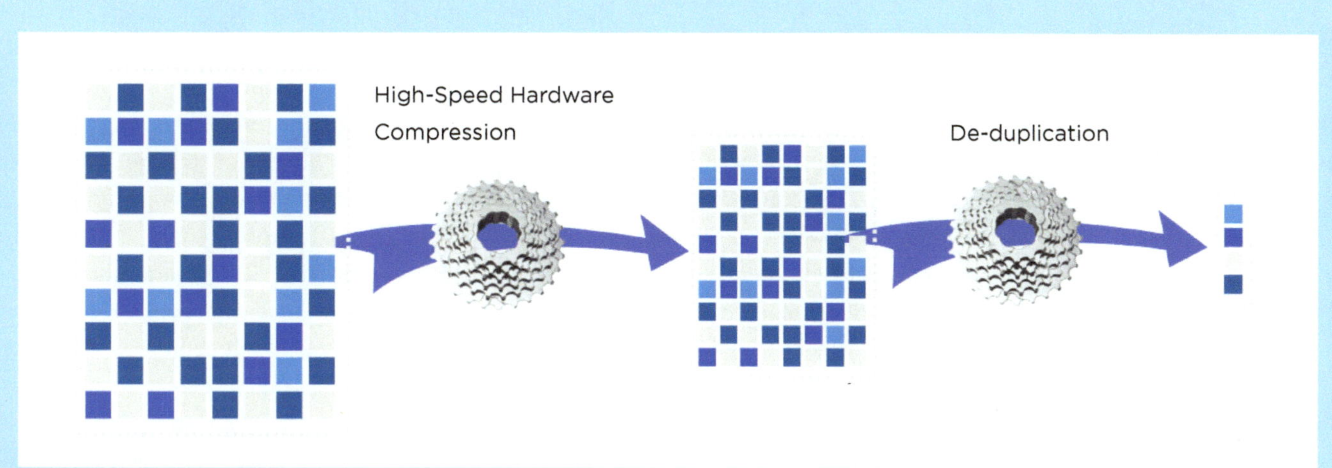

Figure 9. With data de-duplication, data is stored once and referred to with shorter indexes when referenced elsewhere. This lets enterprises get more out of existing storage space and reduces the overall amount of storage needed, cutting capital costs, data management costs and power costs.

Source: NetApp

to the space used in a non de-duplicated environment. Cloud providers are increasingly using de-duplication, along with other storage optimization approaches, but only when possible, as in some countries certain regulated data cannot be stored in any compressed format.

The expanding capacity of storage is also moving towards the edge of computing. The handheld smart phone of today is reaching storage capacities of 32 gigabytes. Small disk arrays with up to 16 *terabytes* of redundant storage are now offered to consumers.[43] SanDisk has even announced that it is working on Security Digital (SD) cards with up to two terabytes of storage — in less than one square inch.[44] The result is that the space to store data is expanding at near exponential rates across all parts of the IT spectrum — and most of that storage will be connected to the Internet.

The space to store data is expanding at near exponential rates across all parts of the IT spectrum — and most of that storage will be connected to the Internet.

SMARTER STORAGE

Simply having more hard drives to store data is not enough. As the amount of data explodes, the industry is working on better ways to access and store that data. In a 2007 Google Labs analysis of the failure rates of over 100,000 hard disk drives, Google found that the failure rates of low-cost HDDs jumped from two percent to over seven percent as the disks reached over two years in service.[45] Disk drive failure is a reality, particularly as drive densities increase.

Drive manufacturers address inherent failure increase that corresponds to higher densities. Most drives today incorporate automatic bad block relocation, error correction codes and other mechanisms to increase drive reliability. The use of RAID (Redundant Array of Independent Disks) technologies has become common in the enterprise, where a system can recover and no data is lost from the failure of up to two drives. In the case of disk arrays, recovery from individual drive failure is usually automatic through "hotspare" drives.

Rather than use a small array of drives as a single unit, Storage Area Networks (SANs) add increasing levels of storage reliability and sophistication by creating the means of sharing a large number of drives in a transparent manner over high-speed network connections. What one server may see as a hard drive may actually consist of a slice of many drives that are shared with hundreds of servers. Similar to how a processor can be shared with many virtual machines, SANs present storage to other systems as virtual storage or virtual drives. Through a combination of aggregated drives, redundant storage controllers, RAID, caching and logical volume management, SANs provide the means to centralize storage for many systems, with increased reliability and speed and reduced per-server storage costs.

SANs, however, are small compared to the data demands faced by companies like Google and Amazon. For massive data scalability, a new set of technologies has been developed, living on top of the SANs or used on top of raw storage technologies. Sun has developed ZFS, a new open source file system technology, which accesses a large pool of drives using I/O pipelining and adds reliability through fast disk snapshots and disk "scrubbing."[46] Furthermore, ZFS automatically caches data on the fastest drives, which enables a high-speed hybrid HDD/SDD storage approach.

To deal with data on hundreds of thousands of drives storing over 40 billion objects in its Simple Storage Service (S3), Amazon uses "buckets" instead of files to store data.[47] (See Figure 10.) Each bucket can store arbitrary types of data objects. S3 is used for a wide variety of storage needs across the Internet, from simple file archiving, supporting popular photo sites such as Smugmug, to storing entire virtual machine image libraries. Amazon designed S3 to be durable (no data loss or corruption), highly available and scalable to virtually infinite storage levels. Although Amazon has had some challenges with S3 availability,[48] Amazon has largely succeeded in storing massive amounts of data on cheap storage hardware through its use of JBOD (just a bunch of disks) rather than sophisticated SANs.

Built to manage the large indexes used for searches, the Google File System (GFS) automatically manages data in triplicate (minimum) 64-megabyte chunks that are managed across thousands of "chunk" servers using multiple redundant

Figure 10 AMAZON'S "BUCKETS" STORE A VARIETY OF DATA TYPES

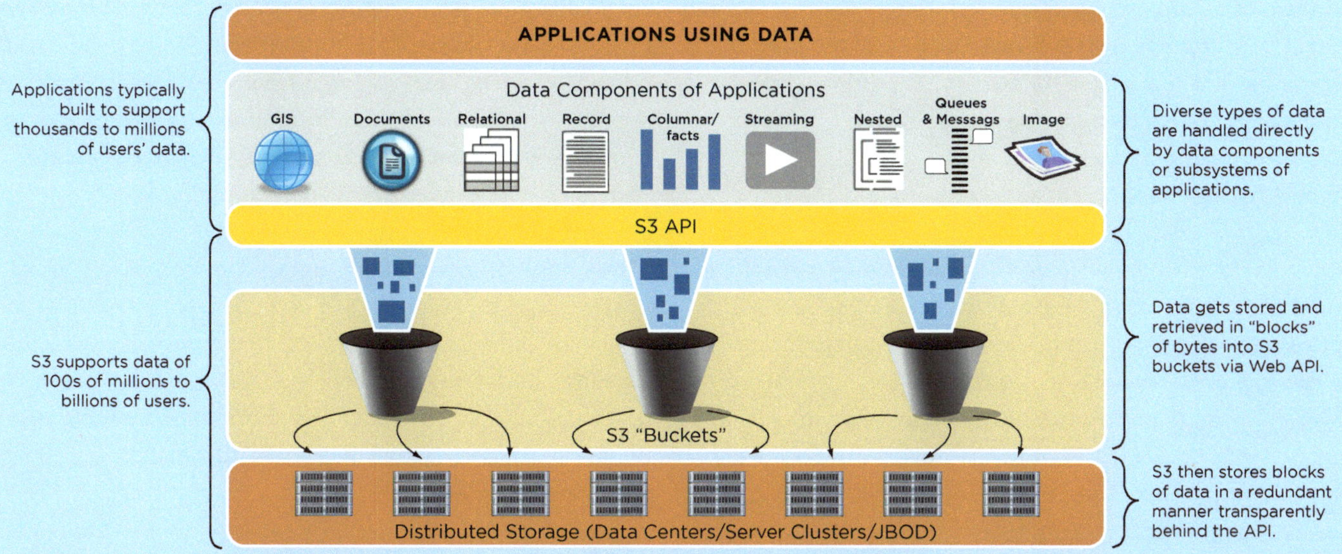

Source: CSC

metadata master servers.[49] Data replicas are created as the data comes into the servers, using parallel network paths. Rather than use the more complex virtual storage approaches of SANs, GFS simply allocates chunks of data to servers based on their disk utilization levels. Although Google has not released its GFS technology, open source projects like Hadoop, actively supported by Yahoo,[50] incorporate similar approaches to distributed data storage. Hadoop is now a popular element in the growing arrangement of cloud technologies for handling large data processing and computational needs.

SMARTER INFORMATION

Even as Amazon and Google are storing massive amounts of data, they do so with little consideration of what the data is. Yet, the usefulness of the data depends on its meaning and content. To take advantage of extreme amounts of data, the IT industry has been hard at work making information smarter — that is, more useful — through XML and database advances.

XML. XML, the eXtended Markup Language, provides a standard way of defining and exchanging data, wrapping content of any type and adding tags to data to expand its meaning. A common means of describing and sharing information on the Internet, XML is a data language that allows people and organizations to define how they share and integrate data. As a result, XML has enabled vast new forms of easily shared and consumed data, from business transaction data to audio podcasts published via RSS (formatted XML). An advanced cousin of HTML, the first language of the Internet, XML is the format for most new data on the Internet (excluding spam). Data either takes the form of XML or is wrapped in XML. XML is a key foundation that enables universal access to information on the Internet and, ultimately, cloud computing. Without XML we would not have Web Services, and without Web Services we would not have cloud computing.

Without XML we would not have Web Services, and without Web Services we would not have cloud computing.

Database Advances. As the amount of data created is shared in different formats based on XML, enterprise database technology has evolved to be smart about XML[51] as well as other data formats. Although all major databases still focus on relational data storage, all major relational database products now provide native support for storing, accessing and even querying data in XML format. These database products have also expanded support for special information types, such as video and spatial (geographic and location) information.

However, once data is encrypted in a database, it must be unencrypted to be used and manipulated. This limits the ability of database products to store data securely for many users or organizations, while still being able to understand the data for indexing and making queries faster. IBM announced research that it hopes will lead to the ability to analyze and manipulate *encrypted* data stored in databases. By using "homomorphic" encryption methods, databases will soon, IBM hopes, be able to act on data while keeping it secure.[52]

But traditional relational databases are still inadequate to support the extremely large scale of the cloud. As Michael Stonebraker, database research pioneer and CTO of Vertica, a leader in column-oriented database technology, says, "The increasing application demands, including the cloud, on DBMSs spell the end of one-size-fits-all."[53] With the highly distributed nature of the cloud, databases have evolved into more specialized approaches. In particular, cloud database technology shares one attribute, "shared nothing," where data stored on one server is independent of data on any other server. Vertica's column-oriented database technology supports this approach and uses massively parallel scale-out technology to meet the needs of ever-expanding database analytics.

Going beyond traditional enterprise databases, computer researchers and major IT players are actively pursuing Very Large Database (VLDB) systems. Not surprisingly, Amazon and Google have been leaders in this emerging area of database technology, as their scale required them to go beyond what available products could provide. Google's Bigtable database is used to store all the index information generated by MapReduce. Like Vertica, Bigtable differs from traditional relational databases in that it stores data in a column-oriented manner, which provides better efficiency for large keyword searches. Using it to store and access petabytes of information, Google describes Bigtable as "designed to scale to hundreds or thousands of machines, and to make it easy to add more machines [to] the system and automatically start taking advantage of those resources without any reconfiguration."[54] Although Google's Bigtable is proprietary technology, the open source community is building similar tools, such as HyperTable.[55]

At the core of most cloud databases is a more simplistic approach, combining "just a bunch of disks" (i.e., not using expensive SANs) with very simple storage structures that differ depending on what the data performance needs are. Block-based and keyed storage are two simple methods being used by cloud providers to enable very simple "bulk" data storage. To support high volume on-line transaction processing (OLTP), emerging database technologies like VoltDB rely on lightweight memory-resident databases with minimal or no locking overhead, reaching two orders of magnitude the transaction performance of traditional DBMSs.[56]

To support data warehousing in the cloud, column-oriented databases like Bigtable or Vertica are proving to be much better suited to retrieve selective data faster than the whole-row approach of traditional relational databases.[57] In the cloud, data will increasingly be stored based on the specific characteristics of the data and how it needs to be accessed. Innovation in cloud databases has just started to bring together new arrangements of data technology; there's more to come in this young area of "scale out" data management.

Innovation in cloud databases has just started to bring together new arrangements of data technology; there's more to come in this young area of "scale out" data management.

UNIVERSAL ACCESS

The foundations of universal power and universal information are only useful when they can be accessed. Over the past decade, the IT industry (in fact, the world) has seen radical changes in the way both humans and systems access information and systems. Universal access goes beyond networking and connectivity, involving new ways enterprises share data and how humans interact with information and each other over networks. The 2006 LEF Report *Connected World* forecast the extent of change we are seeing in communications and access:

Universal access is the circulatory system for the cloud.

> The connectivity landscape — the core network and how we access it — is undergoing a major transformation that is driven by abundant low-cost bandwidth at the core, expansion of wireless capabilities at the edge, and global consensus that the protocol to unify us on all fronts is the Internet Protocol (IP). . . .
>
> Readiness for the connected world is at hand. Next-generation IP networks are ready. The network edge is ready. The content world is ready, working on whole new types of content. Enterprises are adopting new forms of connectedness. Players are entering new markets. Industry groups are pushing for standards. Legacy players are rethinking their position due to new entrant pressure. Imagination is the limit; technology is not.[58]

Universal access is the circulatory system for the cloud. Without universal access to broadband networks, all interwoven into the Internet, cloud computing would not exist. Asserted by Sun's John Gage in the early 1980s, "the network is the computer" has become a prophetic statement as cloud computing starts to deliver universal computing capabilities from anywhere, with the Internet as the centerpiece.[59]

Universal access starts with ubiquitous broadband networks. Cisco has predicted that global network traffic using IP will increase fivefold by 2013, approaching 56 exabytes per month,[60] as shown in Figure 11. This growth, driven by both consumers and industry, will be enabled by unified, faster, smarter networks; new edges to the Internet; and smarter integration capabilities. A breakdown of consumer traffic, which represents the bulk of the growth, is shown in Figure 12.

Figure 11 CISCO FORECASTS 56 EXABYTES PER MONTH OF IP TRAFFIC IN 2013

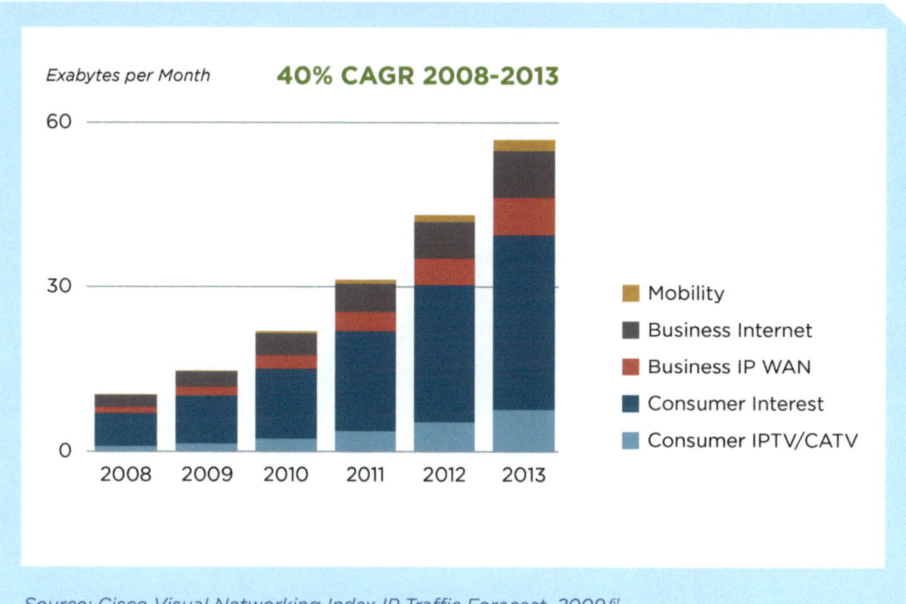

Source: Cisco Visual Networking Index IP Traffic Forecast, 2009[61]

Figure 12 CISCO'S GLOBAL CONSUMER INTERNET TRAFFIC FORECAST THROUGH 2013

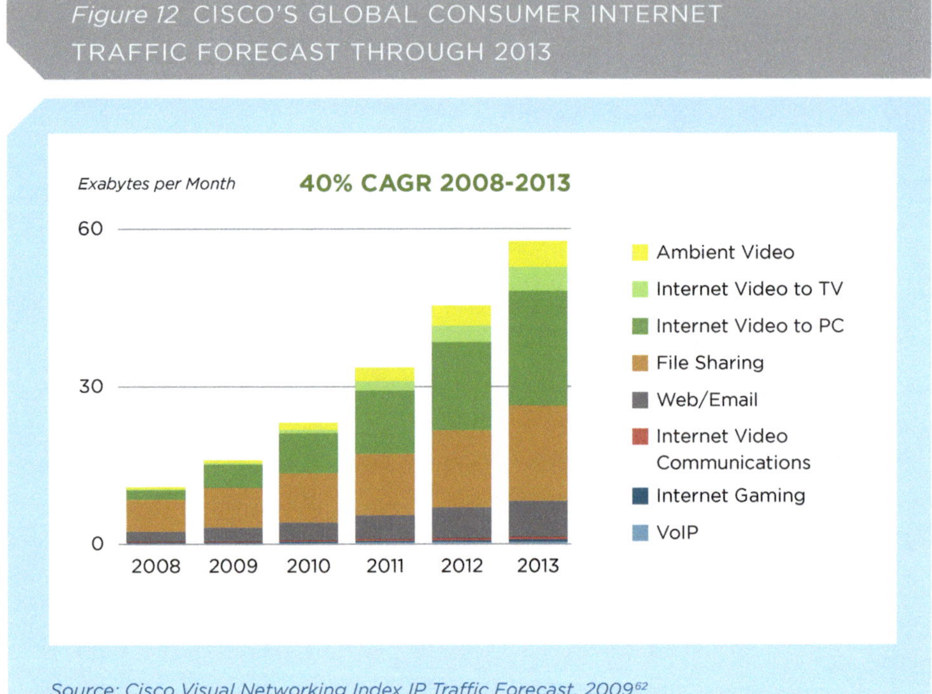

Source: Cisco Visual Networking Index IP Traffic Forecast, 2009[62]

UNIFIED, FASTER, SMARTER NETWORKS

The world, including all of IT, has made a clear decision: the core of all network communications is IP, the protocol used to connect systems and transport data across the Internet. As a result, IP networks have become a common fabric to tie all communication formats together, including voice, video and even fax. Unified Communications is blurring the lines between the phone, TV and computer.

Although VoIP (voice over IP) adoption has been increasing steadily within companies, the impact of Unified Communications is even more apparent in the consumer space, where instant messaging, video conferencing, voice calling, desktop access, document collaboration and even e-mail are all coming together. Not surprisingly, Google is pursuing this new convergence with its Google Voice and upcoming Google Wave technologies.

IP is also becoming the common fabric in the data center. Beyond VoIP, video and Web access, Ethernet networks are reaching speeds of 10 gigabits per second and beyond, which makes it possible to use IP as a backbone for inter-process communication and even for connecting SAN disk arrays. Cisco's Unified Computing System extends the networking fabric so that even virtual machines running on UCS can be assigned dedicated (full-speed) 10 gigabit network connectivity.[63] Soon mega data centers will have massive network pipes to connect thousands of servers as 100 gigabit speeds are just around the corner and terabit Ethernet becomes reality by 2015.[64] In theory, with such super-fast networks, processors and memory can be located in different parts of the cloud; the entire computing package breaks down and the cloud becomes the computing environment.

The cloud is also increasingly relying on ever-bigger broadband "pipes" to and between data centers, enabling the creation of virtual data centers that go beyond a single location. In 2000, Dr. Larry Smarr became founding director of a novel University of California San Diego/University of California Irvine partnership, the California Institute for Telecommunications and Information Technology (Calit2). Calit2 is prototyping a living laboratory across California research universities that foreshadows bringing gigabit broadband to every citizen in California.[65]

Soon mega data centers will have massive network pipes to connect thousands of servers as 100 gigabit speeds are just around the corner and terabit Ethernet becomes reality by 2015.

Calit2 is already investigating with Canadian collaborators the use of energy-efficient 10 gigabit optical networks to enable university research groups to move their processing needs to green cloud data centers, while still meeting their data access performance needs.[66] With ever-increasing bandwidth to and between cloud data centers, applications like the immersive 3D environment StarCAVE (see Figure 13) no longer need to rely on local servers for adequate performance to support the complex user experience.[67] Calit2's goal now is to bring terabit-scale networking within reach, having already achieved network speeds of 320 gigabits per second in its labs at the end of 2008.[68]

Figure 13. Using dedicated gigabit optical networks, StarCAVE allows users in multiple global locations to use 3D "OptIPortal" software environments, with the processing taking place in remote green data centers. Here researchers explore proteins in 3D from the Protein Data Bank, displayed inside the StarCAVE.

Source: Erik Jepsen/Calit2

Today IP networks are used for nearly all aspects of communicating between machines, to humans and between humans. Not only does data flow over IP, but so does data center storage traffic, voice traffic, video, location information, images and control of mechanical devices — even home appliances.[73] Even with some of their historic limitations, IP networks have become one of the primary and pervasive fabrics in our economic infrastructure, alongside electricity and roadways. IP now binds the world's communications together.

NEW EDGES

Much of the attention on cloud computing has been on the growing power, size and flexibility of data centers, servers and storage. Just as important is how these clouds are being accessed and from where. Over the past 15 years, the IT and communications industry has been in a race to provide faster and wider access to the Internet.

From 4800 baud modems and ISDN to now optical fiber in the home and business, the "last mile" connection has seen a major transformation from near-analog, high-cost connections to nearly ubiquitous high-speed broadband global network access. With 63 percent of its population having high-speed access to the Internet in 2009,[74] the U.S. maintains the largest number of broadband network subscribers, although many small and other industrialized nations have higher per-capita broadband usage than the U.S.[75] Most of the world has seen rapid growth in broadband Internet access;[76] China is expected to reach 139 million broadband subscribers by 2010.[77]

As IP networks get faster, they are also getting smarter. Not only can new 10 gigabit copper Ethernet NICs (Network Interface Cards) automatically throttle energy consumption when full bandwidth isn't needed,[69] they can also offload processing for network-based inter-process communications, essentially turning the local Ethernet into a virtual server backplane.[70] Announced in early 2009, Juniper's Project Stratus is designing switches that support thousands of servers in large data centers, not only routing IP traffic but also support the emerging Converged Enhanced Ethernet standards or CEE.[71] CEE, also called Data Center Ethernet (DCE), will enable data centers to use Ethernet, even across locations, for "lossless" data traffic and create parallel network paths for increased throughput.[72]

IP networks have become one of the primary and pervasive fabrics in our economic infrastructure, alongside electricity and roadways.

Connecting the world together is a vast network of fiber optic trans-oceanic cables, many of which were put in place several years ago. Originally much of the cable went unused as "dark fiber," but parts of the trans-oceanic network are expected to be fully used by 2014.[78] New cables are being placed on ocean floors supporting network speeds of 40 gigabits per second[79] to over 100 gigabits per second.[80] NEC has announced undersea cables that each have a capacity of over 10 *terabits* per second.[81] Even within the data center,

10 gigabit Ethernet networks are rapidly becoming common,[82] and, as mentioned earlier, terabit Ethernet is within sight.[83]

But broadband Internet access is no longer bound by cables or wires. Wireless broadband, primarily through the expansion of cellular networks, is readily available in nearly all modern metropolitan areas and, with the help of satellite broadband, is expanding into areas with limited traditional cabled infrastructure.[84] Ovum research has forecast 1,024 percent growth in mobile broadband users globally by 2014,[85] while Verizon is expected to lead the way in making LTE — 4G cellular broadband — common within four years.[86]

Small and Fast — Smarter Devices at the Edge. The rise of wireless broadband has brought with it several new generations of mobile computing devices. Already, portable notebook computers outsell desktop computers in the PC market.[87] Now netbooks are rapidly gaining traction. These smaller, low power, lightweight notebook computers don't have the same capabilities as their bigger siblings, but they offer an inexpensive alternative for those who perform most or all of their daily computer tasks using online services. Netbooks are expected to make further inroads into the enterprise, particularly as an increasing number of applications needed by business users reside entirely on the Web.[88]

Although still met with skepticism by IT departments, the Apple iPhone has arguably had the most impact on how mobile devices on the edge of the network are viewed. The iPhone represents one of the best examples of combinatorial evolution of technology. Exemplifying a novel organization of existing technologies, the iPhone has blurred the lines between computing device, broadband mobile phone, GPS locator and application platform. Major enterprise software vendors, including Oracle and SAP, are releasing networked applications for the iPhone.[89]

Netbooks are expected to make further inroads into the enterprise, particularly as an increasing number of applications needed by business users reside entirely on the Web.

With devices like the iPhone, Google's G1, BlackBerrys and the HP 1501 netbook[90] for the enterprise, expectations are high that in the next few years most enterprise users will more likely be using a mobile device, backed by applications on the Internet, to do the majority of their work.[91] To make the mobile application experience (even in the browser) better, the pas de deux between the mobile device and the application servers on the network is also evolving.

Integrating the Edge with the Center. Even in the early days of the Internet, the use of caching on a PC or a Web server became common, largely to avoid unnecessary network transfers and slower response times. As the Internet became a fundamental network in the world's economic infrastructure, companies like Akamai invented technology to push content, particularly static content, ever closer to the consumer of that content.

Now Content Distribution Networks (CDNs) are being used in an invisible manner by billions of people every day. Particularly with the rise of online video content and consumption, an entire market of CDN providers maintains content on thousands of servers spread across the globe. When a user requests a video or image via a browser, the Web technology transparently finds the closest server that has this content cached. Not only are response times improved, but the approach ensures a more effective use of the networking bandwidth available. During the U.S. Presidential Inauguration in 2009, Akamai alone served over seven million live video streams requiring 800 gigabits per second of bandwidth.[92] The need for CDNs will continue to rise, particularly as video is expected to make up a significant amount of consumer Internet traffic. (Recall Figure 12.)

SMARTER INTEGRATION

Amidst the vast network plumbing of the Internet, business and users access data and servers through applications. These applications often require data from other applications or data sources on networks. In the past, client-server and N-tier system architectures brought together application components but were typically limited to a LAN or company network. The initial years of the Web brought HTML-rendered documents and forms to users but did not effectively support the creation of larger applications, which required integrating components from across the Internet.

At the end of the last century this started to change. The IT industry began inventing the means for easily integrating applications and systems across the Internet, gluing together the Web's primary protocol, HTTP, and the new universal data format, XML. The result was a new approach to integration across the Internet through Service Oriented Architecture (SOA). Based on SOA approaches, Web Services package access to applications, services and data in common API structures (like SOAP and REST), making it easy to assemble multiple services into new composite applications (or even new Web services).

Within the enterprise, IT initially adopted SOA approaches to obtain flexible modularity of business services in the organization. However, over the past few years, SOA and Web services have enabled the integration of business processes across organizational boundaries. At NEHEN (New England Healthcare EDI Network), CSC built the Clinical Data eXchange (CDX), a SOA-based integration system that enables prescriptions and other information to be securely sent and processed between hospitals, insurers and pharmacies via Web services.[93]

CDX is also an example of how businesses are integrating not just data but processes. Harnessing standard process definition languages and flexible data formats such as ebXML, Business Process Management tools are now regularly used to connect Web services across companies to support specific business activities.[94]

As businesses began to connect to each other through SOA over the Web, or Web Oriented Architecture, a new set of controls and standards emerged to help ensure that companies could trust each other when using Web servers and know that the integrity and protection of their data was maintained. Through the use of digital certificates and standards such as the Security Assertion Markup Language (SAML) and WS-Security, companies are using federated security mechanisms to help confirm the identity (and authenticity) of a partner and the integrity of the data being shared.

Web services and the approach of SOA are now the lingua franca for tying together services, applications and even infrastructure control, which are increasingly being delivered as cloud services. SOA has become the delivery vehicle for the cloud; the next step is technology that brings those services together for end users.

Rich Internet Apps. Using the combination of modern browser technology and the ability to integrate application services across the Internet using SOA, the last few years have seen the rise of "Web 2.0." A number of Web 2.0 technologies have evolved that enable Rich Internet Applications (RIAs):

- *Javascript* — The original browser scripting language, Javascript has become the workhorse for interactive Web applications, where pieces of application functionality are sent to and run at the browser.

- *Dynamic HTML* — DHTML takes HTML, the original lingua franca of the Web, and gives it more capabilities to change a page visually without having to communicate to the Web server.

- *AJAX* — Combining XML and Javascript, AJAX (Asynchronous Javascript and XML) allows Javascript to run in parallel in the background, so the browser can communicate with Web servers (via Web services) and make changes incrementally to the Web page, giving the user a seamless interface.

- *Flash/Silverlight* — Adobe's Flash and Microsoft's Silverlight plug-ins for browsers add a complete application platform, supporting anything from animated video to custom applications.

- *HTML 5* — The newest addition to the group, HTML 5 extends the hypertext markup language for Web pages with highly interactive Web application mechanisms, scripting APIs and even native video support.[95] Expected to reach mainstream adoption in the next few years, HTML 5 is already making headlines through the creation of innovative Web applications like Google Wave.[96]

One popular use of these technologies is to create mashups, relatively quick-and-easy Web applications that bring together multiple Web services and applications, mashing them up into unique combinations that provide innovative capabilities. Although mashups originated in the consumer Web space, their use in the enterprise is expected to explode into a $700 million market by 2013.[97]

The impact of mashups has been to enable people to build Brian Arthur's new arrangements of technologies at breakneck speed, where new applications and capabilities — through the gluing together of applications across the Internet — now appear on a daily basis. Cloud computing is often seen by end users in the form of these mashups, where the application itself consists of an innovative assembly of cloud services realized within the browser.

Whether using browser mashups or smart phone applications downloaded from an app store, people will increasingly be using their mobile devices to access consumer and enterprise applications. Although desktop PCs (or even thin client workstations) won't go away anytime soon, people will mainly use applications from where they are at anytime, rather than from a specific location. The combination of sophisticated mobile devices, increasingly ubiquitous high-speed networking, and applications running across the network is leading to a host of new possibilities.

The centerpiece of these new opportunities, then, is the network. The network glues cloud computing together and is the backbone of the Cloud rEvolution. The network is the primary organizing construct around which various arrangements of computing power, information and access, plus applications and processes, are forming to enable a new way of supplying, managing and using information technology.

The network is the primary organizing construct around which various arrangements of computing power, information and access, plus applications and processes, are forming to enable a new way of supplying, managing and using information technology.

A NEW CLOUD ECONOMY

Cloud computing, which represents a morphing of the digital domain, is driving a new era of how computing services are provided and consumed by enterprises and by the world. Figure 14 is another illustration of how the foundational technologies stack together to enable the cloud. The rapid combinatorial evolution of universal power, information and access is creating an exponential effect on the IT industry as well as all parts of the economy dependent on IT — in short, our global economy.

Each digital foundation of the cloud brings a single element that, working together with the others, has an amplifying effect on how these technologies will change the nature of IT and business. In the cloud, all these technologies matter — from hard technology, such as infrastructure and high-speed networks, to realized abstractions of use such as virtualization and cloud APIs.

From the minuscule changes in technology, such as the density of disk storage and multiplication of processing power at 35-nanometer scales, to the large-scale use of computing, including mega data centers supporting billions of consumers, the digital foundations of the Cloud rEvolution show how technology combines into new arrangements to create new technology — which in turn creates new economies and new worlds. The Cloud rEvolution is the next step in how information technology is changing the way we do business. Or as Brian Arthur puts it, "The economy is an expression of its technologies."[98]

The Cloud rEvolution is the next step in how information technology is changing the way we do business.

Many technologies in the Cloud rEvolution are abstract and involve layering new perspectives on existing technologies, further accelerating the rate of change. Arthur describes this effect:

> In talking about structural change then, we need to acknowledge that the set of changes may not all be tangible and may not all be "arrangements." And we need to keep in mind that changes may have multiple causes and a high multiplicity of

> effects. . . .Structural change in the economy is not just the addition of a novel technology and replacement of the old, and the economic adjustments that follow these. It is a chain of consequences where the arrangements that form the skeletal structure of the economy continually call forth new arrangements.[99]

Today's digital foundations — those combining and underlying technologies and new arrangements — are only the beginning of the Cloud rEvolution. To fully understand the cloud — what makes it larger than a set of technologies and what it means to IT and to your business — we require the remaining volumes of this report, starting with Volume 2, ***The Art of Abstraction***, which affects all layers of the stack and lays the groundwork for the ultimate abstraction of the cloud. Volume 3 takes us into ***The Cloud Effect***, outlining the impact the cloud has already had and will continue to have on IT and across all industries. Finally, Volume 4, ***A Workbook for Cloud Computing in the Enterprise***, provides practical guidance for transitioning to the cloud, which is rapidly becoming a question of when and how, not if.

Figure 14 THE GROWTH OF CLOUD COMPUTING

Source: Dion Hinchcliffe, ZDNet, http://blogs.zdnet.com/Hinchcliffe/?p=303

As we'll see in these upcoming volumes, the cloud is more than a sum of the new digital foundations. Today we enjoy access from our myriad enterprise computers and personal devices to ever-bigger, more powerful systems with massive amounts of data and data storage. We have just begun to see what new applications and uses of data are possible in this evolved technology environment. The combinatorial evolution of information technology has given us new digital foundations to build upon, with exciting potential. With these new digital foundations, the sky is the limit.

NOTES

1. "Cloud Computing Is No Pipe Dream," *BusinessWeek*, 9 December 2008. http://www.businessweek.com/technology/content/dec2008/tc2008128_745779.htm

2. W. Brian Arthur, *The Nature of Technology: What It Is and How It Evolves* (New York: Free Press, August 2009), pp. 18-23.

3. Ibid., p. 70.

4. Ibid., p. 145.

5. "Cloud is an operations model, not a technology," James Urquhart, The Wisdom of Clouds blog, CNET News, 28 May 2009. http://news.cnet.com/8301-19413_3-10249486-240.html?tag=mncol;posts

6. Arthur, *The Nature of Technology*, p. 155.

7. "Digital Foundations: Technology's Building Blocks for Business Breakthroughs in the 21st Century," CSC Leading Edge Forum, 2000.

8. Multicore chips were identified by the LEF as a disruptive technology in "Digital Disruptions: Technology Innovations Powering 21st Century Business," CSC Leading Edge Forum, 2008, p. 62. http://assets1.csc.com/lef/downloads/LEF_2008DigitalDisruptions.pdf

9. "Troubled AMD Looks to Pass Intel with 12-Core Chip," InsideTech.com, 24 April 2009. http://www.insidetech.com/news/articles/4662-troubled-amd-looks-to-pass-intel-with-12-core-chip

10. "ARM shows possibly iPhone-bound multicore mobile processor," *AppleInsider*, 16 February 2009. http://www.appleinsider.com/print/09/02/16/arm_shows_possibly_iphone_bound_multicore_mobile_processor.html

11. AMD-Virtualization (AMD-V) Technology, http://www.amd.com/us/products/technologies/virtualization/Pages/amd-v.aspx

12. "Cisco's Unified Computing System — It's not just a blade center," 30 March 2009. http://www.colinmcnamara.com/ciscos-unified-computing-system-its-not-just-a-blade-center

13. "Cisco Unified Computing System Extended Memory Technology Overview," Cisco white paper, March 2009, p. 1. http://www.cisco.com/en/US/prod/collateral/ps10265/ps10280/ps10300/white_paper_c11-525300.pdf

14. "Hoff's Metastructure and the Intercloud," 29 June 2009, http://www.infra20.com/post.cfm/hoff-s-metastructure-and-the-intercloud; and "Inter-Cloud Rock, Paper, Scissors: Service Brokers, Semantic Web or APIs?", 27 July 2009, http://www.rationalsurvivability.com/blog/?s=intercloud.

15. "Inter-Cloud Rock, Paper, Scissors: Service Brokers, Semantic Web or APIs?", 27 July 2009. http://www.rationalsurvivability.com/blog/?s=intercloud

16. "Competitive Advantages: Mainframe," Mainframe Executive, 6 May 2008. http://www.mainframe-exec.com/articles/?p=19

NOTES

17. "Ellison Insists Sun's Sparc Still Has a Future," The 451 Group in Seeking Alpha, 13 May 2009, http://seekingalpha.com/article/137375-ellison-insists-sun-s-sparc-still-has-a-future; and "Rock (processor)," http://en.wikipedia.org/wiki/Rock_(processor).

18. "IBM lifts the veil on Power7 chips," *The Register*, 21 July 2009. http://www.theregister.co.uk/2009/07/21/ibm_power7_details/page2.html

19. Chris Gibson, "Implementing Micro-Partitioning on the IBM p5 595 Server," SysAdminMag.com, 7 May 2008. http://gibsonnet.net/aix/595MicroPartitioning.pdf

20. "On Cloud z," *IBM Systems Magazine*, March-April 2009, http://www.ibmsystemsmag.com/mainframe/marchapril09/ittoday/24328p2.aspx; and "Fujitsu and Sun Boost SPARC Enterprise Server Performance and Virtualization," *Cloud Computing Journal*, 21 July 2009, http://au.sys-con.com/node/1042067/.

21. "IBM and SAP preview live motion between clouds," CNET News, 3 March 2009. http://news.cnet.com/8301-19413_3-10186589-240.html

22. "Rackable Doubles Up Server Density," Internet.com, 24 June 2008. http://www.internetnews.com/hardware/article.php/3754811 Note: Rackable Systems was renamed SGI (Silicon Graphics International Corp.) in May 2009, after acquiring Silicon Graphics, Inc.

23. "Google uncloaks once-secret server," CNET News, 1 April 2009, http://news.cnet.com/8301-1001_3-10209580-92.html; and "Inside A Google Data Center," Google Data Center Efficiency Summit, 1 April 2009, http://www.youtube.com/watch?v=bs3Et540-_s

24. http://www.sgi.com/icecube

25. "Google App Engine Stalled Out for About 6 Hours Today," TechCrunch, 2 July 2009. http://www.techcrunch.com/2009/07/02/google-app-engine-broken-for-4-hours-and-counting

26. "What Went Down At Rackspace Yesterday? A Power Outage And Some Backup Failures," TechCrunch, 30 June 2009. http://www.techcrunch.com/2009/06/30/what-went-down-at-rackspace-yesterday-a-power-outage-and-some-backup-failures/

27. "Google uncloaks once-secret server," CNET News, 1 April 2009. http://news.cnet.com/8301-1001_3-10209580-92.html

28. Cassatt Active Response, Data Center Edition, http://www.cassatt.com/prod_data_center.htm

29. "Clearing the air on cloud computing," McKinsey & Company, March 2009, slide 29. http://uptimeinstitute.org/content/view/353/319 (Requires registration.)

30. Luiz André Barroso and Urs Hölzle, Google Inc., "The Datacenter as a Computer," 2009, p. 2. http://www.morganclaypool.com/doi/pdf/10.2200/S00193ED1V01Y200905CAC006

NOTES

31. Michael Isard, Microsoft Research, "Autopilot: Automatic Data Center Management," April 2007. http://research.microsoft.com/pubs/64604/osr2007.pdf

32. CASCADAS Project Demonstration Event, 28 October 2008. http://www.cascadas-project.org/demo_London.php

33. "Extreme Data: Rethinking the "I" in IT," CSC Leading Edge Forum, 2005, p. 2. http://assets1.csc.com/lef/downloads/1140_1.pdf

34. "HP brings storage, servers into one rack," *Computerworld*, 6 May 2008. http://www.computerworld.com/s/article/9083198/HP_brings_storage_servers_into_one_rack?taxonomyId=19&intsrc=kc_top&taxonomyName=storage

35. "Examine the Digital Storage Market in Consumer Electronics 2008, as Storage Capacity Requirements Could Double Those of the Average User," Reuters, 15 August 2008. http://www.reuters.com/article/pressRelease/idUS153548+15-Aug-2008+BW20080815

36. The data in chart form is at http://www.willus.com/archive/cpu/2006/hard_drive_price_history.png, and this chart appears in PCWorld at http://www.pcworld.com/article/127104-3/the_hard_drive_turns_50.html

37. "Bandwidth: How much is enough?," TelephonyOnline, 1 July 2008. http://telephonyonline.com/access/commentary/how-much-bandwidth-0701/

38. "Hard Disk Drive Market Likely to Go Down in 2009," HubPages, February 2009, http://hubpages.com/hub/Hard-Disk-Drive-Market; and "Worldwide Hard Disk Drive 2009-2012 Forecast: Navigating the Transitions for Enterprise Applications," IDC, February 2009, http://www.electronics.ca/publications/products/Worldwide-Hard-Disk-Drive-2009%252d2012-Forecast:-Navigating-the-Transitions-for-Enterprise-Applications.html

39. "DataSlide Says Revolutionary HD is Closer," StorageSearch.com, 13 July 2009. http://www.storagesearch.com/diskwin.html

40. "How many terabytes can you fit on a 2.5-inch hard drive?," *The Register*, 30 September 2008. http://www.theregister.co.uk/2008/09/30/hdd_areal_density_improvements/page2.html

41. "Sun beefs servers with SSDs," *The Register*, 11 March 2009. http://www.theregister.co.uk/2009/03/11/sun_ssd_servers/

42. "Mass Data Storage Trends: HDD Technology," November 2008. http://www.connectorsupplier.com/tech_updates_MassDataStorageTrends_11-18-08.htm

43. Introducing DroboPro, http://drobo.com/products/drobopro/

44. "SD and Memory Stick cards to hit 2TB: What you need to know," CNET UK, 8 January 2009. http://crave.cnet.co.uk/accessories/0,39101000,49300513,00.htm

NOTES

45. Eduardo Pinheiro, Wolf-Dietrich Weber and Luiz André Barroso, "Failure Trends in a Large Disk Drive Population," Google white paper, February 2007, p. 4. A link to the paper is at "Google's Disk Failure Experience," StorageMojo, 19 February 2007, http://storagemojo.com/2007/02/19/googles-disk-failure-experience/

46. What is ZFS?, OpenSolaris.org, 18 September 2008. http://www.opensolaris.org/os/community/zfs/whatis/;jsessionid=7A34AEE6DAACCB6534BE511593A

47. "Cloud Storage FUD," presentation by Alyssa Henry, General Manager, Amazon S3, USENIX Conference on File and Storage Technologies, 25 February 2009. http://www.usenix.org/events/fast09/tech/ (See video.)

48. "Amazon S3 Storage Service Goes Down, Still Not Up," GigaOM, 15 February 2008. http://gigaom.com/2008/02/15/amazon-s3-service-goes-down/

49. "Google File System Eval: Part 1," StorageMojo, 2006. http://storagemojo.com/google-file-system-eval-part-i/

50. "Hadoop and Distributed Computing at Yahoo!", http://developer.yahoo.com/hadoop/

51. "XML and RDBMS: 10 years on," Simple-Talk, 25 August 2006. http://www.simple-talk.com/opinion/opinion-pieces/xml-and-rdbms-10-years-on/

52. "IBM Researcher Solves In-Cloud Data Encryption Puzzle," Cloud Computing Journal, 26 June 2009. http://cloudcomputing.sys-con.com/node/1015761

53. "The Cloud and the Future of DBMSs," presentation by Michael Stonebraker at TTI Vanguard conference, "Ahead in the Clouds," 19 February 2009, slide 2.

54. "Database War Stories #7: Google File System and BigTable," O'Reilly Radar, 3 May 2006, http://radar.oreilly.com/archives/2006/05/database-war-stories-7-google.html. See also Fay Chang, Jeffrey Dean, Sanjay Ghemawat, Wilson C. Hsieh, Deborah A. Wallach, Mike Burrows, Tushar Chandra, Andrew Fikes and Robert E. Gruber, "Bigtable: A Distributed Storage System for Structured Data," Google white paper, November 2006, http://labs.google.com/papers/bigtable.html.

55. HyperTable, http://www.hypertable.org/

56. Daniel Abadi, Stavros Harizopoulos, Sam Madden and Michael Stonebraker, "Horizontica — A New Approach to OLTP Data Bases," MIT CSAIL Research Abstracts 2007. http://publications.csail.mit.edu/abstracts/abstracts07/stonebraker-abstract2/stonebraker-abstract2.html

57. "Debunking a Myth: Column-Stores vs. Indexes," The Database Column blog, 18 July 2008, http://databasecolumn.vertica.com/2008/07/debunking-a-myth-columnstores.html; and Michael Stonebraker, Samuel Madden, Daniel J. Abadi, Stavros Harizopoulos, Nabil Hachem and Pat Helland, "The End of an Architectural Era (It's Time for a Complete Rewrite)," VLDB '07, 23-28 September 2007, http://cs-www.cs.yale.edu/homes/dna/papers/vldb07hstore.pdf. See in particular section 5.3, Results.

NOTES

58. "Connected World: Redefining the Geography of Business and How We Work and Play," CSC Leading Edge Forum, 2006, pp. 3 and 5. http://assets1.csc.com/lef/downloads/1139_1.pdf

59. "The Network is the Computer," Jonathan Schwartz's Blog, 20 March 2006. http://blogs.sun.com/jonathan/entry/the_network_is_the_computer

60. "New Cisco Visual Networking Index Forecasts Global IP Traffic to Increase Fivefold by 2013," Cisco press release, 9 June 2009. http://newsroom.cisco.com/dlls/2009/prod_060909.html

61. "Hyperconnectivity and the Approaching Zettabyte Era," Cisco white paper, June 2009, Figure 1, p. 4. http://www.cisco.com/en/US/solutions/collateral/ns341/ns525/ns537/ns705/ns827/VNI_Hyperconnectivity_WP.html

62. "Hyperconnectivity and the Approaching Zettabyte Era," Cisco white paper, June 2009, Figure 2, p. 5. http://www.cisco.com/en/US/solutions/collateral/ns341/ns525/ns537/ns705/ns827/VNI_Hyperconnectivity_WP.html

63. Cisco Unified Fabric, http://www.cisco.com/en/US/netsol/ns945/index.html

64. "100 Gigabit Ethernet: Bridge to Terabit Ethernet," *Network World*, 20 April 2009. http://www.networkworld.com/news/2009/042009-terabit-ethernet.html

65. "Add Another Zero: An Interview with Larry Smarr," *Educause Review*, Vol. 38, No. 6, November/December 2003, http://www.calit2.net/newsroom/article.php?id=313; and "CENIC Announces Winners of Its Gigabit Awards," 7 May 2003, http://www.calit2.net/newsroom/article.php?id=552.

66. "UK Company Highlights Role of its 10 Gigabit Ethernet Technology in GreenLight Project," Calit2 press release, 4 March 2009, http://www.calit2.net/newsroom/article.php?id=1482; and "Project GreenLight: Measuring the Energy Cost of Applications, Algorithms, and Architectures," CENIC Awards Presentation, 10 March 2009, http://www.calit2.net/newsroom/presentations/lsmarr/2008/ppt/CENIC_031009.ppt.

67. "3D Virtual Reality Environment Developed at UC San Diego Helps Scientists Innovate," Calit2 press release, 17 September 2008, http://www.calit2.net/newsroom/release.php?id=1383; and "$2,600,000 UC San Diego Energy Efficient Computing Project, Heavily Instrumentation & Monitoring, to Calculate Performance/Watt," Green Data Center blog, 28 July 2008, http://www.greenm3.com/2008/07/2600000-uc-san.html.

68. "First Terabit Speed Computing Technology," The X-Journals, 28 January 2009. http://x-journals.com/2009/first-terabit-speed-computing-technology/

69. "10G Ethernet: can copper cut the mustard?," *Computerworld*, 2 September 2008. http://www.computerworld.com.au/article/258872/10g_ethernet_can_copper_cut_mustard?pp=2&fp=4&fpid=78268965

70. "Copper 10 Gigabit Ethernet NICs unveiled," *Network World*, 18 January 2007. http://www.networkworld.com/newsletters/lans/2007/0115lan2.html

NOTES

71. "Juniper sees data center opportunity despite poor economy," *Network World*, 26 February 2009. http://www.networkworld.com/news/2009/022609-juniper.html?page=2

72. Cisco Data Center Ethernet, http://www.cisco.com/en/US/solutions/collateral/ns340/ns517/ns224/ns783/qa_c67-461717.html

73. "IP-based home automation systems flaunt convergence, scalability," Global Sources, 6 May 2009. http://www.security.globalsources.com/gsol/I/Home-automation/a/9000000104655.htm

74. "US Broadband Penetration Grows to 63% — US Broadband Penetration Jumps to 94.7% Among Active Internet Users," June 2009 Bandwidth Report. http://www.websiteoptimization.com/bw/0906/

75. Broadband Internet Statistics, 2007, http://www.internetworldstats.com/dsl.htm

76. "Broadband Subscriber Total Tops 400 Million," TelecomWeb, 24 November 2008. http://www.telecomweb.com/news/broadband/charts/262012.html

77. "China broadband to reach 139m by 2010," International Telecommunication Union, 4 September 2006. http://www.itu.int/ituweblogs/treg/China+Broadband+To+Reach+139m+By+2010++.aspx

78. "Trans-Atlantic Internet cables may be filled by 2014," TechWorld, 23 June 2009. http://www.techworld.com.au/article/308437/trans-atlantic_internet_cables_may_filled_by_2014

79. "Digital Virtual Concatenation Protocol Enables Super-Wavelength 40G Service Transmission over Trans-Oceanic and High PMD Networks," February 24-28, 2008. http://ieeexplore.ieee.org/Xplore/login.jsp?url=http%3A%2F%2Fieeexplore.ieee.org%2Fiel5%2F4512186%2F4528018%2F04528153.pdf%3Farnumber%3D4528153&authDecision=-203

80. "Cable Technology — Alaska Communication Systems Selects Nortel 40G Optical Network," TMCnet, 4 September 2008. http://cable.tmcnet.com/topics/cable/articles/38803-alaska-communication-systems-selects-nortel-40g-optical-network.htm

81. "NEC's Submarine Cable System," NEC presentation, 5 December 2008, slide 8. http://www.nec.co.jp/ir/en/pdf/081205/081205_01.pdf

82. "Intel dubs 2009 'The Year of 10Gb Ethernet,'" *The Register*, 3 March 2009. http://www.theregister.co.uk/2009/03/03/10gbe_gains_ground/

83. "Terabit Ethernet possibilities," *The Register*, 16 February 2009. http://www.theregister.co.uk/2009/02/16/terabit_ethernet_optics/

84. "Satellite broadband seeing improved adoption across Europe," Top 10 Broadband, 9 July 2009. http://www.top10-broadband.co.uk/news/2009/07/satellite_broadband_seeing_improved_adoption_across_europe/

85. "Mobile Broadband Users and Revenues Forecast Pack to 2014," Ovum Plc, 2 April 2009. http://www.marketresearch.com/product/display.asp?productid=2270654

NOTES

86. "Verizon Wireless to light up LTE in 20 to 30 markets in 2H 2010," Engadget, 15 May 2009, http://www.engadget.com/2009/05/15/verizon-wireless-to-light-up-lte-in-20-to-30-markets-in-2h-2010/; and "LTE to edge out WiMax," ZDNet Asia, 15 January 2009, http://www.zdnetasia.com/insight/specialreports/tech-outlook/2009/0,3800017920,62050038,00.htm.

87. "Notebook Sales Outpace Desktop Sales," eWeek.com, 24 December 2008. http://www.eweek.com/c/a/Midmarket/Notebook-Sales-Outpace-Desktop-Sales/

88. "Netbooks pushing into enterprises in Asia," ZDNet Asia, 11 May 2009. http://www.zdnetasia.com/news/hardware/0,39042972,62053924,00.htm

89. "Five enterprise apps for the iPhone," CNET News, 3 September 2008. http://news.cnet.com/8301-1001_3-10031431-92.html

90. "HP Continues to Create 'Enterprise Netbooks,'" Mobility Site, 30 June 2009. http://mobilitysite.com/2009/06/hp-continues-to-create-enterprise-netbooks/

91. "Study Finds Employees Expect Mobile Access to Enterprise Applications," Open Kernel Labs press release, 5 May 2009. http://www.ok-labs.com/releases/release/study-finds-employees-expect-mobile-access-to-enterprise-applications#

92. "Akamai Delivers Record Streaming and Web Content During Historic Presidential Inauguration," Akamai press release, 20 January 2009. http://www.akamai.com/html/about/press/releases/2009/press_012009.html

93. "e-Prescribing Utility Boosts Massachusetts' Rx Standards," CSC case study, http://www.csc.com/service_oriented_architecture/case_studies/9258-e_prescribing_utility_boosts_massachusetts_rx_standards. See also "CSC Blazing the Trail to a Nationwide Health Information Network," http://www.csc.com/government/ds/11284/12758-csc_blazing_the_trail_to_a_nationwide_health_information_network.

94. "BPM Adoption and Delivered Value/ROI — Market Research and Analysis," Business Process Management (BPM) — Insights blog, 21 November 2008. http://bpmfundamentals.wordpress.com/2008/11/21/bpm-adoption-and-delivered-value-market-research-and-analysis/

95. "HTML 5: Could it kill Flash and Silverlight?," *InfoWorld*, 16 June 2009. http://www.computerworld.com/s/article/9134422/HTML_5_Could_it_kill_Flash_and_Silverlight_?taxonomyId=11&intsrc=kc_feat&taxonomyName=development

96. "Google Wave Drips With Ambition. A New Communication Platform For A New Web," TechCrunch, 28 May 2009. http://www.techcrunch.com/2009/05/28/google-wave-drips-with-ambition-can-it-fulfill-googles-grand-web-vision/

97. "Forrester: Enterprise Mashups to Hit $700 Million by 2013," ReadWriteWeb, 6 May 2008. http://www.readwriteweb.com/archives/forrester_enterprise_mashups.php

98. Arthur, *The Nature of Technology*, p. 193.

99. Arthur, *The Nature of Technology*, p. 198.

ACKNOWLEDGMENTS

Rick Muñoz, Yale Esrock and Doug Neal conducted the research for the *Cloud rEvolution* report series. Working on *Cloud rEvolution* has deepened their appreciation for the innovation, efficiency and untapped potential of cloud computing for the enterprise.

Rick Muñoz (left) is a senior technology architect at CSC and a 2009 LEF Associate. He specializes in emerging information technology platforms and methods, including agile solution delivery using dynamic virtual environments. Rick has delivered technology strategies and IT solutions for many Fortune 500 companies. A member of CSC's Global Business Solutions and Services group, Rick now focuses on developing cloud computing services for clients across multiple industries. rmunoz@csc.com

Yale Esrock (center) is a business process architect in CSC's North American Public Sector and a 2009 LEF Associate. Yale has held key roles in the Program Management Offices of large military and civil government transformation programs, and was a key contributor to the incorporation of Service Oriented Architecture concepts in CSC's Catalyst[SM] methodology. His interest in cloud is on meeting business objectives, while mitigating risk, through the creative application of cloud concepts. yesrock@csc.com

As Research Fellow in the LEF Executive Programme, Doug Neal (right) is responsible for research on "Innovating through Technology." Doug began researching enterprise cloud computing under the guise of IT consumerization. He led cloud computing study tours in Silicon Valley in 2008 and 2009 and consults with enterprises on cloud strategy. Doug's research interests also include green IT, collaborative technologies and Web 2.0. dneal@csc.com

The LEF thanks the many others who contributed to the *Cloud rEvolution* report series.

Jeff Allen, *Cisco*
Jeff Barr, *Amazon*
W. Brian Arthur, *Santa Fe Institute*
Justin Barney, *3Leaf Systems*
Randy Bias, *Stratospheric*
Brian Boruff, *CSC*
Lisa Braun, *CSC*
Jeff Budge, *CSC*
Simon Crosby, *Citrix*
Cees de Groot, *Marktplaats*
Scott Dowell, *CSC*
Mike Dyer, *CSC*
Martin English, *CSC*
Michael Ernesto, *CSC*
Jim Fenner, *CSC*
Chris Fleck, *Citrix*
Glenn Gravatt, *CSC*
Mike Groner, *Appistry*
Phil Grove, *CSC*
Daniel Gubber, *CSC*
Nigel Healy, *CSC*
Randy Hill, *CSC*
Christofer Hoff, *Cisco*
Gabe Kazarian, *CSC*
Bob Lozano, *Appistry*
Mark Masterson, *CSC*
Byron Miller, *CSC*
Daniel Mintz, *CSC*
Jim Moran, *ETS*
Peter Nickolov, *3Tera*
Erika Mir Olimpiew, *CSC*
Purnima Padmanabhan, *MokaFive*
Nicholas Payne, *CSC*
David Pickup, *CSC*
Srinivas Polisetty, *CSC*
Tony Puerto, *CSC*
Bob Quinn, *3Leaf Systems*
Billy Rollin, *CSC*
Robert Rosenwald, *CSC*
Alit Bar Sadeh, *GigaSpaces*
Bob Slook, *CSC*
Larry Smarr, *California Institute for Telecommunications and Information Technology (Calit2)*
Tomas Soderstrom, *NASA Jet Propulsion Laboratory*
Michael Stonebraker, *Vertica*
John Taylor, *ETS*
Simon Wardley, *Canonical*
John Willis, *Cloud Cafe*

Worldwide CSC Headquarters

The Americas
3170 Fairview Park Drive
Falls Church, Virginia 22042
United States
+1.703.876.1000

Europe, Middle East, Africa
The Royal Pavilion
Wellesley Road
Aldershot
Hampshire GU11 1PZ
United Kingdom
+44(0)1252.534000

Australia
26 Talavera Road
Macquarie Park NSW 2113
Australia
+61(0)29034.3000

Asia
139 Cecil Street
#06-00 Cecil House
Singapore 069539
Republic of Singapore
+65.6221.9095

About CSC

The mission of CSC is to be a global leader in providing technology enabled business solutions and services.

With the broadest range of capabilities, CSC offers clients the solutions they need to manage complexity, focus on core businesses, collaborate with partners and clients, and improve operations.

CSC makes a special point of understanding its clients and provides experts with real-world experience to work with them. CSC is vendor-independent, delivering solutions that best meet each client's unique requirements.

For more than 50 years, clients in industries and governments worldwide have trusted CSC with their business process and information systems outsourcing, systems integration and consulting needs.

The company trades on the New York Stock Exchange under the symbol "CSC."

Produced in USA 0469-10 09/09

LEADINGedgeforum 2009

Cloud rEvolution:
The Art of Abstraction

Volume 2

CSC

As part of CSC's Office of Innovation, the Leading Edge Forum (LEF) is a global community whose programs help participants realize business benefits from the use of advanced IT more rapidly.

LEF members work to spot key emerging business and technology trends before others, and identify specific practices for exploiting these trends for business advantage. Members enjoy access to a global network of thought leaders and leading practitioners, and to a powerful body of research and field practices.

LEF programs give CTOs and senior technologists the opportunity to explore the most pressing technology issues, examine state-of-the-art practices, and leverage CSC's technology experts, alliance programs and events. LEF programs and reports are intended to provoke conversations in the marketplace about the potential for innovation when applying technology to advance organizational performance. For more information about LEF programs, visit www.csc.com/lef.

The LEF Executive Programme is a premium, fee-based program that helps CIOs and senior business executives develop into next-generation leaders by using technology for competitive advantage in wholly new ways. Members direct the research agenda, interact with a network of world-class experts, and access topical conferences, study tours, information exchanges and advisory services. For more information about the LEF Executive Programme, visit lef.csc.com.

LEF LEADERSHIP

WILLIAM KOFF (left)

Vice President and Chief Technology Officer, Office of Innovation

A leader in CSC's technology community, Bill Koff provides vision and direction to CSC and its clients on critical information technology trends, technology innovation and strategic investments in leading edge technology. Bill plays a key role in guiding CSC research, innovation, technology thought leadership and alliance partner activities, and in certifying CSC's Centers of Excellence and Innovation Centers.
wkoff@csc.com

PAUL GUSTAFSON (above right)

Director,
Leading Edge Forum

Paul Gustafson is an accomplished technologist and proven leader in emerging technologies, applied research and strategy. Paul brings vision and leadership to a portfolio of LEF programs and directs the technology research agenda. Astute at recognizing how technology trends inter-relate and impact business, Paul applies his insights to client strategy, CSC research, leadership development and innovation strategy.
pgustafs@csc.com

RICHARD DAVIES (left)

Vice President and Managing Director, LEF Executive Programme

Richard Davies directs a global, strategic research and advisory program aimed at helping CIOs and other enterprise IT leaders understand and exploit the ever-expanding intersection between business and information technology. Richard has over 20 years of experience in the IT market and has held a variety of sales and marketing positions both nationally and internationally.
rdavies5@csc.com

DAVID MOSCHELLA (above right)

Global Research Director,
LEF Executive Programme

David Moschella guides a series of strategic research initiatives aimed at helping CIOs and other enterprise IT leaders benefit from the growing intersection between business and information technology. David's key areas of expertise include globalization, industry restructuring, disruptive technologies, environmental strategies, and the co-evolution of business and IT. He is an author and former columnist on IT industry trends.
dmoschella@csc.com

In this ongoing series of reports about technology directions, the LEF looks at the role of innovation in the marketplace both now and in the years to come. By studying technology's current realities and anticipating its future shape, these reports provide organizations with the necessary balance between tactical decision making and strategic planning.

The Cloud rEvolution *report series examines the technology and business aspects of cloud computing. Although each volume is valuable on its own, the full scope of the* Cloud rEvolution *is best obtained by reading all the volumes. To receive the entire* Cloud rEvolution *series, visit www.csc.com/lefreports or subscribe to the LEF RSS feed: www.csc.com/lefpodcast*

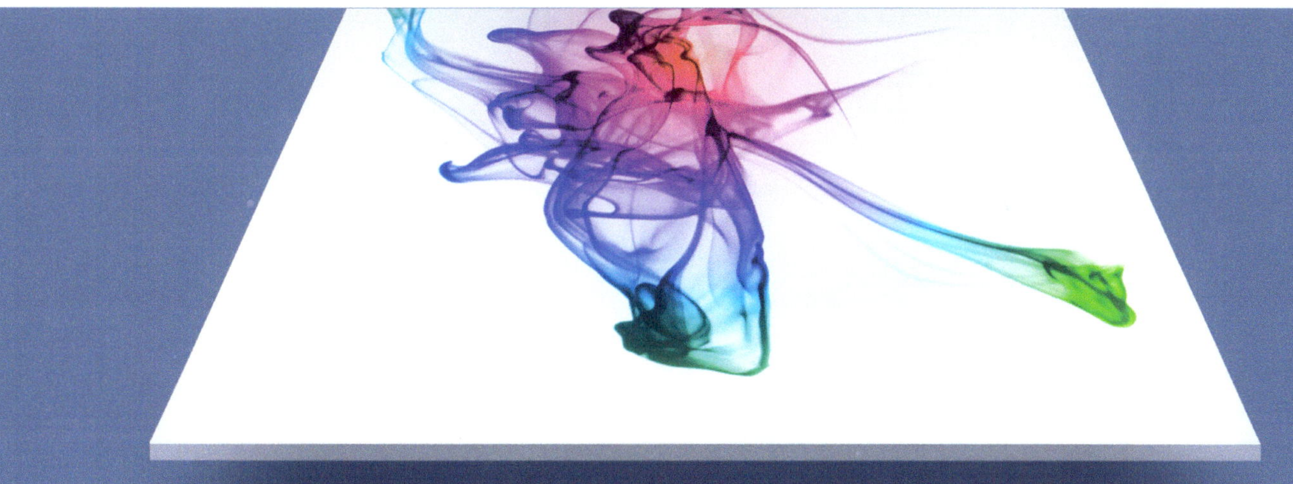

Cloud rEvolution: The Art of Abstraction

Volume 2

CONTENTS

Get all LEF reports by subscribing to the LEF RSS feed: www.csc.com/lefpodcast

Preface

Supercomputers assembled from game stations. Data storage for a few cents per gigabyte. A mobile phone that runs full-scale applications like a computer. A network that spans the globe and extends into space. A server that fragments into multiple virtual machines, each of which can do its own thing and be turned on and off like a light switch. Processor, memory and I/O resources that are liberated from the confines of a single server and shared dynamically across the data center. An entire portable, disposable infrastructure that is comprised of software instead of hardware.

Welcome to the new world of information technology (IT). In this new world, a marketing manager who wants to do a detailed data analysis of national sales can fire up a few virtual machines for half an hour and do it on the spot. No more waiting months for a free server in the data center and being at the mercy of IT to carry out the request. Order up your computing, pay for it with a credit card and run the analysis yourself — all for the cost of lunch.

Sweeping changes underway in IT — namely, cloud computing and its underlying building blocks — are yielding unprecedented speed and agility, the ability to do more with less, and new levels of cost savings. Since the business can only change as fast as IT, these changes are having an enormous impact on the business's ability to unleash innovation and address changing markets and customers ahead of the competition.

The Cloud rEvolution *report tackles these sweeping changes in a four-volume series. Volume 1,* **Laying the Foundation**, *introduces the Cloud rEvolution and explores the digital foundations — the core building block technologies — that lay the groundwork for cloud computing. Volume 2,* **The Art of Abstraction**, *explores how abstraction loosens the IT stack, providing flexibility and efficiency as a precursor to the ultimate abstraction: the cloud. Volume 3 focuses on* **The Cloud Effect**, *describing the impact the cloud is having on IT and business tactically and strategically. Volume 4,* **A Workbook for Cloud Computing in the Enterprise**, *provides practical guidance for transitioning to the cloud, which is rapidly becoming a question of when and how, not if.*

A MORPHING OF THE DIGITAL DOMAIN

As we saw in Volume 1 of the *Cloud rEvolution* series,[1] cloud computing represents a morphing of the digital domain, as described by economist Brian Arthur in *The Nature of Technology: What It Is and How It Evolves*.[2] This morphing has been greatly enabled by abstraction, long used in the world of IT as a way to mask complexity. "Abstraction provides the secret sauce that positions hardware and software for services in the cloud and, in so doing, completely transforms the digital domain," asserts Paul Gustafson, director of the Leading Edge Forum.

As Arthur puts it, "A domain morphs when one of its key technologies undergoes radical change."[3] In this case the key technology is all of IT in its traditional on-premise delivery, radically changed by new combinations of technologies and techniques that lay the groundwork for cloud computing. Abstraction is the catalyst of the new combinations. Abstraction shows the morphing of the digital domain in action.

With abstraction, we can do in minutes what used to take days or weeks.

The digital domain itself facilitates abstraction. Arthur describes this: "Digitization allows functionalities to be combined even if they come from different domains, because once they enter the digital domain they become objects of the same type — data strings — that can therefore be acted upon in the same way."[4] In short, if something in IT can be represented as digital data or software, it can become another abstraction to be manipulated and morphed.

In addition to new combinations, a key benefit of abstraction is reduced cycle times. With abstraction, we can do in minutes what used to take days or weeks. For example, we can replace a virtual server in minutes rather than a physical server in days. Further, we can match IT demand to supply far more accurately, doing away with the excess IT inventory that has plagued the industry. This inventory shake-up is reminiscent of the U.S. manufacturing shake-up that took place when just-in-time

DÉJÀ VU IN IT: FROM JUST-IN-CASE TO JUST-IN-TIME

At one time the U.S. manufacturing industry was the envy of the world. However, with long lead times; "just-in-case" policies that required large safety stocks and resulted in excessive inventory; and a penchant for expensive, complex, high-end machinery, the industry was rocked when formidable competition seemed to come out of nowhere.

Armed with new paradigms such as the Toyota Production System, just-in-time manufacturing, and the use of numerous small, simple, inexpensive machines that could be quickly set up, Japanese companies defied the conventional wisdom of the day and swiftly came to dominate world manufacturing. Using these methods, Japan was able to closely match supply to demand, drastically cut inventories and lead times, and produce high-quality products at relatively inexpensive price points. The rest is history.

That history seems to be repeating itself in the IT industry. Cloud providers such as Amazon, Google and Salesforce.com have seemingly come out of nowhere with new paradigms of IT supply and demand that are causing many to rethink how they do IT. These cloud providers make extensive use of IT abstraction concepts to gain unprecedented benefits and capabilities. As a result, these providers can supply IT capacity quickly, in any amount, at a reasonable price.

Companies availing themselves of these cloud services can:

- avoid upfront purchases of IT resources
- obtain IT resources immediately
- eliminate internal safety stock of unused IT capacity
- closely match their supply of IT capacity to actual demand by obtaining their safety stock from the cloud, and at attractive price points

The result is transformational: business can now match IT demand to supply, with no waiting. As with the manufacturing sector, this changes the game in IT, opening up a whole new world of business opportunities.

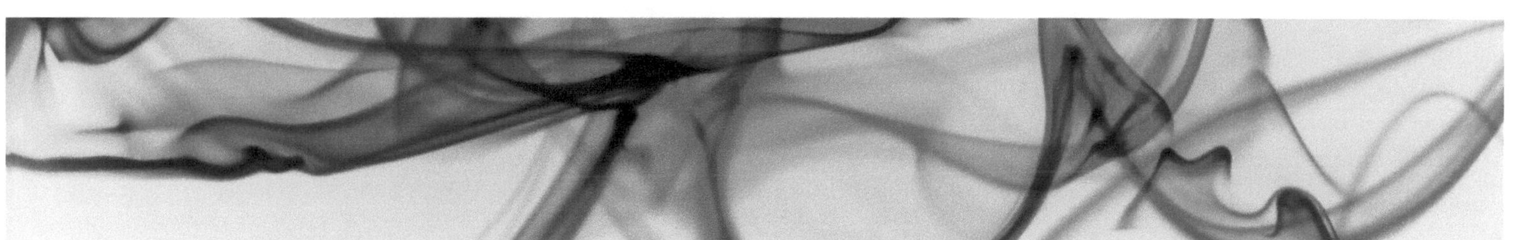

approaches were introduced from Japan in the 1980s. Just-in-time manufacturing has given way to just-in-time IT.

Figure 1 MORPHING THE DIGITAL DOMAIN

Owned/operated here

Accessed/ rented out there

MORPHING THROUGH ABSTRACTION

STAGE 1

TRADITIONAL IT

- Physical IT resources owned by the enterprise
- Tight coupling of dedicated IT products
- Low resource utilization
- On-premise resource delivery

STAGE 2

ABSTRACTED IT

- Virtualized IT resources (e.g., hardware, software, networking and storage)
- Loose coupling of flexible IT resources
- New combinations of abstracted IT resources

STAGE 3

CLOUD-SERVICED IT

- Physical resources owned by third-party provider
- IT resources shared by many independent organizations (e.g., multitenant)
- Remote delivery of abstracted resources via service interfaces
- Resources globally available on demand
- Massively scalable resources "rented" as needed

Source: CSC

That is why abstraction techniques — including various types of virtualization, services and multitenancy — often play a direct role in helping cloud providers manage their massive infrastructure and offer their services cost-effectively.

In addition, when used within the enterprise data center, many of these same abstractions not only have direct, tangible benefits but also help make us comfortable with the notion that we need not always have knowledge of the details of the underlying technical implementation and location. For example, desktop virtualization, a form of abstraction, shows us that our desktop environment can be delivered over the network rather than from our local hard drive. This plants the seed that the desktop can be served from the network, and ultimately the cloud. It is not such a big leap, then, to imagine letting all our IT services be provided from the cloud.

Indeed, services are the big story of abstraction. Virtualization and other forms of abstraction have been at work for some time shifting enterprise IT from products to services, from "owned and operated here" to "accessed and rented out there" on the network. Abstraction, in rendering services, lays the foundation for cloud computing, which is transforming IT from specific technology implementations in the on-premise data center to software-accessible services consumed over the Internet. Figure 1 shows the evolutionary stages from traditional on-premise IT to abstracted IT to cloud.

The *Cloud rEvolution* series parallels these stages. Volume 2, this volume, explores stage 2 by examining abstraction, the core catalyst of the morphing of the digital domain. Volumes 3 and 4 delve into stage 3 through *The Cloud Effect* and *A Workbook for Cloud Computing in the Enterprise*, respectively.

Stage 2 has strengths in its own right, bringing new and important capabilities to IT. Abstraction starts to break down the rigid data center in stage 1. If we peer inside this data center, we see the traditional monolithic IT stack shown in Figure 2. By making the stack more flexible, abstraction paves the way for combining and recombining technology components into numerous uses. These new "arrangements," as Arthur calls them,[5] are the basis for new products, services and efficiencies.

Figure 2 TYPICAL IT STACK

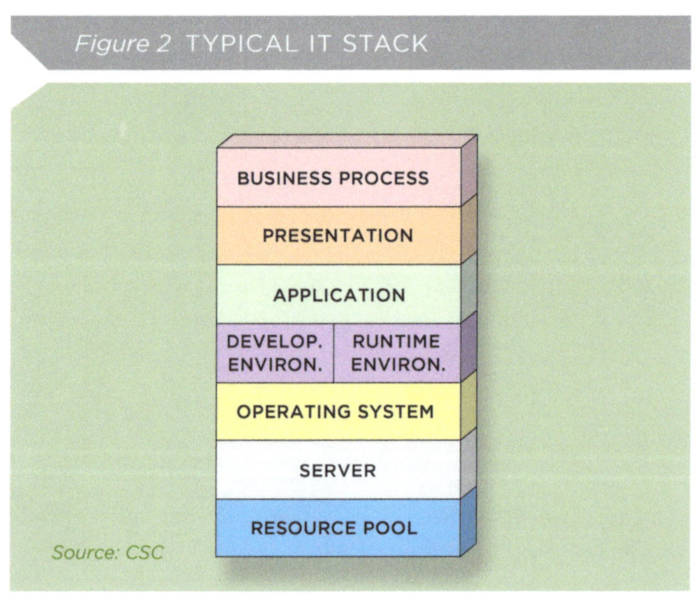

MASKING COMPLEXITY AND FREEING RESOURCES

Abstraction is a way of making something usable without getting caught up in the underlying details. The prototypical "black box" (see Figure 3) is a case in point: you can make full use of a black box without having to understand how it works. Its inner workings are hidden — abstracted — from the user, who only has to focus on inputs and outputs. Put another way, the external interface is decoupled from the box's internal machinery. This "letting go" — abstraction — spreads innovation, allowing non-experts to use the box and combine it with other components.

Figure 3. A black box allows users to focus exclusively on inputs and outputs.

Source: CSC

OUTPUT
?
INPUT
BLACK BOX

The entire digital domain, including the IT industry, is based on building abstractions on top of one another. For example, digital computing itself is based on the basic abstraction of using different voltage levels to represent the "1s" and "0s" of a binary language, and binary values are used to represent complete systems of human intelligence and knowledge. In fact, by applying accepted abstractions, IT has become a universal means for manipulating, storing and using information.

Other illustrations abound. For example, an application programming interface (API) is an abstraction of the actual application, allowing interaction with the application software without knowing its underlying technical details. APIs turn the application into a black box. The Web itself is an abstraction, where HTML — an abstraction of a Web page — is produced by distant servers and then rendered in a browser for people to read.

More recently, Service Oriented Architecture (SOA) concepts have emphasized abstraction by implementing layers of services that are usable by automated consumers that are provided a narrative service description, specification of inputs and outputs, and a Service Level Agreement (SLA) but no physical details of the underlying technology.

Abstraction techniques, primarily in the form of virtualization, have assumed new importance in IT today. Abstraction can be found at all levels of the IT stack and has the effect of "flexing the stack" by separating and buffering the stack layers, freeing them to change and evolve independently. (See Figure 4.)

In essence, abstraction makes computer resources more malleable. Properly implemented, it provides the basis for enhancing IT flexibility, using IT resources more efficiently, reducing IT costs, simplifying resource management, improving reliability, "greening" the data center and minimizing vendor lock-in.

In the remainder of this volume we explore abstraction in more detail, taking an overall look at virtualization, examining hardware and software virtualization in more depth, reviewing other forms of abstraction, and introducing a form of abstraction that assumes increased importance for cloud computing: cloud services.

Figure 4 TYPICAL IT STACK WITH ABSTRACTION

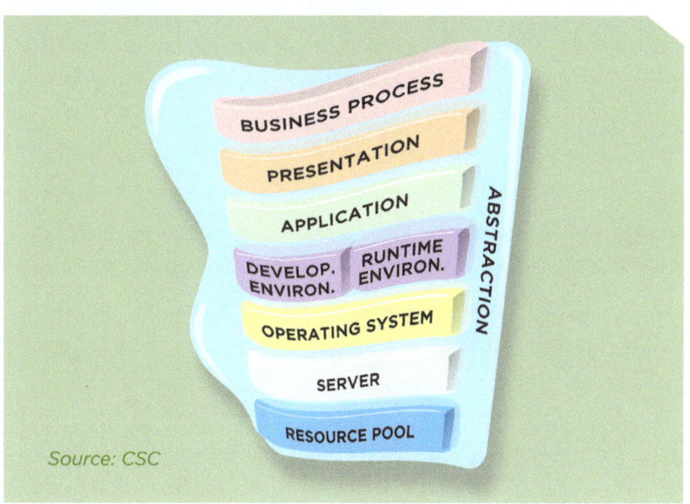

Source: CSC

THE VIRTUAL WORLD OF IT

In the virtual world of IT, nothing is as it seems. One server may appear to be many servers, or many servers may appear to be one. A user's desktop may be running on a server in the data center while the user thinks it is running on his local client device. An application may run on a user's client even though it was never actually installed there. Human or machine users may think they are using a single source of storage when, in reality, the data is on scores of heterogeneous, dispersed storage devices. Geographically dispersed teammates in a work group may appear to enjoy their own private communication network even though they are actually attached to different segments of the general enterprise network. Hardware infrastructure may not be hardware at all but, instead, software representations of the hardware functionality. Welcome to the wonderful world of virtualization.

Although various forms of virtualization have been around since mainframe days, economic and environmental pressures coupled with hardware and software advances are bringing virtualization to the forefront as an important set of technologies available today for use with industry standard, commodity servers. Virtualization has become a powerful way to optimize the use of physical infrastructure and provide more flexibility. It has also become a core strategy for managing infrastructure services provided from the cloud, public or private. (Public and private clouds are discussed in Volume 3, *The Cloud Effect*.) For example, virtualization enables provisioning on demand, a key characteristic of cloud computing.

Analysts have listed virtualization as one of the key strategic technologies for the past couple of years. With these technologies it is now possible to virtualize almost any aspect of enterprise IT. For example, storage virtualization may be used to simplify management of numerous heterogeneous, dispersed storage devices by creating a single virtual storage space (a vdisk) that maps to actual physical storage devices. As another common example, at the infrastructure level virtual private networks (VPNs) are a form of network virtualization that allows external or mobile users to securely access the internal enterprise network, while virtual local area networks (VLANs) can either combine different physical networks into a single virtual network or split a single physical network into multiple, isolated virtual networks.

Already, these kinds of abstractions are being combined to deliver flexible and encrypted networking communications within the cloud. Amazon recently announced the availability of its Virtual Private Cloud (VPC), which combines VPNs, VLANs and other network abstractions to allow cloud-based systems to operate as if they sit inside a customer's own data center.[6] Google's Secure Data Connector and Cohesive FT's VPN-Cubed are two other offerings that securely link corporate data centers to public clouds. (Virtual private clouds are discussed in Volume 3, *The Cloud Effect*.)

In general, virtualization creates a layer of abstraction between layers or components in the stack. This abstraction layer decouples components, allowing them to evolve independently, and providing the opportunity to modify how the components appear to, and interact with, each other. This opens the door to greater innovation since modifying at the component level provides greater flexibility and more potential arrangements of use than modifying at a higher (more monolithic) level. At the same time, virtualization results in implications for decision making that potentially impact the business as well as the technology. By abstracting away lower-level details, we accept those details as given (thus abrogating our decision rights at that level) and can then concentrate on technical and business issues and decisions at higher levels of the stack.

We will now take a more detailed look at some of the forms of virtualization that have the potential to significantly impact operations in both on-premise and cloud data centers.

VIRTUALIZING HARDWARE

Hardware virtualization has emerged as the primary tool for supporting the flexible, efficient, green, dynamic data centers of the future. Virtualization of hardware resources, as described in Volume 1,[7] started with virtual machines, where a single physical machine can run multiple operating systems. Going far beyond simple virtual machines, several hardware virtualization approaches can be applied in enterprise data centers today:

- a single server can be "liquefied" into many independent machines
- the basic resources within a server can be liberated and shared in pools across the data center
- the entire infrastructure can be made portable and disposable by providing its functionality with software instead of hardware.

Many of these same techniques often play an important role in enabling cloud service providers to efficiently manage large infrastructures and offer cloud services economically and safely. Using virtualization, providers can "seal off" portions of their infrastructure, allowing disparate users to employ virtual representations of it without negatively impacting the physical infrastructure itself, and without negatively impacting portions of the infrastructure being used by the provider for other purposes.

THE LIQUID SERVER

Think of a server as a frozen glass of water. The server has traditionally been as rigid as a glass of ice, with the hardware (the glass) and operating system (the water) frozen together as one unit. But when this tight coupling is loosened, that leads to new flexibility. If the operating system is virtualized, its bond with the hardware melts. The original block of ice breaks down into multiple ice cubes, each cube a virtual machine running its own operating system, each separate but still within the confines of one glass (physical server). The tight coupling melts. Each ice cube can even be moved to a different glass.

Thus, the physical server becomes a liquid server by virtualizing the operating system (server virtualization). Server virtualization has rapidly become the key element in transforming the data center and addressing server sprawl. In the past it has been common practice to dedicate one or more physical servers to a specific application. These servers are usually oversized in order to handle peak loads. The result in many data centers is large numbers of servers that:

- take up space, consume power and require cooling (idle computers can consume up to 50 percent of their total power consumption while contributing no value[8])
- must be procured, installed, cabled, configured, repaired and decommissioned
- have a high total cost of ownership (a physical server's total cost of ownership can be 10 times its capital cost due to all the "touch labor" and the procurement and life cycle labor[9])
- have very low average utilization (common estimates are five percent[10]).

Further, when new servers are needed, approval for capital expenditure is required. This can stifle innovation because the need for compute resources must be justified beyond a reasonable doubt, or else risk assumptions must be accepted. In addition, a fairly lengthy procurement and installation cycle can delay availability of new machines for months. A typical procurement cycle alone can take four to 12 months. In some cases, by the time the infrastructure comes online, requirements have changed and the new equipment does not meet the changed needs. The result: utilization is low and business goals are not met.

The Benefits of Liquid. Server virtualization is a solution to many of these issues, providing faster and more flexible deployment than traditional procurement methods. Server virtualization provides an abstraction that liquefies the frozen coupling between operating system and hardware. Using a virtual machine monitor or hypervisor technology, server virtualization partitions a physical host server into multiple guest servers or virtual machines (VMs). Each VM is independent and believes it has its own dedicated hardware. Each VM can be independently and dynamically booted and shut down, and each can run its own applications and operating system, all managed together across many physical servers with VM management tools.

Depending on how virtualization is implemented, each VM may run a different operating system, none of which has to match the host operating system. For example, a Linux 64-bit server can simultaneously host a VM running Unix, a VM running Linux 32-bit, a VM running Windows 32-bit, a VM running Windows 64-bit, etc. Depending on configuration, consolidation can be as high as 30:1 (30 VMs on a single physical server).

Hardware virtualization has emerged as the primary tool for supporting the flexible, efficient, green, dynamic data centers of the future.

Coupled with consolidation is improved utilization. Construction contractor Bechtel Corporation, for example, has achieved 70 percent server utilization using virtualization.[11] Such a high utilization rate enables significant server consolidation and the attendant cost savings. Fewer servers lower capital expenditures, reduce space requirements in the data center, require less power and cooling, and can be managed with fewer people.

Achieving benefits like these drove CSC to create a powerful virtualization solution for a large manufacturer by using Sun Microsystems servers and Sun's Solaris container technology. This was believed by Sun to be the first production implementation of virtual servers using Sun containers. The virtualization consolidated 47 servers onto six, with no reduction in performance or functionality for users, and required only one-eighth the floor space. Patching and daily maintenance activity has been dramatically minimized because of the smaller footprint and how the containers are engineered. Patch one server template and all virtual servers receive the benefits of the patch. Backup is done at a global level, not for each individual virtual machine. Overall, the CSC team expects a 40-60 percent reduction in the cost of ownership for the new environment. And because servers can be provisioned in near real time, this translates to the bottom line since costs drop sooner and business is not held up. The technology can be applied to production, development and test, and proof-of-concept environments. In 2009 the virtualization work was recognized for its technical and business impact as a CSC Chairman's Award for Excellence finalist.

Another example of the dramatic impact of virtualization is the UK's National Health Service. NHS needed a new patient care record system to support over 28 million patients, 540,000 hospital-based health professionals and 15,000 general practitioners in over 6,000 locations. This massive system demanded rapid server deployment and infrastructure provisioning, extreme service availability and information integrity, and high levels of data sharing with comprehensive provisions for security and access control.

The solution to these complex issues, developed by a CSC-led alliance, relies on a healthy dose of virtualization. NHS operates approximately 8,000 servers. Of these, approximately 4,200 are virtual servers hosted on some 360 physical servers (averaging 11:1 VMs on a single physical server). The virtual servers run VMware ESX, making this one of the world's largest single installations of VMware ESX. Nearly 80 percent of the servers (virtual and physical) are in production or near-production environments.

In addition to server virtualization, NHS takes advantage of presentation virtualization, a form of application virtualization. (Presentation virtualization is discussed on pages 61-63.) There are over 1,300 Citrix XenApp presentation servers in production, each delivering business applications to the equivalent of 50-100 concurrent users depending on the application.

OASIS PROVIDES SERVER SPRAWL RELIEF

To virtualize or not to virtualize — that is the question. How do you know the answer?

CSC has created an assessment, the Optimization Assessment and Systems Integration Study (OASIS), to help enterprises answer the virtualization question and others in an effort to combat server sprawl and optimize IT resources. OASIS assesses the IT environment and provides a five-year roadmap for how to maximize investment, whether through virtualization, database stacking, right-sizing or other techniques.

An OASIS study analyzes 12 key data elements about the enterprise's IT environment (servers, storage, networks) and issues four reports: a site breakdown report, a platform breakdown report, an environmental report ("green report") and an ROI report. The reports are used to create an enterprise view of current and future IT states and contain data on server frame and operating system counts, square footage, racks, power, cooling and carbon dioxide emissions. The ROI report helps enterprises prioritize IT expenditures and focus on the optimization paths that will have the most positive impact on the business. Recommendations are based on the cost of implementing the technique relative to the overall savings estimated over five years.

The heart of OASIS is its rules engine, which analyzes the 12 data elements. The engine contains optimized sets of rules, based on CSC best practices and industry standards, to assess the data in areas such as location, availability, work stream, architecture, storage, backups, archives and usage. Recommendations are customized to the client's environment, unlike the one-size-fits-all solutions common in the industry.

OASIS can scan the entire enterprise environment and provide a baseline inventory in 24 hours. A full assessment can be performed and results returned in one to two weeks. (Similar analyses in the past have taken from three to six months.) To date, over 20 assessments have been conducted, covering more than 20,000 servers. In one case, OASIS recommended virtualizing two-thirds of the client's environment, for a potential savings of $4 million.

"OASIS takes an enterprise view of the overall infrastructure, not a silo view, to provide guidance on how to maximize IT investment," says Billy Rollin, OASIS model designer. OASIS received the CSC Chairman's Award for Excellence in 2009.

OASIS provides relief when trying to optimize the vast desert of IT servers, storage devices and networks.

Architecture Recommendations

Tiered Storage

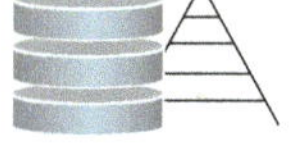

Archival Recommendation

Data Protection

Availability

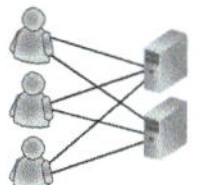

Standardized Architecture (PODs)

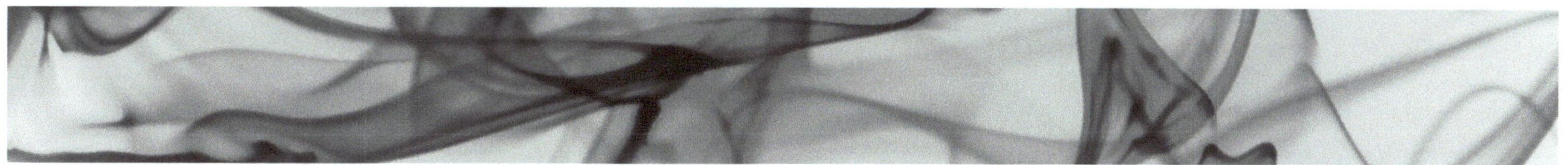

The results of the solution are significant. At the time of deployment, data center improvements included 480 fewer racks, 720 fewer square meters of floor space, power savings of over 80 million kilowatt-hours, and carbon dioxide savings of 48 million kilograms annually (equivalent to removing more than 8,200 20-mph cars from the road).[12]

These types of benefits are attractive to any large enterprise, including military organizations. In the Consolidated Network Operations Center (CNOC) that supports both the U.S. European Command (USEUCOM) and the U.S. Africa Command (USAFRICOM), CSC supported enterprise consolidation by implementing server virtualization. Some 40 percent of 250 servers were virtualized. Most of these virtual servers, created with help from CSC, were consolidated onto just eight physical servers.

In addition to saving money, electrical power and server rack space, a major benefit was faster provisioning and reduced labor costs for building and maintaining servers. Labor for building virtual servers was reduced by using templates that were already patched, configured and compliant with Defense Information Systems Agency security guidelines. Instead of building a physical server from scratch, a point-in-time snapshot of the virtual machine could be captured, a copy of which could be deployed at any time. This saved valuable time when bringing new servers online.

The impact on the IT administrator is reduced time to restore servers in a virtualized environment. A copy of the server configuration is stored and can be applied to another virtual server in a fraction of the time (less than an hour) it would take to rebuild and configure a new server (approximately eight hours). This was critical in an operational environment like USEUCOM/USAFRICOM, which had limited tolerance for downtime. With any virtual environment, new requirements and expansion can be met quickly with minimal impact; the only requirement is having enough software licenses to support the new capabilities in the virtual environment.

Recognizing the many benefits of server virtualization — reductions in hardware, provisioning time, maintenance costs, excess capacity, power consumption and cooling requirements — CSC has implemented a Virtualization First policy in its data centers. Virtualization First aggressively imposes virtualization on all new systems (using an exception process). In 2008, Wintel server virtualization rates were eight to nine percent. Virtualization First targets 60 percent virtualization by mid-2012 for all existing Wintel systems.

Virtualization is already a common foundation for many emerging cloud service providers. Amazon uses the open source hypervisor Xen,[13] Microsoft uses its own Hyper-V, and Rackspace[14] uses a mix of VMware, Xen and other enterprise hypervisors to provide cloud services. Virtualization gives these companies the means to divvy up their massive hardware resources into an abundance of VMs that can be started and stopped at any time.

LIBERATING SERVER RESOURCES

A traditional server is a self-contained piece of hardware constructed from various modules such as processors, memory and I/O boards. These basic resources are integral to the server and are available for use only by the server. If the server does not fully use its resources, those resources are wasted.

What if, however, the resources within a server could be liberated? What if these basic compute resources could be "extracted" from each server and aggregated together into data-center-wide resource pools that could be drawn from as needed? This would simplify management since entire resource pools could be managed instead of large numbers of individual servers. Spikes in demand could be more easily accommodated. And, resource usage would be improved since pool resources could be dynamically allocated to form virtual servers with various characteristics as needed. Servers would no longer be limited to just their internal resources. Virtual servers with very large amounts of memory or processing power could be constructed on-the-fly and could grow and shrink on demand without needing a reboot.

This type of technology is demonstrated by 3Leaf Systems with its Virtual Compute Environment (VCE), which harnesses the resources of many commodity x86 servers to deliver variable performance levels. (See Figure 5). Using both ASIC and software technologies, commodity switch fabrics of up to 20 gigabits per second of networking bandwidth per server, and processor interconnects from both AMD and Intel, VCE allows a single guest operating system to span multiple cores and physical servers with shared memory across servers. The result is a flexible computing fabric that can deliver small server or supercomputer performance.

Figure 5. 3Leaf Systems' Virtual Compute Environment frees compute resources from the confines of individual x86 servers and shares them in pools across the data center.

Source: 3Leaf Systems

This type of capability proved valuable to a large supercomputing center that was looking to build out a new high performance computing (HPC) environment. Traditionally, such a high capacity, shared memory environment would have required investing in expensive, non-x86, proprietary hardware (i.e., "Big Iron"). However, a recent benchmark showed that 3Leaf's commodity hardware approach combining 128 processor cores and 512 gigabytes of memory on 32 x86 processors performed as well as a 144 core non-x86 machine costing several times the price.

"3Leaf has created a low-cost x86 technology that allows an unmodified Linux or Windows operating system to scale from one CPU core and a small amount of memory all the way to 128 cores and one terabyte of memory, totally on-the-fly. Computing resources can respond to changes in demand, including spikes, by instantaneously assigning just enough resources to service the load. This creates a new level of agility not found in today's data centers," declares 3Leaf chairman, founder and chief technology officer Bob Quinn.

PORTABLE, DISPOSABLE INFRASTRUCTURE

Not only can servers be liquefied and server resources liberated, but the entire underlying hardware infrastructure — including application servers, switches, routers, firewalls, storage and other infrastructure components — can be provided by virtual infrastructure appliances. These appliances contain software that duplicates the functionality of specific pieces of hardware. The software runs in self-contained environments packaged in virtual machines that can be deployed on any virtualization environment, thus eliminating the need for specialized physical hardware. Using this approach, the entire infrastructure needed to support an application can then be packaged together with the application as a single object or component. The infrastructure is implemented by deploying this component onto a grid of commodity servers, where each appliance boots into a usable piece of infrastructure. The result: a functional infrastructure rendered in software that actually runs as if specialized hardware components were in place.

This functional infrastructure is both portable and disposable, and has its own resource requirements such as maximum CPU, memory and bandwidth usage. Because the software infrastructure is packaged with the application, the application along with its entire supporting infrastructure can be easily cloned to another node on the network. This could be a node in the on-premise data center or in another data center across the globe. When the application is shut down, the functional infrastructure releases its resources back to the grid for use by other applications. (See more on virtual appliances in "Virtual Appliances: Software Stack to Go" on pages 65-66.)

3Tera's AppLogic Cloud Computing Platform software accomplishes this in a very intuitive way. Described as "a grid operating system for Web applications," AppLogic creates a disposable infrastructure that exists for the duration of the application and then is "dissolved" — i.e., given back to the resource pool.[15] AppLogic uses virtual software appliances that contain software implementations of infrastructure components complete with an operating system and everything the component needs to run. 3Tera not only provides its own infrastructure appliances but also an app store from which users can select a wide variety of third-party appliances.

Using a Visio-like interface, the user drags and drops icons representing the infrastructure appliances onto a palette to construct a diagram of the desired infrastructure. (See

Figure 6.) The icons are preconfigured with certain operational characteristics, such as resource requirements, and can be modified with the click of a mouse. When the diagram is complete, a single click is all that is needed to actually assemble and deploy the designed infrastructure onto a grid of commodity servers, either in the internal data center or over the network at a third-party site. When the application is no longer needed, the infrastructure dissolves and the grid nodes are freed up. In its simplified, component-style assembly, AppLogic is like a modern version of a CASE tool or a scripting language — an innovative, contemporary packaging of software components to create virtual infrastructure.

When the application is no longer needed, the infrastructure dissolves and the grid nodes are freed up.

International News Media (INM), an Internet marketing and content delivery company, is taking advantage of disposable infrastructure via AppLogic. As an Internet-based services company whose offerings include IPR Wire, a press release service, and I BLOG IT, a business blogging platform, INM must be able to cost-effectively manage and scale infrastructure to meet rapidly growing demand in a competitive market. According to INM CTO Gabriel Kent, "We moved all of our applications from a colocation provider into a virtual private datacenter [using AppLogic] and never looked back. Everything needed to create and deploy Web-scale infrastructure, including gateways, load balancers, Web servers, clustered storage and databases, is available within a mouse click. Now, if I want, I can even manage our datacenter, deploy new applications and add resources while sitting at the corner coffee shop."[16]

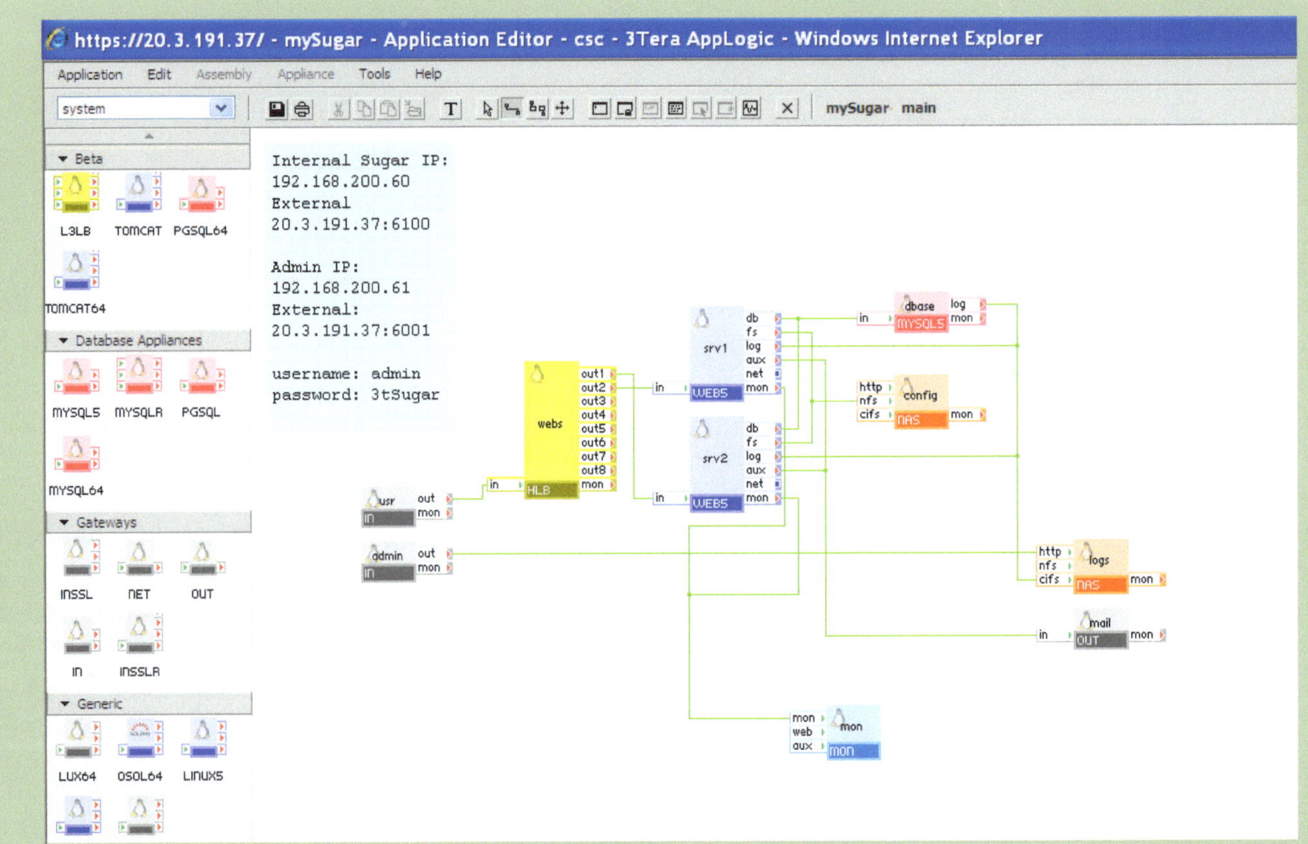

Figure 6. This disposable infrastructure for a Customer Relationship Management application shows input and output gateways (gray), a load balancer (yellow), two Web servers (blue), a shared storage device (orange, top) and a database (pink). The infrastructure is modeled using 3Tera's AppLogic software, which uses drag-and-drop techniques to configure and modify the infrastructure. When the application is no longer needed, the infrastructure is freed up for other applications.

Source: CSC

VIRTUALIZING SOFTWARE

The typical enterprise uses hundreds if not thousands of pieces of software including business applications, productivity software, system software, middleware and utility software. In addition to software installed on the server, there is software installed exclusively on client devices as well as client-server software that may, in a thick client implementation, have substantial functionality installed on the client as well. Most of this software is developed to run in specific environments targeted at specific types of hardware devices using specific software stacks. This severely limits flexibility and makes software distribution and management difficult.

With the rise of the Internet and the Web, several technologies emerged that partially addressed this limitation. The use of "applets," small application components in Java, allowed some automatic shifting of application capabilities so they could run inside the browser. JavaScript, Flash and AJAX are now all staples of creating richer Web interfaces, where small pieces of the application are shifted to the browser to enhance the user's experience. However, the use of these thin-client technologies has not eliminated the need for a full desktop system with many locally running applications. Even as the Web begins to offer limited versions of desktop applications (like Google Docs), the need for full desktop environments has not significantly diminished in the enterprise IT world, where hundreds of millions of PCs or similar client devices are still deployed.

Because of the large number of client devices in the enterprise, client-side software management has often been a significant burden. Desktop administration — including provisioning, securing and maintaining large numbers of desktops — is often a huge, costly, ongoing task for many organizations. Distribution and installation of applications on the desktop is another related issue. A common historical approach has been the heavily tested Standard Operating Environment (SOE), but this comes with performance issues (e.g., long time to boot) and long lead-times spent in testing, with applications often taking up to a year to be rolled out. Compounding the problems is an increasingly mobile workforce that needs access to its computing environment from many different venues outside the enterprise using an increasing array of mobile devices.

Server-side software management issues also abound, and specific stacks are required for software to function. These types of problems affect not only the enterprise but also software vendors. A developer bringing a product to market faces a conundrum: either develop the software to run on one specific operating system (in which case a large number of potential customers may be excluded), or develop different versions for different operating systems (in which case development and maintenance costs are high).

These types of issues are difficult to address in traditional software environments due to the nature of the prevailing architecture. If layers of the IT stack can be separated and buffered, however, this provides flexibility to implement new architectures and provide new options such as those that better address mobility. Virtualization does just that. Various forms of virtualization — including application virtualization, desktop virtualization and virtual appliances — can be combined to begin resolving thorny software distribution and management issues. Further, they open the door to ultimately managing and distributing software from afar — from a cloud.

Virtualization opens the door to ultimately managing and distributing software from afar — from a cloud.

APPLICATION VIRTUALIZATION

Application virtualization helps to break apart the stack by abstracting the application from the underlying operating system and hardware, or separating the application interface from the application logic. With application virtualization, applications are centralized instead of being installed locally on the client device. The application is installed on servers in the data center, where it can be monitored, controlled, updated and secured from a single console. No need for IT to manage each client device individually. In addition to improving IT management, application virtualization improves the quality of the user experience because isolating the application in its own virtual environment can provide a more stable environment for the application to run in.

Application virtualization can be deployed in two ways: client-side application virtualization and server-side application virtualization, depending on whether the application executes on the client or on the server.

Client-Side Application Virtualization. With client-side application virtualization, a master instance of the application is managed centrally in the data center, and a copy runs on the client device even though it is never actually installed there. This approach makes updating and patching applications more efficient (patch once, run everywhere) and helps ensure that users always have the correct software version. To accomplish this trick, application streaming and application isolation are used.

With application streaming, the application is delivered to the client device either in whole or in part. If delivered as a whole, the user may disconnect and work offline, if needed. If delivered in parts, the user must remain connected while working.

In either case, the application runs in isolation. Here's how it works: The application is first virtualized using a one-time packaging or sequencing process. This process creates an abstraction layer that serves as a private virtual environment for the application. The abstraction not only separates the application from the operating system but also isolates the application from other applications that might be running on the same machine. The abstraction layer can be installed on the client operating system — an approach used in Microsoft Application Virtualization (App-V), Symantec Altiris SVS, Citrix XenApp and Trigence AE products — or packaged with the application to form a single executable, as is the case with VMware ThinApp.

Either way, the application itself is never installed on the client but is cached on the client when needed from the master version in the data center, and runs as though it were actually installed. Prepackaging the application and abstraction layer makes the application more portable because it can be executed from any device, including a USB stick.

Client-side application virtualization has come in handy for an application development department creating advanced data analysis applications for the U.S. Secretary of Defense.[17] In its environment, networks are secured and computers locked down so end users don't have administrative privileges to install applications or register code components. This presented a challenge for the group, because the applications had to run flawlessly regardless of the Windows version, which varied from Windows 98 to XP. The applications needed to be able to run from the secured intranet or the computer without installation, and give the end user a consistent and polished experience.

The Department of Defense implemented VMware ThinApp to address the demanding deployment requirements, using it for applications developed in a range of code frameworks and third-party libraries including legacy applications built on Microsoft Access 97, Java, Visual Basic, OpenSource and .NET. Later, the implementation was broadened to encompass commercial applications that were not able to be installed on the locked down desktops. As a result of this approach, installation conflicts, which had run as high as 20 percent, were eliminated; applications were secured due to their own isolated ThinApp environment; the need for regression testing was slashed by 70 percent; the time to release applications was reduced from weeks to hours; and legacy applications were given new life since, without the need for installation, they could now run on new Windows platforms.

In contrast to the DoD approach, which copied (cached) the entire application to the client, applications can also be streamed in a piecemeal fashion. For many applications, only a small portion of the code is actually used at any one time. In this case, the sequencing process determines what portions of the code are commonly needed, when, and in what order. When a user requests the application, only the portions needed for start-up are sent from a streaming server in the data center to the client. More of the application is streamed as needed based on what the user is doing.

For example, with App-V, Microsoft provides just the parts of the software you need, when you need it, over the network, to run on the PC. (See Figure 7.) This is a major departure from Microsoft's mainstay packaged software business. With App-V, nearly any Windows application can be packaged to be streamed in pieces. The resulting applications operate within their own "sandboxes," isolating any system changes from being made directly to the local machine.

Figure 7 MICROSOFT APP-V ARCHITECTURE FOR CLIENT-SIDE APPLICATION VIRTUALIZATION

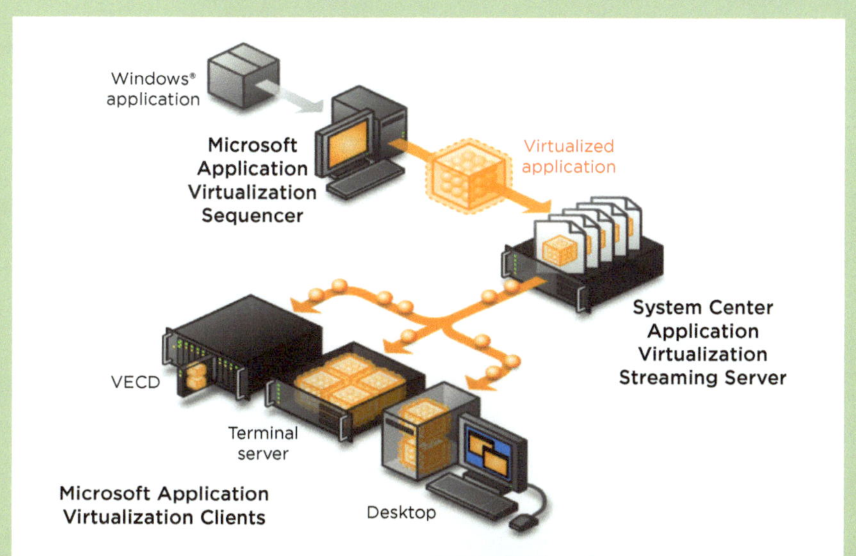

Microsoft App-V architecture consists of an application sequencer (virtualizes the application), one or more streaming servers (delivers the application) and the App-V client (runs the application). Applications are virtualized by the sequencer and stored on central servers for streaming to client devices. Applications execute in an isolation environment on the client without actually being installed on the client — a great boon to IT management.

Source: Microsoft Corporation[18]

As many other vendors are attempting, Microsoft is looking at combining multiple virtualization mechanisms to provide even further abstraction between applications and the hardware. App-V, combined with MED-V (Microsoft Enterprise Desktop Virtualization), combines both application and operating system virtualization, allowing enterprises to dynamically run applications on multiple versions of Windows on a single platform. With further application platform abstractions, such as .NET and Silverlight, Microsoft is moving towards running any application on any operating system on any hardware platform.

Server-Side Application Virtualization (a.k.a. Presentation Virtualization). As described in Volume 1,[19] the Web enables applications to extend their reach through a combination of technologies, from the original HTML to new Web 2.0 tools. Applications running on servers use this combination of technologies to present the application's user interface in the user's browser. Although not a form of virtualization, this abstraction of user interface and interaction has shown how the network extends the reach of applications. Many consumer cloud services are now based on the effective use of Web user interfaces, often rapidly recombined in mashups (new applications assembled from existing ones).

However, the Web interfaces used in the browser are limited to the capabilities of what can be supported by the basic protocols and client-side browser capabilities. For many applications this isn't enough, particularly for those with very expressive and rich user interfaces that are typically only available by having a combination of computation and graphics resources on the local desktop computer (and installing or sending the application, via application virtualization, to run on the client system). What's needed is a way of extending the application's visualization and interface from the server while allowing the application to be accessed from anywhere — to virtualize the application's presentation itself.

Server-side application virtualization (i.e., presentation virtualization) does just that, breaking apart another aspect of the stack by separating an application's presentation interface from its functionality. Instead of sending the application to the user's device, only the presentation interface is sent, and only the user's keystrokes, touches and other interactions are returned.

This improves application management and security because applications and data reside solely in the data center. Worker productivity increases as well because workers can effectively access any application from any device. Since the client device does not need to process the application at all, this frees the application from client-side dependencies and opens the door for running the application on numerous devices.

Citrix provides a good example of presentation virtualization, shown in Figure 8. The master application is copied to and runs on a presentation server in the data center, which also runs the virtualization software Citrix XenApp. XenApp intercepts all of the application's display data and, using the Independent Computing Architecture (ICA) protocol, sends the encrypted display to the client device, which runs a client agent for ICA. The user's interactions (keystrokes, mouse clicks, touches, etc.) are returned to the application on the server.

Figure 8 THE POWER OF PRESENTATION VIRTUALIZATION: WINDOWS ON THE iPHONE

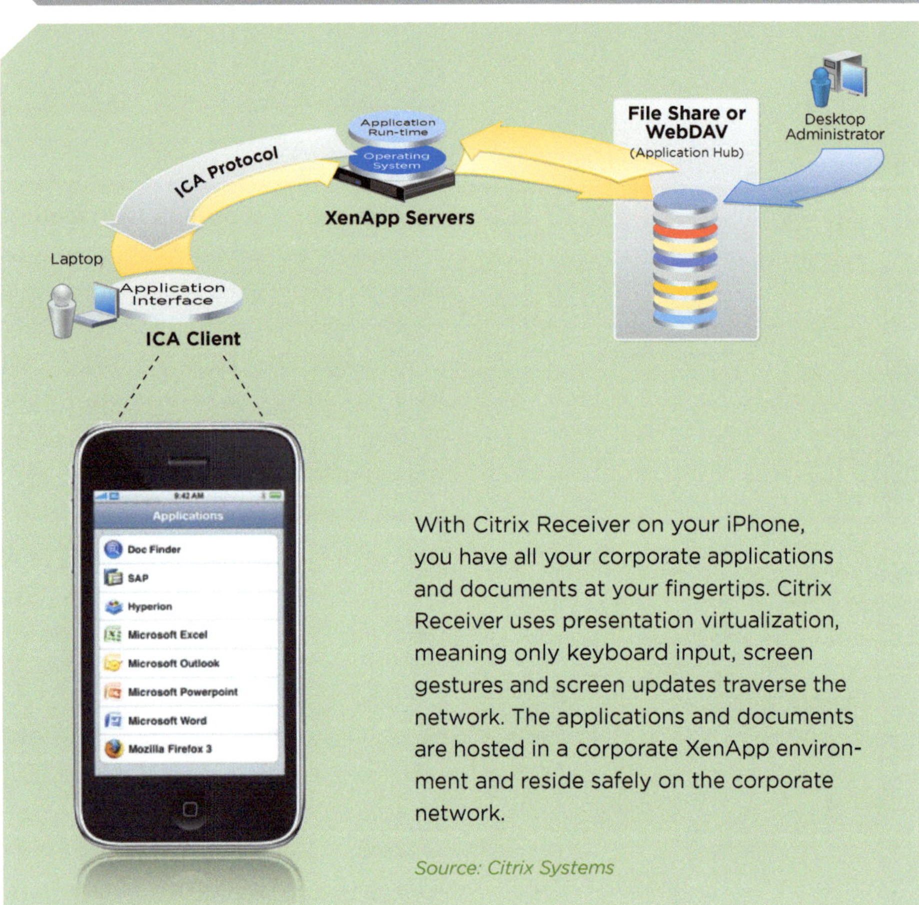

With Citrix Receiver on your iPhone, you have all your corporate applications and documents at your fingertips. Citrix Receiver uses presentation virtualization, meaning only keyboard input, screen gestures and screen updates traverse the network. The applications and documents are hosted in a corporate XenApp environment and reside safely on the corporate network.

Source: Citrix Systems

Presentation virtualization is an extremely useful approach because it allows any application to be accessed by any type of device that runs the ICA client agent, even an intelligent mobile device like the iPhone. With an iPhone running Citrix Receiver (the ICA client agent), you can access your corporate applications and documents from the iPhone, meaning you can edit Microsoft Word documents and PowerPoint presentations on a completely different platform in the palm of your hand. Both you and the iPhone become even more versatile because of this cross-platform capability.

Presentation virtualization is also extremely well-suited to client-server applications. Both the client and the server software run centrally on a server that has more processor, memory and storage capacity than a typical client device. As a result, overall performance is usually improved in spite of a slightly increased amount of network latency. (Note that presentation virtualization can typically work well at a continental level but not a global level due to round-trip speed-of-light issues.)

Outside the enterprise, presentation virtualization is making its mark where you'd least expect it: video games. In late 2009, OnLive is planning on delivering high-end 3D video games with intensive graphics demands to TVs and PCs with limited graphics capabilities. OnLive has developed compression technology that enables it to render the 3D graphics on the server end and then transmit them via video streaming to the end-user device, fast enough to keep the game going as if all the processing was being done locally on a high-end PC. Real-time 3D graphics has traditionally only been possible with local graphics processors. OnLive aims to change that common convention by becoming the first cloud gaming platform.

While OnLive is focusing on the consumer gaming market, traditional enterprise vendors are also exploring the use of server-based realtime graphics rendering for business applications demanding high-end graphics. One example is HP Remote Graphics Software, which extends the Remote Desktop Protocol to support presentation virtualization for CAD/CAM and other 3D applications.[20] Now Autodesk and other engineering software companies are moving to put even the highest-end 3D graphics applications into the cloud.[21]

Presentation virtualization provides a bridge to the cloud. With presentation virtualization technology, cloud providers have started stepping beyond traditional Web-based applications and providing transparent access to applications by virtually extending the presentation from the server, giving users a complete "native" interface while applications continue to reside in the cloud.

Presentation virtualization provides a bridge to the cloud.

DESKTOP VIRTUALIZATION

Virtualization has opened the door to a new managed approach not just for applications but for the entire desktop environment. Traditionally, the corporate desktop environment has been locked down, often through the establishment of standard operating environments and corresponding disk images. Under this approach, specific system environments are provided and changes to it are limited, if not prohibited. This makes the desktops easier to manage — especially when the corporation may have tens of thousands of desktops — but comes at the cost of user flexibility.

Today, however, desktop virtualization can free us from the traditional locked-down desktop. Like the server, the client can be "liquefied" through virtualization to provide a more flexible environment, bringing more freedom to the end user while preserving the need to manage desktops centrally. Desktop virtualization is a step on the journey to cloud computing, for it is about rendering desktop images from the network rather than the local laptop. Virtualization of the desktop environment, like virtualization of individual applications, occurs in two ways: client-side desktop virtualization and server-side desktop virtualization.

Desktop virtualization can free us from the traditional locked-down desktop.

Client-Side Desktop Virtualization. With client-side desktop virtualization, the desktop environment resides on the client but is managed centrally from a master image in the data center. The advantage of this is that users can work offline — they do not need a live connection to the data center — and IT can still manage applications and system software centrally. A timing mechanism can be included that requires users to reconnect after a certain period to ensure that they are using the latest desktop versions. The same timing mechanism is also used to enforce the latest policies, including, for example, the disabling of a desktop environment when a device is stolen or an employee is terminated.

MokaFive provides client-side desktop virtualization in a unique way that combines centralized management with end-user customization. MokaFive refers to its approach as "dynamic compositing" of the desktop. MokaFive's LivePC engine creates a virtual desktop that can be downloaded to any end point, such as a laptop, smart phone or memory device such as a USB stick

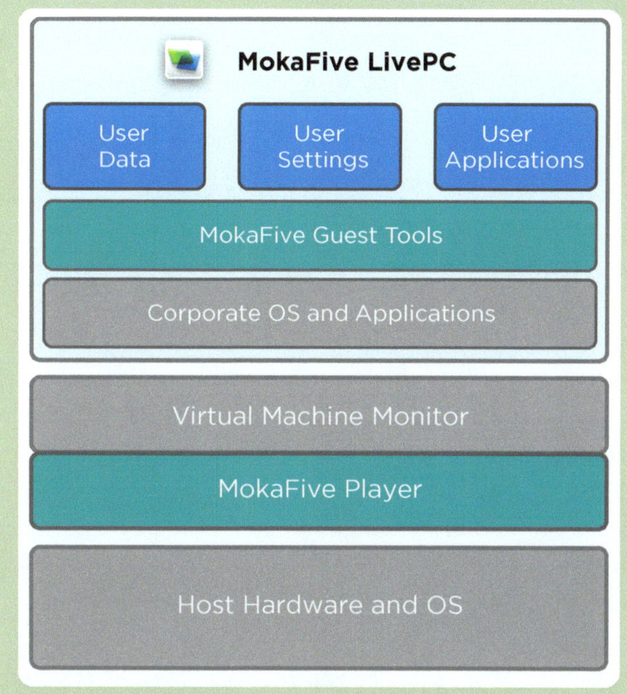

Figure 9. MokaFive LivePC for desktop virtualization breaks the desktop environment into logical layers, separating the corporate environment from the personal environment. Each layer can be managed and delivered independently, creating a device-independent desktop. With LivePC installed in the data center, IT can provide users with their desktops anywhere (work, home, on the road), anytime (online or offline), and on any device (corporate or personal), customized with their personal data, settings and applications.

Source: MokaFive

or memory card. This dynamic compositing of the desktop, on-the-fly, keeps updates and patches to the underlying corporate system current but enables users to customize their settings, personal applications and data. This approach moves desktop management into the cloud, for it enables provisioning and delivery of desktop services from the network, not the end point.

To do this, MokaFive breaks the desktop environment into logical layers, separating the corporate environment from the personal environment. (See Figure 9.) "The user benefits from having a local desktop with his or her customizations, while the IT department benefits from having central management," explains Purnima Padmanabhan, vice president of products at MokaFive. "Personalization will be the key to adoption of the virtual desktop, reflecting the fact that lock-down never really worked."

She continued, "Client-side desktop virtualization accommodates different user needs. You can combine work and personal, Mac or Windows, a laptop or a BlackBerry. It's more like a liquid client."

Server-Side Desktop Virtualization. In server-side desktop virtualization, also called Virtual Desktop Infrastructure (VDI), the desktop environment is hosted and managed centrally in the data center while providing the user with the illusion of a full, client-resident desktop experience. With VDI, the entire client desktop environment, preferences, settings, operating system and applications are hosted on a physical or virtual server in the data center. Each time the user logs in, a fresh desktop image is created and personalized with the user's settings. The user accesses the desktop image using presentation virtualization. Citrix XenDesktop, Sun VDI, Parallels VDI and VMware View provide this type of functionality.

By deploying server-side desktop virtualization, CSC helped the Royal Mail Group in Britain provide its partners with access to Royal Mail's CRM system quickly, flexibly and without sensitive customer information ever leaving Royal Mail's data center.

Using external telesales agencies to support its mailing campaigns gives Royal Mail the flexibility to scale resources up and down as demand fluctuates, but presented Royal Mail with the challenge of how to collaborate effectively. Traditionally, the agencies would be e-mailed spreadsheets, but that was inefficient and a potential security risk. Royal Mail wanted these external sales agents to have access to the same CRM system as its own staff so that performance could be analyzed as one, as well as access to parts of its intranet for detailed product information. The challenge was to provide this access securely, and to be able to scale it quickly.

The solution was CSC Dynamic Desktop, an offering in the CSC Virtual Desktop Services (VDS) family. CSC Dynamic Desktop allows Royal Mail to create virtual desktops with access to only the subset of systems it wants to share, and deliver those applications to the agents remotely. The agents can access their Royal Mail desktops using any computer, over any Internet connection, without any special software. Their desktops, complete with all their personal settings and preferences, are instantly assembled and presented to them when they log in.

Security is built in; nothing is downloaded to users' machines. The only things transmitted are screen changes and user instructions (keystrokes and mouse actions), encrypted using SSL. All the data remains in the Royal Mail data center, where it is easiest to secure.

CSC provides Dynamic Desktop to Royal Mail as an on-demand, managed service. Royal Mail pays only for what it uses. Paul Shepherd, service excellence manager at Royal Mail, says, "The great thing about CSC Dynamic Desktop is that it gives users the fast, personalizable performance they're used to, while we get very fine-grained control over who has access to what and can easily create new partner relationships or sever existing ones if necessary."

CSC is also using server-side desktop virtualization in its business process outsourcing (BPO) centers that service insurance and banking clients. In 2009 CSC intends to replace more than 2,500 desktop computers at 17 BPO sites with virtualized desktops. Workers will access their desktops via ultra-thin clients and will be able to work securely from anywhere, because none of the operational data or software applications is transmitted to or stored outside the data center. The virtualization, called CSC Anywhere Desktop[22] (also a VDS offering), uses Sun Ray ultra-thin clients with built-in smart cards, Sun VDI, Sun Secure Global Desktop Software for Web access to virtual desktops, and Sun servers. Administrators will host and centrally manage the virtual desktops from servers in the data center, while users enjoy a full desktop experience from a thin client that consumes only about four watts of energy.[23] The deployment is part of a larger CSC initiative to enhance security, reduce costs and save energy.

Server-side desktop virtualization is well-suited for call centers and office workers whose IT environment is relatively static. It is also handy for when these workers are mobile.

Server-side desktop virtualization is well-suited for call centers and office workers whose IT environment is relatively static. It is also handy for when these workers are mobile. With virtual desktops, data de-duplication and data mirroring, users can roam the planet and access an exact replica of their desktop. No matter where they are, mobile workers can tap into their corporate desktop, securely and as they last left it. While workers travel, small changes in their desktops are replicated globally. The virtual desktop masks network latency and yields a robust global desktop strategy. At the same time, as illustrated in Figure 10, a server-side virtual desktop strategy lowers the total cost of desktop ownership.

VIRTUAL APPLIANCES: SOFTWARE STACK TO GO

When software is installed, the correct stack — including the correct versions of operating system and higher-level software — must be present. These software layers must be licensed, installed, configured, integrated, tested and managed, or the software won't work properly, if at all. This complexity may be eliminated, however, using pre-packaged software stacks in the form of virtual software appliances. As we have seen, virtual software appliances enable portable, disposable infrastructure. Here we explore virtual software appliances in general and discuss how they make working with software easier because you don't have to worry about the underlying software stack.

Figure 10 TOTAL COST OF OWNERSHIP WITH CSC VIRTUAL DESKTOP SERVICES CAN BE REDUCED BY ABOUT 20 PERCENT

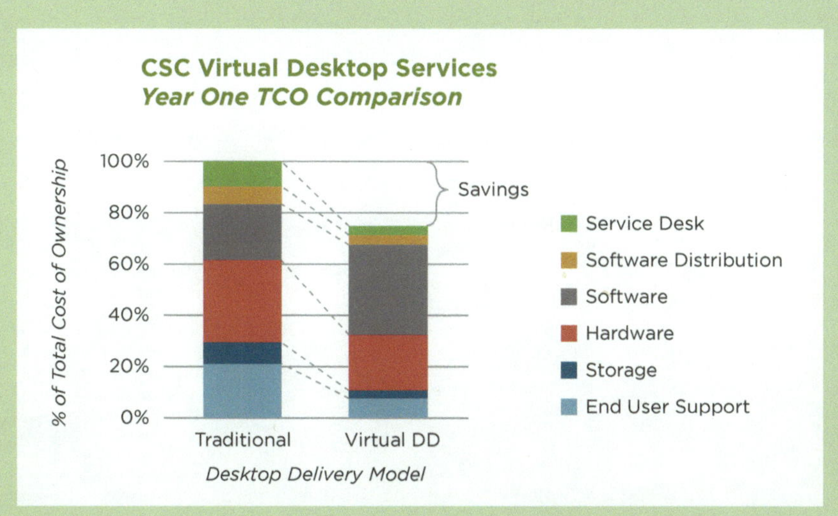

ASSUMPTIONS:

- Traditional desktop is cost baseline for savings
- 5,000 users and a five-year contract
- Per user file storage is five GB
- Windows OS is OEM moving to stand-alone licensing
- Break/fix decreases from 10% to 5% due to device simplicity
- Service calls decrease from 12 to seven calls per year

CAUTIONS:

- This comparison assumes no pre-existing operation.
- Stranded assets are not considered.
- Your depreciation schedule may differ.
- Service options you may select may differ.

Source: CSC

An appliance, like a refrigerator or toaster, performs a specific function and is ready to use "out of the box." A virtual appliance also performs a specific function and comes ready to use. A virtual appliance is a self-contained, pre-tested software environment that is packaged with an application and designed to run on a virtual machine. The appliance contains everything the application needs, including a bare bones "Juice" version of the operating system (i.e., JeOS — just enough operating system), and runs on top of a hypervisor. For example, MediaWiki, the software that underlies Wikipedia, is available as an appliance and contains "all the necessary software, including operating system, database and MediaWiki, to run a wiki installation as a black box."[24] Using the appliance relieves developers from manually installing MediaWiki, which can be time consuming. If you install the MediaWiki appliance on a virtual machine, you have a virtual appliance.

This format is especially useful when software is licensed from a vendor. The vendor can develop, maintain and distribute his application more efficiently by packaging it as a virtual appliance. The customer can implement the application quickly and easily, knowing it will run properly without having to worry about building, installing and configuring the underlying software stack. Distribution of the application is a snap since the appliance is ready-to-go out of the box. Instances may be deployed by simply copying the appliance.

Virtual appliances also provide flexibility and choice in the data center by abstracting the application from the data center operating environment. Because it is already packaged with its own operating system, a virtual appliance does not care what operating system is used in the data center. Within the appliance, the application is developed to work with a specific operating system, yet the appliance can run anywhere regardless of operating system.

A good example of these concepts is the JumpBox Open Collection, a set of open source Web applications packaged as virtual appliances that will run on almost any virtualization platform or hypervisor. JumpBoxes are available for project management, Web site management, customer relationship management, IT infrastructure management, and a host of others. JumpBoxes are even available on Amazon's EC2 service through the Cloud Gear service.[25] rPAth's rBuilder, on the other hand, is a product that allows custom packaging of virtual appliances for any purpose, optimized to run on any hypervisor.

Open source vendor Zenoss used rBuilder to make its IT management software easier to install.[26] Zenoss needed to get its Linux-based software up-and-running in front of potential customers as quickly as possible for effective sales demonstrations. This ease of installation also had to transfer to the implementation of the product in the customer's working environment. However, many Zenoss customers lacked the knowledge to install and administer Linux. This knowledge gap discouraged potential customers from considering Zenoss, despite their appreciation of the product's features. On the flip side, those customers that used Linux and Unix often required the software to be ported to each platform and Linux distribution. This sapped resources from Zenoss engineers, who had to worry about operating system compatibility instead of focusing on new features.

Zenoss realized that the virtual appliance approach was the best way to quickly enter its target markets without extra engineering effort. Using rBuilder has enabled Zenoss to demonstrate a working instance of a very complex enterprise product in a few minutes. This same quick installation experience is then available to customers. For customers wary of Linux, they can install Zenoss in a virtualized environment running on Windows (VMware ESX, Citrix XenServer or Microsoft Hyper-V) without having to tackle an unfamiliar operating system. The virtual appliance allows Zenoss's customers to run the solution on their platform of choice. Knowledge of Linux is no longer a barrier. The operating system detail has been abstracted away.

OTHER ABSTRACTIONS

Although virtualization is one of the most widely used forms of abstraction, other abstractions — cloud desktops, Web abstractions, multitenant architectures, warehouse-size computer grids and managed code platforms — are freeing up IT resources for new combinations that support the rise of the cloud.

CLOUD DESKTOP

Once we accept the data center managing the desktop in a virtualized way, from the network, the next stop is the cloud (see Figure 11). We can expect an entire industry to form to deliver and manage these new desktop arrangements.

For example, a number of companies are looking at abstracting the desktop into the cloud, not through desktop virtualization but by storing in the cloud all aspects of what the user thinks of as the desktop. The result is that the user's "desktop" is available on all devices, not just installed on a single PC or available through a virtual client running on a server. Instead of a virtual desktop, this is an *abstracted* desktop, where the essence of

Figure 11 DESKTOP EVOLUTION TO THE CLOUD

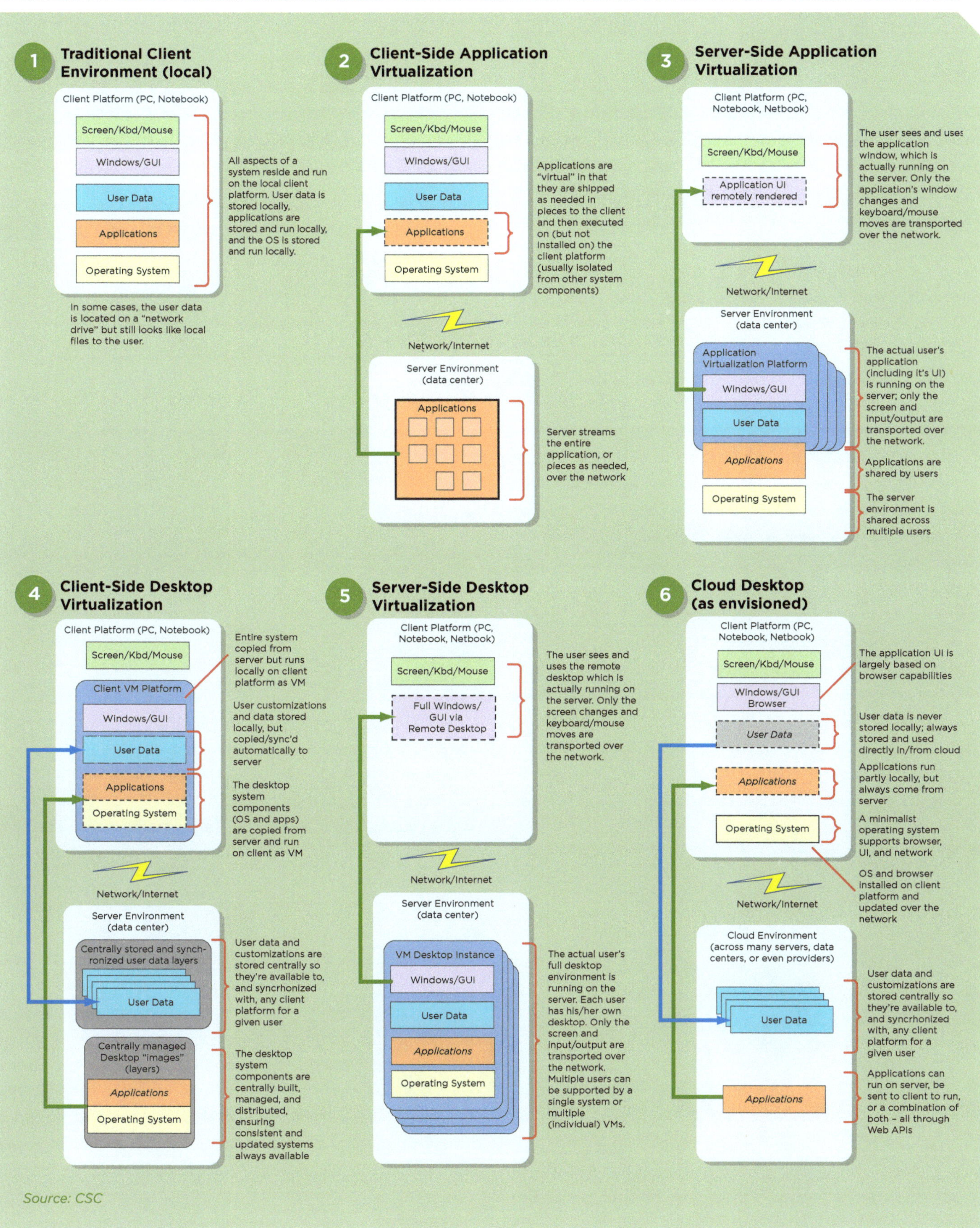

Source: CSC

the user's environment, including all the settings, applications and documents, is managed as data that, through the use of a "cloud desktop" interface, shows up the same on all of the user's cloud-connected devices.

These new cloud desktops are actually a special form of distributed application — more like application virtualization, but with all the data still residing on the server. The result is an illusion: the desktop is actually running locally but only exists as data on the server. Unlike server-side desktop virtualization, where the "whole brain" (desktop environment including applications) is on the server side, cloud desktops use more of a "split brain" approach. Applications can run in the cloud (i.e., on the server), be sent to the client to run locally, or a combination of both (all through Web APIs).

The start-up company Good OS is working on a cloud desktop environment called Cloud 1.0. Using a netbook running Cloud 1.0,[27] everything a user does is stored and managed from the cloud; no data is stored locally that isn't already in the cloud. Another start-up, Jolicloud, calls its cloud desktop an "Internet operating system," where the user interacts with a desktop that comes from the Internet rather than residing locally on the netbook or notebook computer.[28]

Now Google has entered into the cloud desktop arena through the announcement of its development of Chrome OS, a standalone version of the Chrome browser that brings its own operating system with it and is used only with cloud-based applications such as Google Docs. For those applications that store data locally, Chrome OS will allow offline application use and will automatically synchronize that data with the cloud when online again. Chrome OS aims to move all but a very minimal set of software into the cloud, with *all* data and applications living in the cloud except the browser (which itself is updated from the cloud).

Unlike server-side desktop virtualization, where the "whole brain" (desktop environment including applications) is on the server side, cloud desktops use more of a "split brain" approach.

As Google puts it, "Google Chrome OS won't be a traditional operating system, it will just be a wrapper for the cloud."[29]

Whether using application or desktop virtualization, or the new cloud desktops, the nature of "running applications" on our PC, netbook or even smart phone is changing rapidly, with the cloud blurring the lines in terms of how and where we interact with computers.

Whether using application or desktop virtualization, or the new cloud desktops, the nature of "running applications" on our PC, netbook or even smart phone is changing rapidly, with the cloud blurring the lines in terms of how and where we interact with computers.

WEB ABSTRACTIONS, MULTITENANCY, WAREHOUSE GRIDS

As mentioned earlier, the traditional Web itself is a combination of abstractions: document abstraction through HTML and XML, API abstraction through SOAP or REST, and interface abstraction through JavaScript and AJAX. These are just some of the examples of how the Web's abstractions are enabling the cloud.

In addition to using the abstractions of the Web, several leaders in cloud computing are using a combination of abstractions that enable them to provide applications and other services transparently via the Internet. A well-known example is Salesforce.com, which implements its cloud services not through virtualization of servers or machine resources but by creating a multitenant environment, where customers are given the illusion of having their own resources even though they are actually running on the same systems. This illusion is achieved through the use of abstraction in the database, where data from multiple customers is kept separate in the running application through a comprehensive meta-data architecture.

Another example is Microsoft, which is also using multitenant architecture to cloud-enable several of its products. For example, Microsoft's e-mail platform, Exchange, has been made multitenant so that a single Exchange installation can support the hosting of e-mail for many organizations, not just one.[30] Microsoft has even provided architectural guidance to its customers on how to build multitenant applications that are ready for the cloud.[31] (For more on multitenant architectures, see Volume 3, *The Cloud Effect*.)

Taking an alternate approach, Google supports its cloud capabilities using a different set of abstractions than the server virtualization techniques adopted by its competitors. In fact, Google is moving in the opposite direction of server abstraction. Rather than dividing its hardware servers into many servers, it deploys large data centers filled with cheap, generic computers that create a single "warehouse-sized" computer,[32] and it uses software that treats these collections of servers as a single computational system or grid. Google's abstraction is to operate many small servers as one.

MANAGED CODE PLATFORMS

Another type of abstraction that is increasingly used is "managed code" platforms, where the application code is not tied to the particular hardware, but is instead abstracted into software that is either run or compiled by another piece of software — a managed code platform. Examples of these "managed code" (or dynamic language) platforms are Microsoft's .NET, Sun's Java, Python, PHP and Ruby. An increasing number of Web applications are built and deployed using these platforms.

Sometimes called software-based virtual machines, these platforms allow for better portability and automatic deployment of application components. Microsoft's Azure cloud environment is in part enabled through the use of .NET, where application components built using .NET can be easily scaled by simply replicating them across many more physical or virtual servers. Appistry is another company that leverages this application code portability to dynamically distribute and scale applications across available server resources.

MOVING PARTS

Whether virtual server, virtual application, virtual appliance, virtual desktop, cloud desktop, Web abstraction, multitenant architecture, warehouse grid or managed code platform, the many forms of abstraction are having a dramatic impact on enterprise IT and, now, the cloud. They break rigid bonds in the IT stack, allowing increased flexibility, options and arrangements of use. We go from a situation of knowing exactly what is happening where, to one where things may not be exactly as they seem. Where is my application running — on my client device or on a server? Is it on a physical machine, a virtual machine on a server I don't know about? Is my infrastructure real hardware or is it software? As an increasing number of IT resources move to the cloud, these questions will become both harder to answer and, for many, no longer relevant. The many forms of abstraction are dissolving the boundaries between what was hardware and what is now software.

The many forms of abstraction are dissolving the boundaries between what was hardware and what is now software.

Thus the static, purely physical nature of IT past does not necessarily apply to IT present and IT future. In fact, if resources can be in different forms in different locations, why maintain physical resources internally at all? Why not just have them provided as services from the cloud?

FROM IN-HOUSE PRODUCTS TO CLOUD SERVICES

Indeed, the cloud is where it's all heading. It is true that with in-house physical products the enterprise has a high degree of control over IT as well as a level of security that is perceived to be fairly high. However, this comes at a significant cost in terms of dollars invested as well as time spent understanding all the technical details and maintaining the systems — many of which may not be core to the enterprise business.

This is where cloud, with its move from IT owned-and-operated products to IT services out on the network, comes in. This trend has been germinating for some time, seeded by virtualization, hosted services, outsourced services and Service Oriented Architecture. Today, cloud has taken on a life of its own.

THE ULTIMATE BLACK BOX

Almost everyone is familiar with consumer applications such as auctions, movie rentals and driving directions that are delivered over the Internet as services. What is new now is that services are beginning to abstract the physical products in the data center that provide business and technical functionality, turning these products into software black boxes that are delivered over the network. (See Figure 12.) Think of the ultimate black box as the IT stack in the cloud.

Such services imply a two-sided interaction. A service provider hosts the service and makes it generally available for use. In addition to the actual service, the provider also makes available a description of the service (its functions, inputs, outputs, terms of use), its pricing, a service level agreement covering such things as expected availability and response, and a standard API through which the user can connect to the service. On the other side of the interaction, service users obtain the functionality provided by the service by connecting through the API and complying with the description and terms of use. The service user does not need to own the service. The service user does not need to know the technical details of

Figure 12 SERVICES ABSTRACT IT PRODUCTS

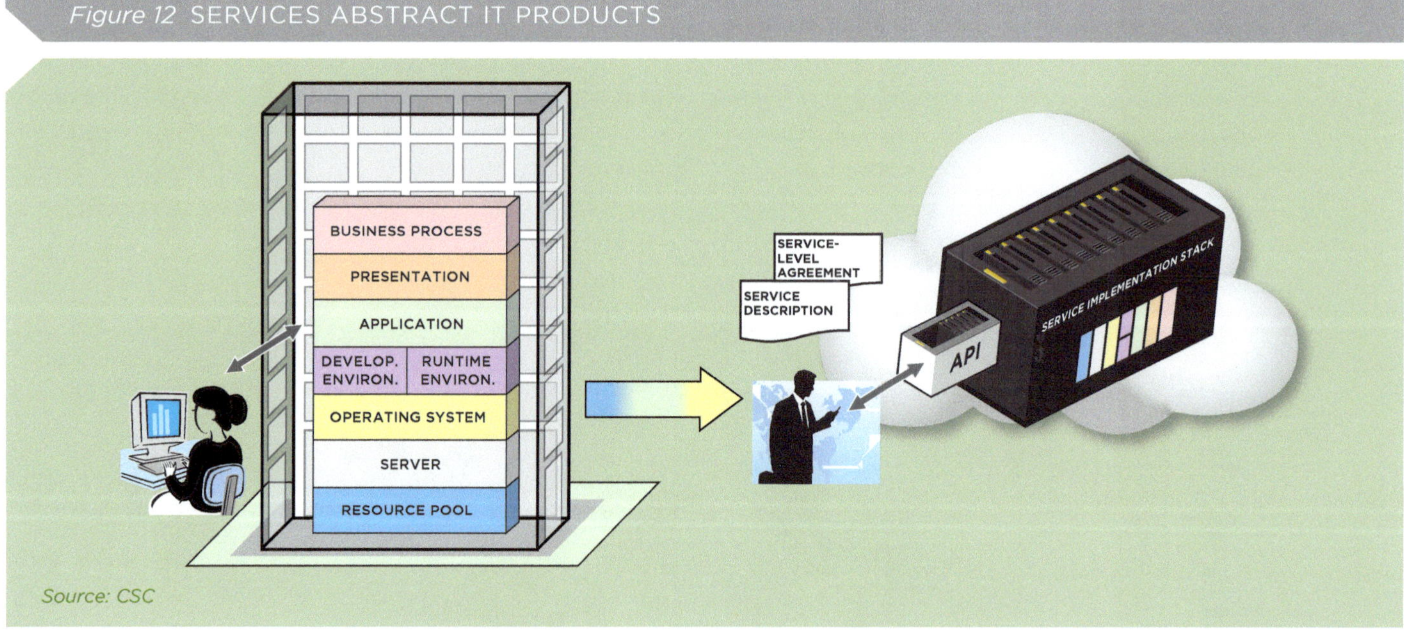

Source: CSC

how the service is actually implemented by the provider. And the service user (in most cases) does not need to know the location from which the service is provided.

Yet, in the end, applications and data — whether provided via physical products in the data center or as services over the network — require hard IT. Data center resources must reside and run somewhere. So long as the resources are abstracted as black boxes, they may be provided as services from anywhere, be it the on-premise data center or a third-party data center. In the latter case, the user can enjoy the functionality without having to invest in, manage or maintain the service, and service improvements may be received automatically. Such services allow enterprises to concentrate on core functions while ceding non-critical functions to service providers. This sets the stage for IT functions to migrate to the network and ultimately float off into the cloud.

IT SERVICES AS DYNAMIC, ABSTRACTED RESOURCES

The rise of the cloud is bringing with it the availability of nearly all IT capabilities — applications, software, platforms and infrastructure — as dynamic resources accessible through a set of agreed upon abstractions, with the Internet and Web services providing the conduit. Abstractions have evolved so that IT itself has become an abstract entity — just software and processes, now made available through the cloud.

The cloud has shifted our view of IT from hardware-centric to software- and services-centric, with the entire IT stack now abstracted into APIs accessed through the Internet. With IT assuming a more software-centric posture, innovation can be faster because software can be manipulated much faster than hardware and can be accessed transparently and quickly as services. Returning to Brian Arthur, this means combinatorial evolution can occur more quickly as software is combined and recombined into new arrangements (with or without hardware).

ONWARD AND UPWARD: TO THE CLOUD

There is no doubt that the resurgence of abstraction concepts and technologies is providing unprecedented benefit and opportunity to IT. And it is clear that abstractions have paved the sometimes bumpy road to cloud computing. Let's review the key connections and how they fit in the *Cloud rEvolution* discussion.

For starters, clouds themselves are abstractions. They provide us with shared IT resources from afar as if they were our own personal resources at our very fingertips. The nature of the cloud abstraction will be explored in detail in Volume 3, *The Cloud Effect*. The types of abstractions explored here in Volume 2, along with another, multitenancy, are often prime enablers of the entire cloud proposition, helping deliver on cloud IT and business benefits that will be examined in Volume 3.

At the same time, abstractions are often the source of major concerns that are preventing some enterprises from taking advantage of cloud computing. When we can't be sure what is going on, real as well as perceived fears arise. We are used to having IT resources that we can see, touch, hear and smell in our own data centers. Their tangible presence is a comfort because we are in control. In contrast, having phantom IT resources made available from who knows where in a cloud makes many enterprises squeamish (hence the concerns). In addition, abstractions create very real issues for areas such as security. Various forms of abstraction not only create areas of security concern that didn't previously exist but also invalidate some security measures that used to work just fine. These concerns will be discussed in Volume 3 as well.

With IT assuming a more software-centric posture, innovation can be faster. . . . Returning to Brian Arthur, this means combinatorial evolution can occur more quickly as software is combined and recombined into new arrangements.

Paradoxically, although abstractions may give rise to concerns, they can also have a psychological effect that helps pave the way for acceptance of the cloud operating model. Implementation of abstraction techniques in our on-premise data centers not only has tangible benefits for the enterprise, but also helps condition us to the notion of having IT capabilities supplied by intangible resources. Once we see that abstracted IT capabilities perform reliably and often better than before, the notion of those capabilities coming from a cloud may then be less disturbing.

So, let's continue this journey on a road where things are not always as they seem. Next stop: the cloud!

NOTES

1. "Cloud rEvolution: Laying the Foundation," CSC Leading Edge Forum, Volume 1, *Cloud rEvolution* series, September 2009, "Cloud: A Morphing of the Digital Domain," pp. 10-11. http://assets1.csc.com/lef/downloads/LEF_2009CloudRev_Vol1_Foundations.pdf

2. W. Brian Arthur, *The Nature of Technology: What It Is and How It Evolves* (New York: Free Press, August 2009), p. 150.

3. Ibid.

4. Arthur, *The Nature of Technology*, p. 206.

5. Arthur, *The Nature of Technology*, p. 192.

6. "Amazon to Offer 'Private Cloud' via VPN," Datamation, 27 August 2009. http://itmanagement.earthweb.com/netsys/article.php/3836451/Amazon-to-Offer-Private-Cloud-via-VPN.htm

7. "Cloud rEvolution: Laying the Foundation," CSC Leading Edge Forum, Volume 1, *Cloud rEvolution* series, September 2009, "Virtual Machines and Portable Code: Stacking Up Applications," pp. 16-19. http://assets1.csc.com/lef/downloads/LEF_2009CloudRev_Vol1_Foundations.pdf

8. "Energy Management vs. Power Management in the Data Center, Take 2," The Server Room Blog, 19 August 2009. http://communities.intel.com/community/openportit/server/blog/2009/08/19/energy-management-vs-power-management-in-the-data-center-take-2

9. "Server TCO: The Price Tag Is Just the Beginning," bMighty Server How-To Center, http://www.bmighty.com/how-to_server/converted/tco-serverpg3.jhtml

10. "Virtualization Basics," 2virtualize.com, http://www.2virtualize.com/index_files/virtualizationbasics.htm

11. "Cloud Computing to the Max at Bechtel," *CIO*, 7 October 2008, http://www.cio.com/article/453214/Cloud_Computing_to_the_Max_at_Bechtel; and "The Googleization of Bechtel," *Network World*, 29 October 2008. http://www.networkworld.com/news/2008/102908-bechtel.html

12. Note: The savings would be different if the virtualization were deployed today. Deploying today would involve Blade servers getting anywhere from 32 to 64 servers per rack. In the original deployment, there were 8-16 servers per rack. Hence the number of racks would decrease substantially if purchased today. Floor space would also decline. However, the savings in power and carbon dioxide emissions would not be as great since the Blade racks consume more power than the original racks.

NOTES

13. "Amazon launches Xen-powered virtual datacenter on demand," virtualization.info, 26 August 2006. http://www.virtualization.info/2006/08/amazon-launches-xen-powered-virtual.html

14. "Rackspace Private Cloud Leverages VMware for Enterprise Computing Offering," Virtualization.com, 7 August 2009, http://virtualization.com/news/2009/08/07/rackspace-private-cloud-leverages-vmware-for-enterprise-computing-offering; and "After VMware also Rackspace wants a piece of Amazon cloud computing business," virtualization.info, 23 October 2008, http://www.virtualization.info/2008/10/after-vmware-also-rackspace-wants-piece.html

15. AppLogic Technology in a Nutshell, http://www.3tera.com/Technology/

16. Featured AppLogic Customers, http://www.3tera.com/Customers/

17. "The US Department of Defense maintains application security and eliminates software conflicts when deploying both custom and commercial applications to locked down desktops," VMware case study, 2008. http://www.vmware.com/files/pdf/customers/DoD_ThinApp_snapshot.pdf This paragraph and the next are from this case study.

18. "Microsoft Application Virtualization 4.5," Microsoft Corporation, 2008, http://download.microsoft.com/download/5/b/c/5bc966bc-47d8-41df-95f2-fa9a2d816258/Microsoft%20Application%20Virtualization%204.5.zip, p.11 of the doc or slide 12 of the ppt.

19. "Cloud rEvolution: Laying the Foundation," CSC Leading Edge Forum, Volume 1, *Cloud rEvolution* series, September 2009, "Smarter Integration," pp. 32-34. http://assets1.csc.com/lef/downloads/LEF_2009CloudRev_Vol1_Foundations.pdf

20. HP Remote Graphics Software, http://h20331.www2.hp.com/hpsub/cache/286504-0-0-225-121.html

21. "Event Report: Autodesk University 2008, Part 2: Cloud computing in the forecast for desktop-dominated CAD market," Cadalyst, 10 December 2008. http://www.cadalyst.com/management/news/event-report-autodesk-university-2008-part-2-8101

22. "CSC Announces Virtual Desktop Services Line of Cross-Industry Solutions," press release, 3 April 2009. http://www.csc.com/newsroom/press_releases/24886-csc_announces_virtual_desktop_services_line_of_cross_industry_solutions_

NOTES

23. "CSC Advances BPO Operations with Desktop Virtualization Technology Built on Sun Ray Thin Clients," press release, 4 February 2009. http://www.csc.com/newsroom/press_releases/21389-csc_advances_bpo_operations_with_desktop_virtualization_technology_built_on_sun_ray_thin_clients

24. "Virtual Appliance," Wikipedia, 15 May 2009. http://en.wikipedia.org/wiki/Virtual_appliance

25. JumpBox Cloud Gear (Early Access), http://www.jumpbox.com/cloud-gear

26. "Zenoss Teams Up with rPath to Create Virtual Appliances," rPath case study, 2008. http://www.rpath.com/corp/images/stories/case_studies/zenoss_casestudy.pdf This paragraph and the next are from this case study.

27. Good OS and Cloud, http://www.thinkgos.com/cloud/index.html

28. The Jolicloud Manifesto, http://www.jolicloud.com/idea

29. "You're Already Running Google Chrome OS," Google Operating System blog, 1 September 2009. http://googlesystem.blogspot.com/2009/09/youre-already-running-google-chrome-os.html

30. "Microsoft Releases SP1 for Exchange Server 2007," PCWorld on ABC News, 30 November 2007. http://abcnews.go.com/Technology/PCWorld/story?id=3933546

31. MSDN Architecture Center, Multi-Tenant Data Architecture, http://msdn.microsoft.com/en-us/library/aa479086.aspx

32. "What we talk about when we talk about cloud computing," Official Google Enterprise Blog, 28 April 2009, http://googleenterprise.blogspot.com/2009/04/what-we-talk-about-when-we-talk-about.html; and Xiaobo Fan, Wolf-Dietrich Weber and Luiz André Barroso, "Power provisioning for a warehouse-sized computer," International Symposium on Computer Architecture, Proceedings of the 34th annual international symposium on computer architecture, 2007, pp. 13-23, http://portal.acm.org/citation.cfm?id=1250662.1250665&CFID=51016747&CFTOKEN=12800990

ACKNOWLEDGMENTS

Rick Muñoz, Yale Esrock and Doug Neal conducted the research for the *Cloud rEvolution* report series. Working on *Cloud rEvolution* has deepened their appreciation for the innovation, efficiency and untapped potential of cloud computing for the enterprise.

Rick Muñoz (left) is a senior technology architect at CSC and a 2009 LEF Associate. He specializes in emerging information technology platforms and methods, including agile solution delivery using dynamic virtual environments. Rick has delivered technology strategies and IT solutions for many Fortune 500 companies. A member of CSC's Global Business Solutions and Services group, Rick now focuses on developing cloud computing services for clients across multiple industries. rmunoz@csc.com

Yale Esrock (center) is a business process architect in CSC's North American Public Sector and a 2009 LEF Associate. Yale has held key roles in the Program Management Offices of large military and civil government transformation programs, and was a key contributor to the incorporation of Service Oriented Architecture concepts in CSC's Catalyst^{SM} methodology. His interest in cloud is on meeting business objectives, while mitigating risk, through the creative application of cloud concepts. yesrock@csc.com

As Research Fellow in the LEF Executive Programme, Doug Neal (right) is responsible for research on "Innovating through Technology." Doug began researching enterprise cloud computing under the guise of IT consumerization. He led cloud computing study tours in Silicon Valley in 2008 and 2009 and consults with enterprises on cloud strategy. Doug's research interests also include green IT, collaborative technologies and Web 2.0. dneal@csc.com

The LEF thanks the many others who contributed to the *Cloud rEvolution* report series.

Jeff Allen, *Cisco*
Jeff Barr, *Amazon*
W. Brian Arthur, *Santa Fe Institute*
Justin Barney, *3Leaf Systems*
Randy Bias, *Stratospheric*
Brian Boruff, *CSC*
Lisa Braun, *CSC*
Jeff Budge, *CSC*
Simon Crosby, *Citrix*
Cees de Groot, *Marktplaats*
Scott Dowell, *CSC*
Mike Dyer, *CSC*
Martin English, *CSC*
Michael Ernesto, *CSC*
Jim Fenner, *CSC*
Chris Fleck, *Citrix*
Glenn Gravatt, *CSC*
Mike Groner, *Appistry*
Phil Grove, *CSC*
Daniel Gubber, *CSC*
Nigel Healy, *CSC*
Randy Hill, *CSC*
Christofer Hoff, *Cisco*
Gabe Kazarian, *CSC*
Ron Knode, *CSC*
Bob Lozano, *Appistry*
Mark Masterson, *CSC*
Byron Miller, *CSC*
Daniel Mintz, *CSC*
Jim Moran, *ETS*
Peter Nickolov, *3Tera*
Erika Mir Olimpiew, *CSC*
Purnima Padmanabhan, *MokaFive*
Nicholas Payne, *CSC*
David Pickup, *CSC*
Srinivas Polisetty, *CSC*
Tony Puerto, *CSC*
Bob Quinn, *3Leaf Systems*
Billy Rollin, *CSC*
Robert Rosenwald, *CSC*
Alit Bar Sadeh, *GigaSpaces*
Bob Slook, *CSC*
Larry Smarr, *California Institute for Telecommunications and Information Technology (Calit2)*
Tomas Soderstrom, *NASA Jet Propulsion Laboratory*
Michael Stonebraker, *Vertica*
John Taylor, *ETS*
Simon Wardley, *Canonical*
John Willis, *Cloud Cafe*

Worldwide CSC Headquarters

The Americas
3170 Fairview Park Drive
Falls Church, Virginia 22042
United States
+1.703.876.1000

Europe, Middle East, Africa
The Royal Pavilion
Wellesley Road
Aldershot
Hampshire GU11 1PZ
United Kingdom
+44(0)1252.534000

Australia
26 Talavera Road
Macquarie Park NSW 2113
Australia
+61(0)29034.3000

Asia
139 Cecil Street
#06-00 Cecil House
Singapore 069539
Republic of Singapore
+65.6221.9095

About CSC
The mission of CSC is to be a global leader in providing technology enabled business solutions and services.

With the broadest range of capabilities, CSC offers clients the solutions they need to manage complexity, focus on core businesses, collaborate with partners and clients, and improve operations.

CSC makes a special point of understanding its clients and provides experts with real-world experience to work with them. CSC is vendor-independent, delivering solutions that best meet each client's unique requirements.

For more than 50 years, clients in industries and governments worldwide have trusted CSC with their business process and information systems outsourcing, systems integration and consulting needs.

The company trades on the New York Stock Exchange under the symbol "CSC."

Produced in USA 0469-20 10/09

LEADINGedgeforum

2009

Cloud rEvolution:

The Cloud Effect

Volume 3

CSC

As part of CSC's Office of Innovation, the Leading Edge Forum (LEF) is a global community whose programs help participants realize business benefits from the use of advanced IT more rapidly.

LEF members work to spot key emerging business and technology trends before others, and identify specific practices for exploiting these trends for business advantage. Members enjoy access to a global network of thought leaders and leading practitioners, and to a powerful body of research and field practices.

LEF programs give CTOs and senior technologists the opportunity to explore the most pressing technology issues, examine state-of-the-art practices, and leverage CSC's technology experts, alliance programs and events. LEF programs and reports are intended to provoke conversations in the marketplace about the potential for innovation when applying technology to advance organizational performance. For more information about LEF programs, visit www.csc.com/lef.

The LEF Executive Programme is a premium, fee-based program that helps CIOs and senior business executives develop into next-generation leaders by using technology for competitive advantage in wholly new ways. Members direct the research agenda, interact with a network of world-class experts, and access topical conferences, study tours, information exchanges and advisory services. For more information about the LEF Executive Programme, visit lef.csc.com.

LEF LEADERSHIP

WILLIAM KOFF (left)

Vice President and Chief Technology Officer, Office of Innovation

A leader in CSC's technology community, Bill Koff provides vision and direction to CSC and its clients on critical information technology trends, technology innovation and strategic investments in leading edge technology. Bill plays a key role in guiding CSC research, innovation, technology thought leadership and alliance partner activities, and in certifying CSC's Centers of Excellence and Innovation Centers.
wkoff@csc.com

PAUL GUSTAFSON (above right)

Director,
Leading Edge Forum

Paul Gustafson is an accomplished technologist and proven leader in emerging technologies, applied research and strategy. Paul brings vision and leadership to a portfolio of LEF programs and directs the technology research agenda. Astute at recognizing how technology trends inter-relate and impact business, Paul applies his insights to client strategy, CSC research, leadership development and innovation strategy.
pgustafs@csc.com

RICHARD DAVIES (left)

Vice President and Managing Director, LEF Executive Programme

Richard Davies directs a global, strategic research and advisory program aimed at helping CIOs and other enterprise IT leaders understand and exploit the ever-expanding intersection between business and information technology. Richard has over 20 years of experience in the IT market and has held a variety of sales and marketing positions both nationally and internationally.
rdavies5@csc.com

DAVID MOSCHELLA (above right)

Global Research Director,
LEF Executive Programme

David Moschella guides a series of strategic research initiatives aimed at helping CIOs and other enterprise IT leaders benefit from the growing intersection between business and information technology. David's key areas of expertise include globalization, industry restructuring, disruptive technologies, environmental strategies, and the co-evolution of business and IT. He is an author and former columnist on IT industry trends.
dmoschella@csc.com

In this ongoing series of reports about technology directions, the LEF looks at the role of innovation in the marketplace both now and in the years to come. By studying technology's current realities and anticipating its future shape, these reports provide organizations with the necessary balance between tactical decision making and strategic planning.

The Cloud rEvolution *report series examines the technology and business aspects of cloud computing. Although each volume is valuable on its own, the full scope of the* Cloud rEvolution *is best obtained by reading all the volumes. To receive the entire* Cloud rEvolution *series, visit www.csc.com/lefreports or subscribe to the LEF RSS feed: www.csc.com/lefpodcast*

Cloud rEvolution:
The Cloud Effect

Volume 3

CONTENTS

Get all LEF reports by subscribing to the LEF RSS feed: www.csc.com/lefpodcast

Preface

Supercomputers assembled from game stations. Data storage for a few cents per gigabyte. A multicore mobile phone that runs full-scale applications like a computer. A network that spans the globe and extends into space. A server that fragments into multiple virtual machines, each of which can do its own thing and be turned on and off like a light switch. Processor, memory and I/O resources that are liberated from the confines of a single server and shared dynamically across the data center. An entire portable, disposable infrastructure that is comprised of software instead of hardware.

Welcome to the new world of information technology (IT). In this new world, a marketing manager who wants to do a detailed data analysis of national sales can fire up a few virtual machines for half an hour and do it on the spot. No more waiting months for a free server in the data center and being at the mercy of IT to carry out the request. Order up your computing, pay for it with a credit card and run the analysis yourself — all for the cost of lunch.

Sweeping changes underway in IT — namely, cloud computing and its underlying building blocks — are yielding unprecedented speed and agility, the ability to do more with less, and new levels of cost savings. Since the business can only change as fast as IT, these changes are having an enormous impact on the business's ability to unleash innovation and address changing markets and customers ahead of the competition.

The Cloud rEvolution *report tackles these sweeping changes in a four-volume series. Volume 1,* **Laying the Foundation**, *introduces the Cloud rEvolution and explores the digital foundations — the core building block technologies — that lay the groundwork for cloud computing. Volume 2,* **The Art of Abstraction**, *explores how abstraction loosens the IT stack, providing flexibility and efficiency as a precursor to the ultimate abstraction: the cloud. Volume 3 focuses on* **The Cloud Effect**, *describing the impact the cloud is having on IT and business tactically and strategically. Volume 4,* **A Workbook for Cloud Computing in the Enterprise**, *provides practical guidance for transitioning to the cloud, which is rapidly becoming a question of when and how, not if.*

REVOLUTION IN THE AIR

Cloud computing, the next major phase in the evolution of IT, has revolutionary potential. When a major pharmaceutical company like Eli Lilly looks at doing drug discovery analytics in the cloud, or a major media company considers webcasting a worldwide sporting event from the cloud, change is underway. For Lilly, getting enough servers up and running quickly — in *one day* rather than the typical three months — was crucial. For the media company, or any company with spiky demand, the cloud represents a way to handle peak loads or one-off events efficiently without having to invest in excess IT capacity that is used occasionally but otherwise stands nearly idle. That is the beauty of the cloud: being able to dial up IT resources as needed, and — perhaps more importantly — being able to dial them down when finished. (See Figure 1.)

This elasticity is a result of fixed resources (hardware and software) that have been turned into malleable ones (services). Provisioned over a network, these malleable cloud services are available to all. Any organization, whether commercial or government, large or small, can take advantage of the cloud. And that, says economist Brian Arthur, spells the making of a revolution. "Cloud computing, along with sensor networks and the digitization of the economy, brings a revolution as significant as the Industrial Revolution. All businesses will be deeply affected by this," Arthur says.

Cloud computing, along with sensor networks and the digitization of the economy, brings a revolution as significant as the Industrial Revolution. All businesses will be deeply affected by this.

Reflecting on his latest book, *The Nature of Technology: What It Is and How It Evolves,* Arthur emphasizes cloud's impact on business change: "Businesses now have access to something that makes much more sense economically: the cloud. All business processes suddenly have access to cloud computing and a very different set of economics, triggering new processes and services. We go way beyond simply doing things cheaper. We need to think about what cloud can do that couldn't be done before."

Having highly scalable, ever-accessible, powerful computing available on-the-fly is unprecedented. Business functions will be designed, deployed and managed in entirely new ways. As more business activity takes place in the cloud, business and IT will become increasingly intertwined and co-evolutionary. Hence business and IT leaders need to understand and adapt to this rapidly changing management and technology paradigm.

Figure 1 Cloud computing is about dialing up IT resources according to business needs and — more importantly — dialing them down when finished.

Source: CSC

JOURNEY TO THE CLOUD

We saw in Volumes 1 and 2 of the *Cloud rEvolution* report series how abstraction helps mobilize core IT technologies, loosen the IT stack, and facilitate new technology "arrangements" (Arthur's term) that enable innovation.[1] Now we look in detail at the ultimate abstraction: the cloud.

At the core of cloud computing is the Internet, that supremely disruptive technology that is manifesting its disruption once again. In this sense, cloud represents the next phase of the Internet: delivering IT resources on demand. Thus our prior focus on the "network effect"[2] (the compounding effect of the Internet on IT resources and business processes) has evolved to the "cloud effect." Paul Gustafson, director of the Leading Edge Forum, explains: "The cloud effect is the influence of cloud computing — of on-demand, elastic, pay-per-use IT — on IT and the business."

CLOUD EFFECTS

This influence is significant and far-reaching. To understand it better, CSC has identified six cloud effects impacting IT and business:

1. The Stack Transforms to Services
2. Structural Deepening Expands the Cloud Ecosystem
3. Cloud Enables New IT Options
4. Mega Data Centers Power It All
5. Cloudonomics Provide Financial Incentive
6. Cloud Drives Business Value

As the cloud effects will demonstrate, the cloud's impact is powerful and varied. Its allure is different to different people. To some, the cloud is a sandbox for software development and testing. To others, the cloud is surplus capacity for handling peak loads. To some, the cloud is private infrastructure for critical applications. To others, the cloud is backup. To some, the cloud is public infrastructure. To others, the cloud is a hybrid. To others still, it is simply a collaboration tool.

Thus, although the U.S. National Institute of Standards and Technology (NIST) is working on a cloud definition,[3] if you ask 20 people for a definition of cloud you will get 20 different answers. While having a common definition may be beside the point — the enterprise will avail itself of at least some cloud services no matter what they are called — a working definition provides common ground for understanding and clarity for making an investment in cloud.

In this spirit, we offer the following general description: cloud is an abstraction that provides an operating model for delivering and consuming IT resources and services. More specifically:

Cloud computing is the latest major phase in the evolution of information technology, in which all the major components of computing — hardware, software, storage, networking, data, information and expertise — are abstracted as scalable services, available globally and on-demand from either "multitenant" public or single-customer private facilities, typically through some type of subscription, pay-per-use or other variable cost model.

Cloud computing is transformational. It will alter IT and the business in untold ways, much the way machinery and mass production ushered in the Industrial Revolution. In this case, cloud is the new machinery, which enables a slicing and dicing of IT to match demand while putting this power in the hands of every enterprise, large or small.

Cloud computing is transformational. It will alter IT and the business in untold ways, much the way machinery and mass production ushered in the Industrial Revolution.

Our first step into the cloud has us thinking about cloud computing as a series of layers that allows IT to choose where to specialize and how much control to retain.

Cloud Effect 1

THE STACK TRANSFORMS TO SERVICES

As mentioned in the conclusion of Volume 2,[4] a primary impact of the cloud is to abstract the IT stack — IT capabilities delivered by physical products in an on-premise data center — into services delivered remotely over the Internet. The cloud ecosystem encompasses a broad array of services that continues to grow. In fact, some tout the notion of "everything as a service," a scenario in which consumers obtain personalized information, social interaction and entertainment from the cloud, and enterprises look to the cloud to meet their most demanding computing requirements.[5]

IT has been moving towards services throughout the evolution of the Internet. Now we have a more mature services environment. While there is great variety to these services, the cloud services landscape, or "cloudscape," has coalesced around a few familiar categories: infrastructure services, platforms services, application services and process services.

Figure 2 shows a services framework that maps the service categories to the traditional on-premise IT stack. Unlike a traditional stack, however, the service categories are not tightly bound. Users may select services from any, or multiple, layers of the framework. This choice, however, results in a tradeoff. The higher the service is in the framework, the more freedom a user has to not be concerned with details at lower levels of the underlying IT stack. On the other hand, the user must accept decisions that have been made by the service provider at these lower stack levels.

Figure 2 also provides a representative sample of service providers at each level of the framework. Note that providers often offer only a subset of these services or services that cross levels.

INFRASTRUCTURE SERVICES

Collectively referred to as Infrastructure as a Service (IaaS), these services provide access to various components of IT infrastructure on demand. This may include any infrastructure components but commonly consists of a subset of virtualized hardware (Hardware as a Service), storage (Storage as a Service) and networking (Network as a Service). Amazon Web Services (AWS)

Figure 2 CLOUD MORPHS THE MONOLITHIC IT STACK INTO SERVICES

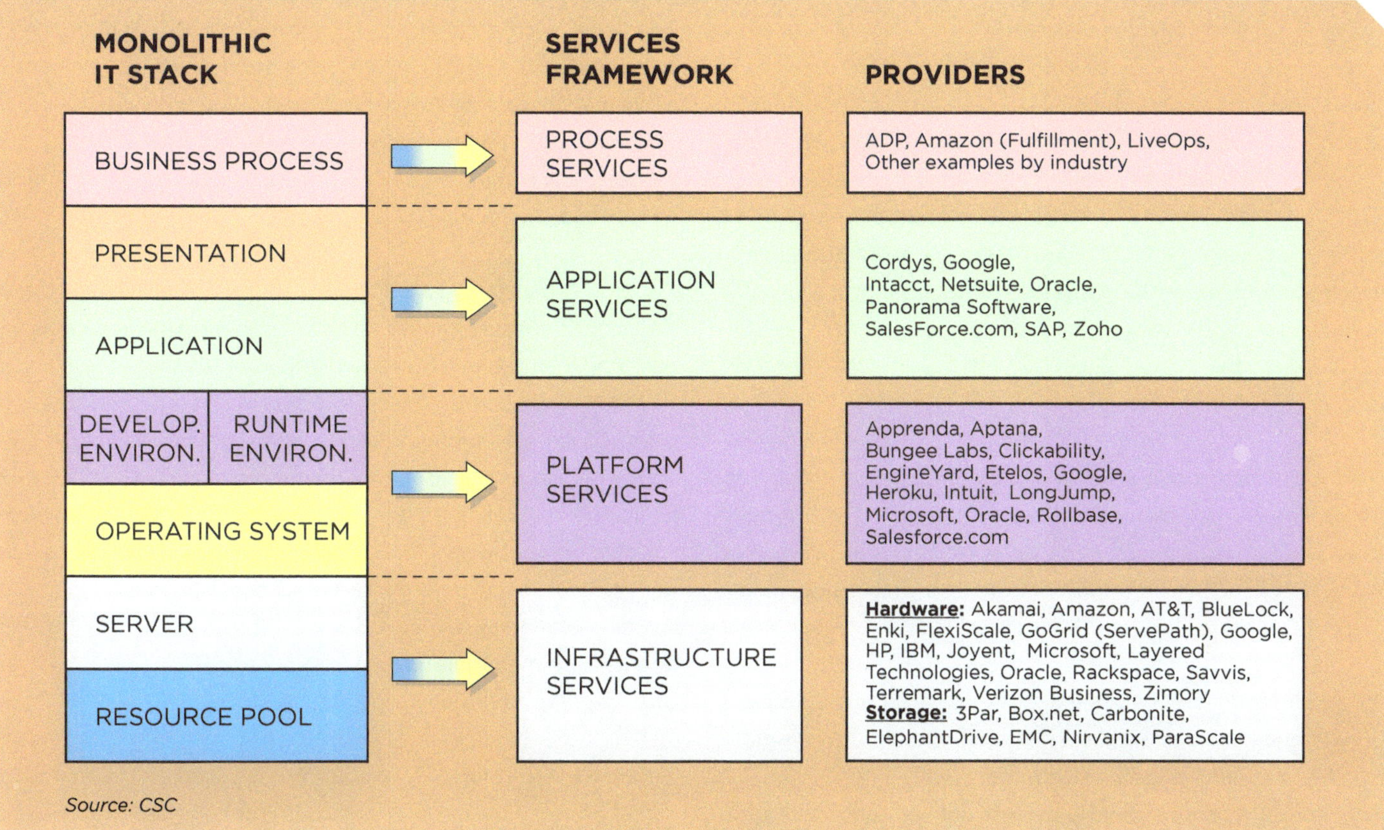

Source: CSC

is the poster child for IaaS, with its Elastic Compute Cloud (EC2) compute service, Simple Storage Service (S3), SimpleDB database service, Simple Queue Service, CloudFront content delivery service, Elastic MapReduce service for creating and processing very large-scale databases, and more. Once an infrastructure service is obtained, it can be used for any purpose, but the user must provide the necessary software and data.

The on-demand nature of IaaS (and all cloud services) is a radical departure from the fixed, all-or-nothing IT of the past. Key to making on-demand work is having a simple user interface. Figure 3 illustrates the user interface for building and managing an infrastructure in the GoGrid cloud. The interface provides an easy mechanism for creating a customized infrastructure consisting of load balancers, Web and application servers, database

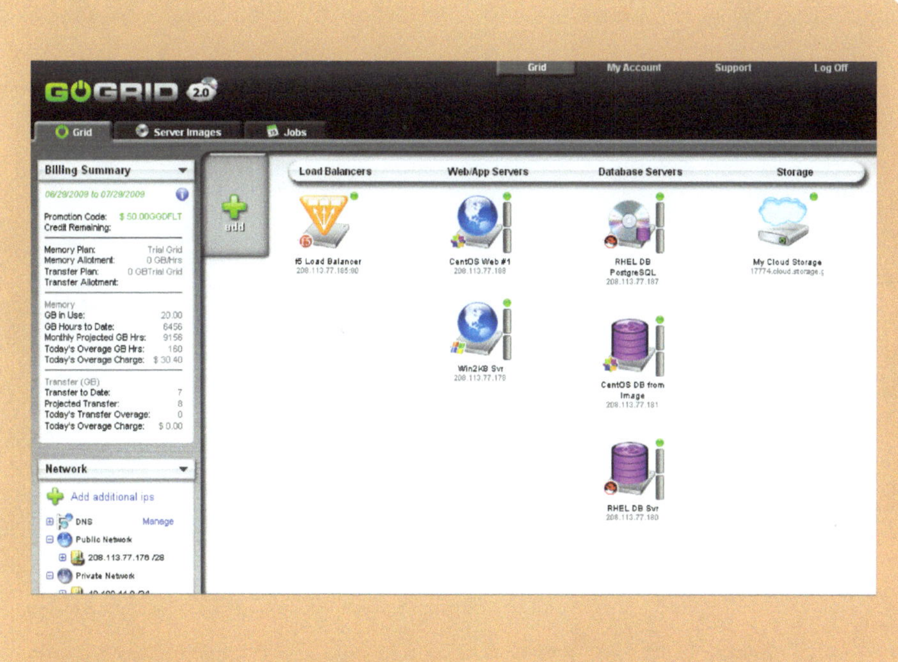

Figure 3 GoGrid provides a simple graphical interface for creating a customized cloud infrastructure on demand.

Source: GoGrid

servers, storage and network resources, and it displays an up-to-the-minute billing summary. (GoGrid is a division of managed hosting provider ServePath.)

Another IaaS player is BlueLock, which offers IT infrastructure (servers, routers, firewalls, switches, storage devices), 24/7/365 full-service management, monitoring and support, as well as an integrated disaster recovery system provided from two SAS 70 certified data centers. BlueLock offers an SLA promising 99.99 percent uptime as well as time-to-resolution, and can enable conformance with various compliance standards such as ISO, PCI, Sarbanes-Oxley, FDA 21CFR11 and HIPAA via proven, pre-configured templates.[6]

In the IaaS arena, cloud storage is a popular type of infrastructure service. In fact, many individuals make use of this type of cloud service regularly to back up their personal computers. With services such as Carbonite, backup of any amount of data is performed automatically and securely and has easy restoration.

Cloud storage is also beginning to be used by the enterprise. The Nirvanix Storage Delivery Network (SDN), for example, provides a highly secure environment with SAS 70 Type II certification, and intelligently stores, delivers and processes storage requests in the network location that provides the most optimal user experience. Data may be stored in up to five geographically dispersed locations according to user policies.[7] NASA is using Nirvanix's storage cloud as a disaster recovery site for data NASA is collecting from the moon.[8]

Indeed, the highly security-conscious government sector is looking to the cloud for storage for many areas. Case in point: Google recently announced a government cloud to be available in 2010 for use by federal, state and local governments to store public data.[9] This is in keeping with the idea of a more open and transparent government; cloud is recognized as a means to that end — as a way to reach out to all.

PLATFORM SERVICES

Commonly referred to as Platform as a Service (PaaS), these services provide a development environment for creating new applications or a runtime environment for executing applications that have been developed (or both). Services in this category, which can vary widely, sometimes overlap into additional functionality that addresses such areas as system monitoring, provisioning, load balancing and security. While such services can significantly ease the process of developing and deploying applications, developers are tied in to using the specific tools and software stacks (which may be fairly common or highly proprietary) prescribed by the PaaS provider.

Perhaps the best known PaaS products are Salesforce.com's Force.com, which provides the ability to quickly develop business applications and, if desired, integrate them with Salesforce CRM, and Google App Engine, which provides a secure, scalable, cloud-based development and runtime environment for Java and Python applications. Microsoft has also joined this space with its Windows Azure platform. (See "Incumbents Retool Around Services" on page 88.) The Windows Azure platform is hosted in Microsoft cloud data centers and consists of the Windows Azure operating system (provides development, service hosting and service management environments) as well as a number of prepackaged applications and services.

Because the Windows Azure platform is based on the Microsoft Visual Studio development environment and .NET Framework, it is compatible with the tools many developers are already familiar with and use in-house. As a result, the Windows Azure platform enables multiple scenarios. In addition to still being able to develop and run applications in-house, IT can develop an application in-house and deploy it in the Microsoft cloud, develop an application in the cloud and then move it back

Figure 4 THE WINDOWS AZURE PLATFORM PROVIDES MULTIPLE DEVELOPMENT AND RUNTIME OPTIONS

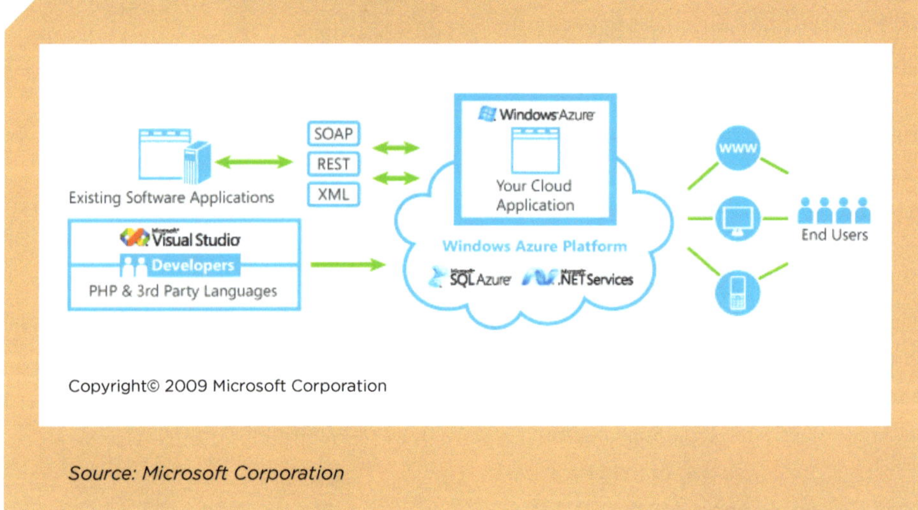

Source: Microsoft Corporation

in-house, and enhance existing applications to run in the cloud. The Windows Azure platform can be used to build a wide variety of applications that are Web-based, PC-based, server-based or mobile, and also supports PHP, Java and Eclipse. (See Figure 4.)

In contrast to Microsoft are start-ups such as Rollbase. The Rollbase platform allows companies to create enterprise-level SaaS applications using do-it-yourself tools in a standard Web browser. Designed from the ground up as a purely metadata-driven, multitenant, on-demand application development and delivery platform, Rollbase provides a unique underlying application execution, serialization and publishing model. Rollbase brings the power of rapid application development to businesses that may not have the time, resources or expertise to create on-demand applications using traditional software development methods. In conjunction with the Rollbase Platform, the Rollbase Application Directory is an on-demand application sharing service where users can browse, test and install business applications built and published by experienced Rollbase users and partners with a single click.[10]

APPLICATION SERVICES

Application services include those termed Software as a Service (SaaS) that provide use of pre-packaged software applications managed by the provider and run on the provider's hardware. The pioneer for the enterprise is Salesforce.com, which made doing customer relationship management in the cloud popular. Today, SaaS vendors and products are available to address almost any aspect of a business including sales, marketing, financial, accounting, manufacturing, engineering, inventory, warehouse and human resource functions.

For those companies looking to address more than a single business area, pre-integrated suites of applications are also available with a SaaS model. SAP Business ByDesign is an example. Another prominent example is Intacct. Intacct is a provider of on-demand financial management and accounting applications. Companies of all sizes can remotely access FASB-, Sarbanes-Oxley- and GAAP-compliant Intacct applications to manage and share financial, supply chain and professional services information. Intacct automates key business processes from order entry through cash collection, and from procurement through vendor payment. This includes financials and accounting, contracts and revenue management, order management, project management, financial consolidation, real-time dashboards and financial reporting applications.[11]

SaaS is also commonly used to provide productivity and collaboration tools to businesses and consumers. Most consumers are regular cloud patrons; Gmail, Flickr and other popular Web sites are examples of cloud-based SaaS applications. In the mobile world, SaaS is *the* method of application delivery, as the iPhone and the Android software platform for mobile devices show.

These kinds of consumer-friendly cloud applications are finding their way into business too. Zoho, for example, is a relatively small SaaS provider from India that offers a staggering array of productivity, collaboration and business applications that are used not just by small start-ups but also by industrial giants like General Electric, which switched its over 400,000 desktops to the use of Zoho applications in the cloud. In the government arena, the city of Washington, D.C. has moved its 38,000 desktops from Microsoft on the desktop to Google Apps in the cloud.[12] In a similar move, the City of Los Angeles announced in October 2009 that, with the help of CSC, it will switch its e-mail, calendar, online chatting and other services for 30,000 city employees to Google Apps.[13] This deal looks to be the bellwether for big city governments (and enterprises) considering switching to the cloud; it will be closely watched.

PROCESS SERVICES

Sometimes referred to as Process as a Service (PraaS) or Business Process as a Service (BPaaS), process services represent the highest level in the cloud services hierarchy. They are complete end-to-end business processes executed by providers in the cloud using a combination of provider-owned software, personnel and (sometimes) business facilities. Think of it as the Internet-age version of service bureaus such as ADP payroll processing.

Process services are at the intersection of SaaS and business process outsourcing (BPO). SaaS concepts such as single instance, multitenancy, and pay-as-you-go pricing are extended and applied to processes. With traditional BPO, the outsourcer executes a long-term contract with the client, takes over the client's actual process and supporting software, and over time may make improvements to the process. With cloud-based process services, the provider has its own process that has been standardized based on best practices. A single instance of this process is often made available in multitenant fashion to many different companies, sometimes with limited customization via metadata. The process is available on-demand and paid for as used by subscription, transaction or another similar mechanism. Long-term contracts are usually not necessary, and when the service is no longer needed, it can simply be turned off. This enables significant business agility, flexibility and scalability. For example, a company's internal order processing capability could be instantly and temporarily scaled up using a cloud process service to cover a short-term demand increase due to an advertising or promotional campaign.

Another example comes with LiveOps, which offers call center services staffed by an army of home volunteers. The company's rapid response to Hurricane Katrina illustrates the power of process services:

> When Hurricane Katrina hit the Gulf Coast of the U.S. in 2005, a toll-free communications centre was urgently needed to put victims in touch with their families. Every other outsourcer that was approached to provide communications services declined to take on the project, because they couldn't mobilize agents fast enough. Within three hours, LiveOps launched a call centre with over 300 independent, home-based agents ready to help reunite victims of Hurricane Katrina with their family members. The virtual call centre, with no fixed investment in buildings or technology infrastructure, was established with skill[ed] workers in hours and then subsequently wound down when work was done.[14]

While similar to SaaS, a process service is more than just SaaS. With SaaS, the enterprise uses provider-owned software to execute a business process, but it is still the enterprise that is running the business process. As illustrated by the LiveOps example, a process service usually has a SaaS component to it, but it is not just software that the customer accesses. It is also people and sometimes facilities. Provider employees actually perform the business process on behalf of the customer and are responsible for the end result. And, depending on the service, use of provider facilities such as call centers, warehouses or stores may be part of the service. Often a mix-and-match hybrid capability is offered, whereby a customer can choose the degree to which provider resources are used. For example, part of a process could be executed completely internally, part internally using the provider SaaS application, and part using the SaaS application accessed by provider personnel.

Another example of the process service in action is Amazon Fulfillment Web Service (FWS).[15] Using this service, depicted in Figure 5, a business can send its products to Amazon, which handles the entire fulfillment process. Amazon stores the product in its warehouses and manages the inventory. Orders are accepted either directly by Amazon on Amazon.com or submitted to Amazon by the seller. The order is picked, packed, shipped and tracked by Amazon. Follow-up return and other customer service is provided by Amazon as well, all coordinated through the Amazon Web site and internal systems. Amazon FWS front-ends the fulfillment service (called Fulfillment by Amazon) and helps companies integrate it directly into their own Web sites or other sales channels.

Figure 5 Process as a Service, such as Amazon Fulfillment Web Service, combines processes, systems, facilities and people.

Source: CSC

SELF-SERVICE IS THE ORDER OF THE DAY

The ready availability and ease of use of cloud-based services is creating a new phenomenon that impacts both IT and the business alike. When it comes to the cloud, self-service is the order of the day.[16] Instead of relying on IT, users can help themselves. No more waiting for the server person, the network person, the storage person, the security person. Just fill in a few fields on your browser, click, and presto — instant IT. Through self-service portals, entire scalable server arrays can be created in the cloud with a few clicks.

Thus, for the IT department, enabling cloud means enabling self-service interfaces. Users need easy-to-use, intuitive interfaces that equip them to manage their own service delivery life cycle. This includes being able to create, scale, modify, pause, restart and shut down virtual servers, from individual machines to entire server arrays. In fact, everything from low-level infrastructure to high-level applications can be available via self-service, whether they reside in a private or a public cloud.

Enterprise applications are also being made available to users in convenient, self-service formats. This includes the ability to access and use personal and enterprise applications from any place on any device, including intelligent mobile devices. In Volume 2, we saw how Citrix Receiver allows even enterprise applications to run on an iPhone.[17]

Now, a complement to Receiver — Citrix Dazzle — enhances the user's self-service experience.

Citrix Dazzle is described as the first self-service "storefront" for enterprise applications. For enterprise customers already using Citrix Delivery Center products like XenApp and XenDesktop, Dazzle gives corporate employees 24/7 self-service access to the applications they need to do work. IT is in control, instantly and easily advertising the existing offline and online Windows applications and Web applications with XenApp's "app publishing" interface. Adding, updating and removing applications and IT services takes minutes — not days, weeks or months. When users launch Dazzle, the store will be fully stocked with all the applications IT has to offer.[18]

Even the U.S. federal government has an application store, Apps.Gov (www.apps.gov). For use by federal employees conducting federal business, the Apps storefront is run by the General Services Administration and includes (or will include) a variety of business applications, productivity software, services like storage and Web hosting, and social applications.[19]

Clearly, self-service IT is the way of the future. Self-service in the cloud contributes to the rise of "double deep" employees who are both business and IT savvy. This powerful combination opens the door to new levels of innovation and agility, for the enterprise can get things done faster and has more flexibility to experiment. For the IT department, self-service heralds a shift in power to the user and a more strategic role for IT.

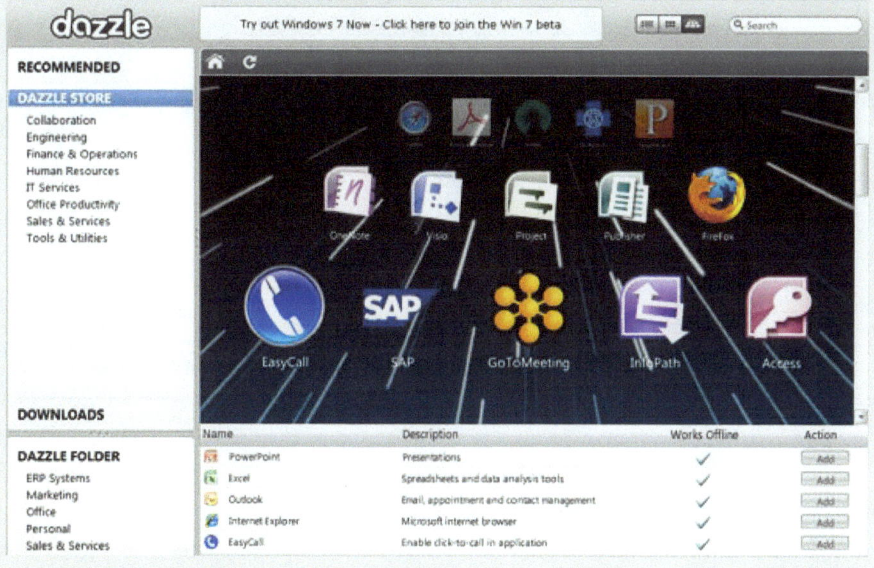

Citrix Dazzle offers a rich, intuitive user experience that requires no training. If you've used DirecTV or Apple iTunes, you already know how to use Dazzle. *Source: Citrix Systems*

INCUMBENTS RETOOL AROUND SERVICES

The morphing of on-premise IT products to cloud-based services is resulting in a new IT landscape where non-traditional vendors have clout, and nimble new vendors flock in to fill niches that didn't previously exist. This is creating pressure for the traditional leaders of the client-server era to keep pace. As a result, mainstay IT players such as Microsoft, Oracle, IBM, HP and SAP are retooling for the cloud.

Microsoft Hedges Its Bets. With a strategy dubbed Software + Services, Microsoft has adopted a two-pronged approach that offers customers the option of obtaining Microsoft products as traditional software on the desktop or as on-demand services in the cloud — for example, through Microsoft Business Productivity Online Suite (BPOS), which includes Exchange Online, SharePoint Online, Office Communications Online and Office Live Meeting.

In addition, in a major move, Microsoft has introduced the Windows Azure platform. As mentioned in "Platform Services," this PaaS product provides many tools including the Windows Azure cloud operating system and cloud-based development and runtime environments.

In July 2009 Microsoft and CSC announced a strategic collaboration around the Windows Azure platform, which includes the formation of a dedicated CSC Global Competency Center in Vietnam specializing in Windows Azure.[20] The two companies will jointly market Windows Azure to enterprises and independent software vendors. CSC is poised to support large-scale development projects with the cloud computing benefits delivered by Windows Azure. CSC is also a reseller of the BPOS cloud-based solutions.[21] "Microsoft and CSC are bringing new cloud propositions to the market," says Brian Boruff, vice president of CSC's cloud computing and software services. "Microsoft's software plus CSC's development and integration expertise will deliver the benefits of cloud computing to large customers and ISVs."

Oracle Buys In. Subscription-based, on-demand access to Oracle products including CRM and PeopleSoft has been offered by Oracle OnDemand Apps, but primarily in a dedicated hosting environment as opposed to a multitenant, pure SaaS model. However, in May 2008, Oracle announced plans to open a $280 million, 200,000 square foot data center in Utah to support its SaaS business.[22]

Then, in September 2008, at the same time that Oracle announced availability of a set of Amazon Machine Images (AMIs) for Oracle Database 11g, Oracle Fusion Middleware, and Oracle Enterprise Manager, Oracle CEO Larry Ellison's famously quoted anti-cloud rant appeared in The Wall Street Journal.[23]

Things later changed with Oracle's acquisition of Sun, a vigorous nod to cloud. Blogging on ZDNet, Dana Gardner, president of Interarbor Solutions, reflects that Oracle's acquisition of Sun "bodes well for cloud computing too, as Oracle just about overnight becomes a cloud force to reckon with."[24] This conclusion is echoed in Gerson Lehrman Group's analysis of the acquisition: "Now with Oracle fighting to be a number one competitor and eventually the go-to vendor in the SaaS space, the strategic move to incorporate cloud computing into its mix of all its future offerings makes it a force to be reckoned with in terms of HaaS competing with Amazon, IBM, and Salesforce.com."[25]

IBM Divvies Up the Cloud. IBM has expanded its cloud-based offerings with LotusLive, SaaS versions of existing on-premise IBM meeting, messaging and collaboration products. Examples include LotusLive Notes (formerly Lotus Notes) for e-mail and LotusLive Engage (formerly Bluehouse) for social networking, Web conferencing, chat, file sharing and storage for enterprise collaboration, with more to come. More recently, IBM extended this by offering a Web-based version of Notes, called LotusLive iNotes, which directly challenges Google Apps.[26] IBM also offers a series of products that can be run on private clouds or hosted in IBM data centers.

IBM refers to the strategy behind these products as hybrid computing. With this strategy, IBM takes a divide-and-conquer approach to computing, providing products that are preconfigured to create clouds for specific enterprise tasks. Development-and-test clouds are an early example, with others, such as clouds to support business analytics, to follow.[27]

In addition, IBM and SAP have demonstrated a new cloud technology called "real-time application mobility" that enables workload portability. IBM and SAP have demonstrated the live migration of SAP applications across remote physical servers, regardless of location.[28] The demonstration used IBM POWER6 systems, making this one of the few examples of non-x86 cloud architecture. Is a specialized, non-x86 cloud on the horizon?

HP Adapts to Cloud. HP offers Adaptive Infrastructure as a Service (AIaaS). AIaaS makes on-demand infrastructure available as a service from HP data centers. Initially these services are optimized for Microsoft Exchange Server, SAP and other business critical applications. Users continue to own and manage their own applications while HP manages infrastructure and application operations. In addition, HP has announced a product called Cloud Assure, a SaaS application that helps users assess cloud security, performance and availability.

On another front, HP has joined forces with Intel and Yahoo to create a Cloud Computing Test Bed. This open source project will consist of data centers around the globe to promote open collaboration among industry, academia and governments by removing the financial and logistical barriers to research in data-intensive, Internet-scale computing.[29]

SAP Moves Early. SAP, long dominant in the ERP market, ventured into the cloud in 2007. Business ByDesign, SAP's on-demand offering for the small and midsize enterprise (SME) market, is priced on a per-user-per-month basis and is aimed at competitors such as Salesforce.com and NetSuite. Complete rollout of the product, however, was delayed for over a year, and has seen numerous fits and starts as SAP continues to figure out how to engineer and make a satisfactory profit with a SaaS product.[30] Although some announcements continue to be made (e.g., Business ByDesign will soon be made available on mobile devices[31]), it does not appear that complete product ramp-up will occur for awhile.[32]

Going forward, cloud services will continue to align around the IT stack, with mainstay and new players jockeying for position as they refine and reshape the cloud marketplace.

Cloud Effect 2

STRUCTURAL DEEPENING EXPANDS THE CLOUD ECOSYSTEM

As we saw in "The Stack Transforms to Services," a plethora of cloud services and providers has emerged, making services for infrastructure, platform, applications and processes readily available. Sometimes these services can be used as is; for example, a business may be able to use a standalone SaaS application. But what if that application needs to work with another cloud-based or in-house application?

Similarly, it is easy to obtain a preconfigured virtual machine such as an Amazon Machine Image (AMI), but this is of no use unless it is loaded with software and can be managed. What if better control of scaling is needed? How can everything be made to work in a coordinated process that supports the business? What if we need to coordinate between different clouds? What if additional security measures are needed? What if we simply don't trust the cloud?

Although some of these issues are addressed by the primary cloud service providers, additional functionality is often needed to weave together capabilities offered by the primary providers so that these capabilities can be used by enterprises in a flexible and reliable manner. Think of this additional functionality as middleware for the cloud. Often it is called orchestration. Whether provided on-demand as a cloud-based service, or as a software application or appliance installed in the enterprise data center, orchestration products and services are emerging to help enable effective use of cloud computing by the enterprise.

The result is a burgeoning ecosystem of cloud providers, services and products. Brian Arthur calls this "structural deepening" — when a technology overcomes its limitations by adding subsystems or assemblies that "(a) enhance its basic performance, (b) allow it to monitor and react to changed or exceptional circumstances, (c) adapt it to a wider range of tasks, and (d) enhance its safety and reliability."[33] The technology, more of an organism, "develops through its constituent parts and subparts improving simultaneously."[34]

In this cloud effect we will discuss three types of structural deepening of basic cloud services (see Figure 6):

- bolstering basic cloud service capabilities, making them easier to use and manage
- coordinating basic cloud services, combining and integrating them across service and cloud types
- providing additional confidence in cloud services

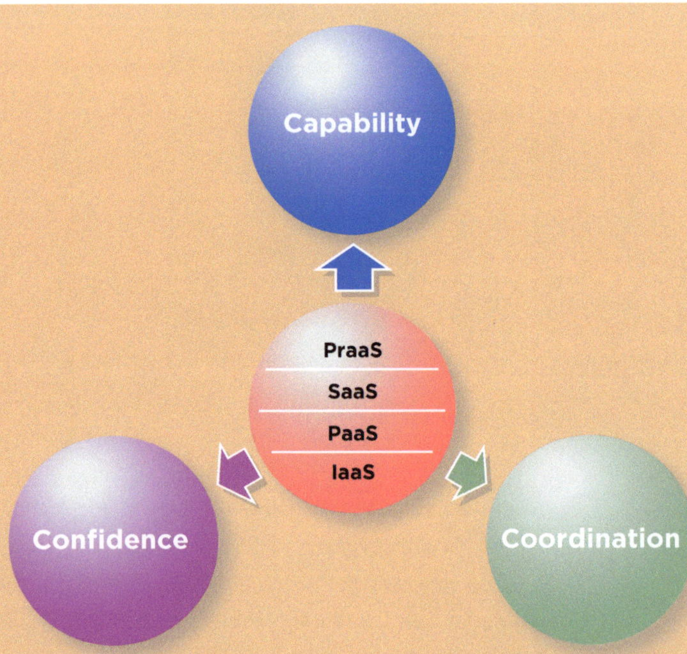

Figure 6 Structural deepening of basic cloud services occurs in three areas: bolstering cloud capabilities, coordinating multiple cloud services and creating confidence in the cloud. The result is a growing ecosystem of cloud services, vendors and products.

Source: CSC

BOLSTERING CLOUD SERVICE CAPABILITIES

While the primary providers of cloud services make a wide variety of IT capabilities available, enterprises sometimes find that the ability to use and manage these capabilities in an acceptable manner is lacking. Some of this is being remedied over time as cloud services and their providers mature. In the interim, additional sources must often be tapped to plug the gaps, particularly for life cycle management, dynamic scaling, application deployment, load balancing and metered billing.

Life Cycle Management. Additional functionality is often needed to provide or augment capabilities offered by primary service providers to manage the life cycle of virtual infrastructure resources both in the cloud and in the on-premise data center. This includes fast and easy creation of virtual machines and clusters, flexible provisioning and deployment of these resources, and pausing and restarting machines when needed.

Attention must be paid, as well, to end-of-life. It is ironic but perhaps not unexpected that server virtualization — once hailed as a panacea for server sprawl — often results in a new epidemic: virtual machine sprawl. Particularly when many enterprise users are allowed to create their own virtual machines in a cloud, those machines often end up being forgotten. The result is large numbers of virtual machines that are untended and unused. Detecting and deleting these unused machines is an important function provided via additional infrastructure management.

Provisioning of virtual machines provides a good example of the need for additional life cycle management capability. When a new physical machine is brought into the cloud network, it must be provisioned with an operating system and other needed system software. Provisioning brings a raw virtual machine to a state where it is ready to be used. Clouds such as Amazon EC2 provide one or more preset server images from which a user can choose. Often, however, this is not sufficiently flexible. Users need more choice and the ability to easily custom provision servers with different performance characteristics and software stacks. The ability to easily provision and manage customized virtual machines is provided by vendors such as RightScale, CohesiveFT and rPath.

Another product that provides a unique provisioning and deployment approach is FastScale Stack Manager. FastScale builds what it calls logical servers — essentially, virtual appliances that package applications together with the software stack needed to run them — and deploys and manages these logical servers across virtual, physical and cloud-based infrastructures. Stack Manager automatically creates a JeOS (just enough operating system) component within the appliance, resulting in a logical server that is extremely compact and self-contained.[35] (For more on virtual appliances, see Volume 2.[36])

Figure 7 DYNAMIC SCALING AUTOMATICALLY MATCHES SUPPLY TO DEMAND

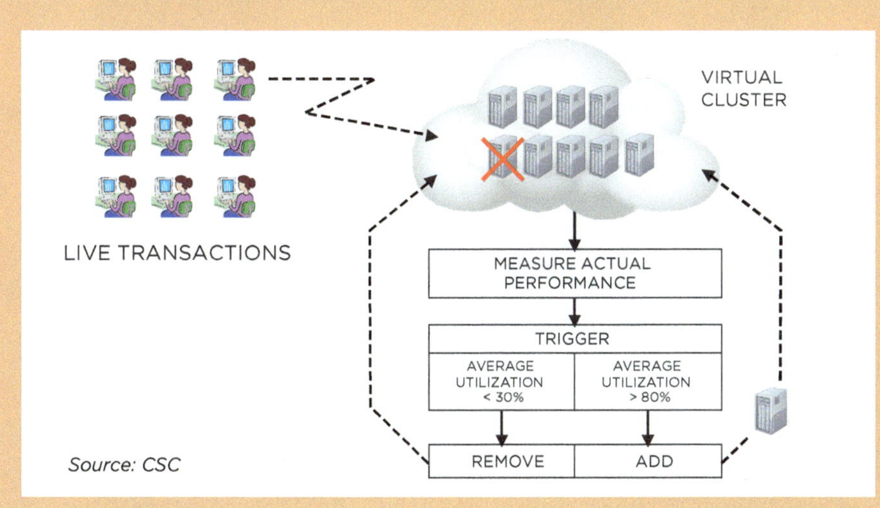

Source: CSC

Dynamic Scaling. Once established, the virtual infrastructure may or may not be an appropriate size to handle the volume of actual demand. The enterprise can continually monitor performance and manually add and delete servers as needed. However, the ability to dynamically handle scale-out of the cloud infrastructure is another key aspect of cloud functionality. This type of elastic scaling is crucial to the incremental matching of IT supply to demand. Automated scaling can occur at the machine level by increasing and decreasing the number of virtual machine instances according to user-specified parameters and actual demand. While some cloud infrastructure providers will do some automatic scaling of your infrastructure, more direct control is often needed. RightScale, for example, provides such an auto-scaling capability, as does Amazon, which has recently bolstered its EC2 service with a separate, user-controlled scaling capability. With user-controlled scaling, trigger parameters are established so that if some performance metric (e.g., average response time or utilization) exceeds a certain amount, a virtual machine is automatically added to the infrastructure. Conversely, if the metric falls below a certain value, a machine is automatically removed. (See Figure 7. For more on scaling, see "Designed to Scale" on page 118.)

Elastic scaling is crucial to the incremental matching of IT supply to demand.

Application Deployment. Creating virtualized infrastructures either internally or in a public cloud has many potential benefits, but those infrastructures are useless unless they can actually do something that is of value to the business. They need software. The ability to distribute applications across the virtual infrastructure is not straightforward, and is an important piece of additional cloud functionality.

If a single instance of the application will run on a single virtual machine, application deployment is fairly simple, and cloud infrastructure providers have mechanisms for uploading software to machine images. The situation is more complex if multiple application images must be deployed to multiple cores in a single machine or across multiple machines. The goal is to have multiple application images that can scale and work together in a coordinated manner yet seem to the user to be a single application.

Accomplishing this is often complex and is impacted by the architecture of both the infrastructure and the application itself. Providers such as 3Tera, Appistry and GigaSpaces address complexities of application deployment both in the enterprise data center and in the cloud. (For more on 3Tera, see Volume 2.[37] For more on Appistry and GigaSpaces, see "Architecting for the Cloud" on page 109.)

Load Balancing. Once application images have been deployed to the infrastructure, transactions from users must be intelligently routed to the best available machine for processing. Automated load balancing does this using numerous algorithms that take into account the level of demand versus available processors, and selects the best machines to maximize performance, utilization or other specified criteria. Load balancing capability may be provided either as a separate hardware or software appliance inserted as part of the infrastructure (e.g., Citrix NetScaler, 3Tera or HaProxy, an open source load balancer used by RightScale), or as an integral part of the functionality offered by Appistry, GigaSpaces and other similar vendors.

Figure 8 GoGrid displays cloud usage right on the interface screen.

Source: GoGrid

Metered Billing. Pay-as-you-go, utility-style billing is a hallmark of the cloud. However, while this is easy in concept, it is not so easy in practice, and is an issue for cloud providers and users alike. For providers, automated tools are required to track usage of processing, storage and I/O by customer and convert this usage into bills at published rates. Users, on the other hand, want to avoid unpleasant surprises when the monthly cloud bill is issued. They often require a more fine-grained look in real time at charges being accrued, and need their own independent verification of resource usage and charges. The ability to meter the cloud to determine valid charges is a crucial but often underestimated cloud function.

Multiple aspects of cloud usage must be metered and combined into an overall chargeback or customer bill. This includes such things as CPU usage (typically charged on a per-hour basis for a virtual machine instance), storage usage (this may include a charge per gigabyte of storage per month with additional charges for I/O requests), data transfer (may include charges for both transfer in and transfer out), and, in the case of SaaS, charges per transaction processed.

Even this, however, is not straightforward, and may have many variations that hinder both understanding what you are really getting as well as comparing charges from one provider to another. For example, for Amazon EC2, the amount of CPU that is allocated to a particular instance is expressed in terms of EC2 Compute Units. Amazon explains that it uses several benchmarks and tests to manage the consistency and predictability of the performance obtained from an EC2 Compute Unit. How does this compare, however, with what you get from another IaaS provider? It may well be difficult to know and compare since there are no standards for cloud capacity.[38]

Capability to meter and bill cloud services, of course, exists and is provided in several manners. Cloud providers themselves often, of necessity, build this capability into their services. While some may only provide the results to users on a monthly basis, others, such as GoGrid, make the results of metering and billing readily visible at all times. We have seen Figure 8 before (recall Figure 3). This time, however, the focus is on the upper left corner, to see a real-time summary of RAM usage and data transfers.

Metering and billing capabilities are provided in other forms by other vendors. Some, such as the eVapt On-Demand Monetization Platform, Aria A+ Billing and Zuora Z-Force, provide these capabilities to companies such as IaaS and SaaS providers. Others, such as Tap In Systems, allow users to monitor usage of their systems in the cloud.

COORDINATING CLOUD SERVICES

Often, a single cloud service is not sufficient to address a complex business need. Multiple types of services at different levels

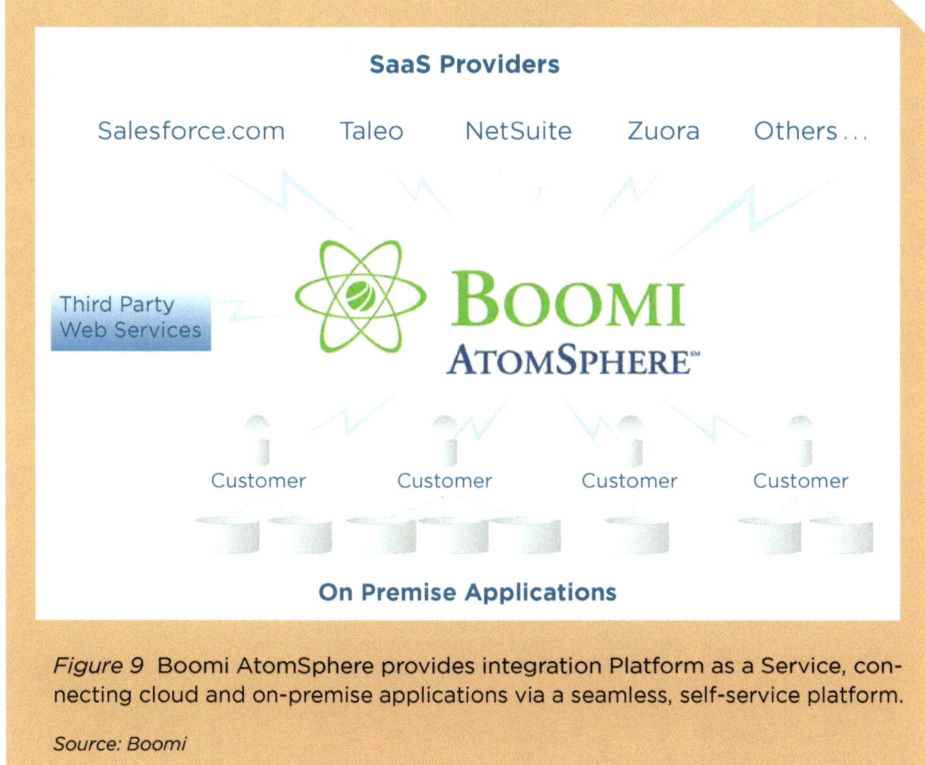

Figure 9 Boomi AtomSphere provides integration Platform as a Service, connecting cloud and on-premise applications via a seamless, self-service platform.

Source: Boomi

of the service hierarchy may be required; services in different clouds may be required; and integration with the on-premise data center is frequently needed. The ability to sort out the possibilities and assemble a single cohesive solution calls for additional functionality that is often crucial to being able to derive significant value from the cloud.

Application Integration. While some SaaS software may be used as a standalone application, often there is a need to integrate with other applications in the same cloud, in a different cloud, or on premise. The ability to integrate cloud-based applications is a critical piece of additional cloud functionality. Various integration approaches are used by different vendors such as Appirio, MuleSource, Pervasive Software, SnapLogic and Boomi (see Figure 9).

Process Integration. Enterprises carry out their business by executing business processes. These processes define and monitor the flow of work and coordinate the use of required resources. Business Process Management (BPM) is a coordination activity that addresses this area.

BPM is not new and has been implemented within the enterprise data center for several years. Now cloud-based BPM is available. What is crucial here is that some business processes or parts of processes will be hosted in a cloud, and some applications supporting processes will be hosted in a cloud. The ability to coordinate all of this into a cohesive end-to-end business process is the key challenge.

BPM can be used to orchestrate complete, end-to-end, composite processes that may invoke numerous other processes as needed. Completely automated activities (no human intervention), semi-automated activities (human input to a system), and completely manual activities can all be coordinated within the same workflow. To enable individual activities within the workflow, system functionality can be accessed, as needed, from any application, including cloud-based Web 2.0 applications and on-premise legacy applications.

Additional capabilities may augment the basic BPM. For example, Business Activity Monitoring (BAM) can be used to measure process performance and identify problems and bottlenecks. Process simulation may then be used to test process improvements, which can be implemented on-the-fly.

Figure 10 APPIAN PROCESS MODELER

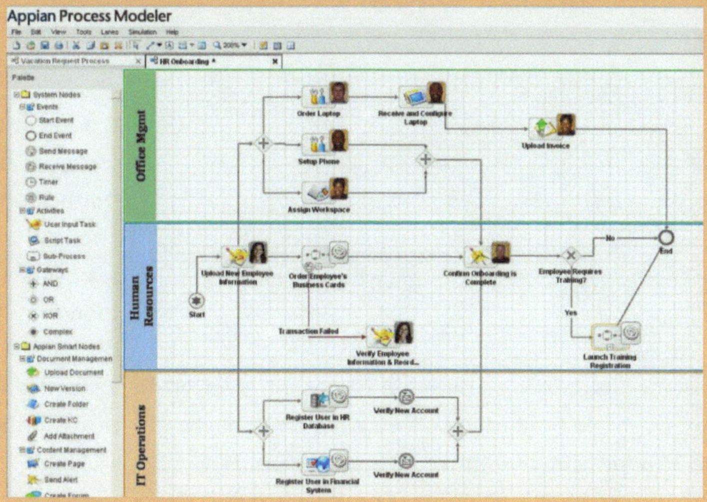

Source: Appian

End-to-end process coordination via cloud-based BPM is provided by vendors such as Appian, Cordys, Itensil, ProcessMaker and Skemma. Figure 10 illustrates the modeling of a typical business process. With many products, such models are directly translated into working processes that can be used to run the business without additional coding.

Brokering. Cloud is supposed to be simple — so straightforward that little instruction is needed, even for non-technical personnel, to take advantage of its many benefits. And, for simple tasks like firing up a virtual machine or using a standalone SaaS application, it is surprisingly easy. Many systems, however, are very complex. Accomplishing what needs to get done may require coordination of multiple cloud services, data integration, and making decisions among multiple alternative cloud providers. These types of issues are as complex as they have always been in traditional IT, if not more so. This is where the role of cloud brokers comes in.

According to Data Center Knowledge, "As enterprises struggle to sort out the array of cloud computing options and services, analysts see a growing opportunity for 'cloud brokers' to serve as intermediaries between end users and cloud providers. These cloud middlemen will help companies choose the right platform, deploy applications across multiple clouds, and perhaps even provide cloud arbitrage services that allow end users to shift between platforms to capture the best pricing."[39]

These cloud middlemen will help companies choose the right platform, deploy applications across multiple clouds, and perhaps even provide cloud arbitrage services that allow end users to shift between platforms to capture the best pricing.

Cloud brokers (or cloud service brokers) represent functionality that may be implemented in software, as an appliance, or, ostensibly, as a function performed by a person. In different scenarios, the broker functionality may be located with the provider of the broker service, in the enterprise data center, or in a cloud independent from both the provider and the enterprise.

The purpose of the broker is to facilitate use of the best resources for a job, whether those resources are located internally as part of a private cloud, or externally as part of one or more public clouds. Enterprises should expect a cloud broker to provide several functions:

- have a single interface for interacting with multiple clouds;
- operate outside of the clouds it controls and monitor those clouds;
- detect cloud failures and react in some appropriate way to those failures;
- move infrastructure elements from one cloud (public or private) to another.[40]

A cloud broker can improve reliability and decrease lock-in by spreading infrastructure across multiple clouds, and can enable disaster recovery into a secondary cloud. In its ultimate evolution, a cloud broker would be able to dynamically move system components from one cloud to another based on user-defined criteria such as cost, availability, performance or quality of service.

An extension to this type of functionality is sometimes provided by a *cloud brokerage*, which provides consulting services to help clients select the types of cloud services and components needed to solve a particular problem, select the best providers of these services and components, negotiate contracts and SLAs as needed (though in the cloud both of these tend to be minimal), and ensure integration of services and data across the entire solution.

Cloud broker functionality is beginning to become available today in various degrees. An example is the newly announced Deltacloud being developed by Red Hat. Deltacloud will allow applications, tools and scripts to work across different clouds. A business could start one instance on its internal cloud and then fire up another on an external cloud. A Deltacloud Web portal will provide an interface for users to migrate those instances from one cloud to another and to view, manage and provision images across all clouds. Public clouds supported include EC2 and (soon) Rackspace, while Red Hat enterprise Virtualization and VMware ESX are supported on the private cloud side.[41]

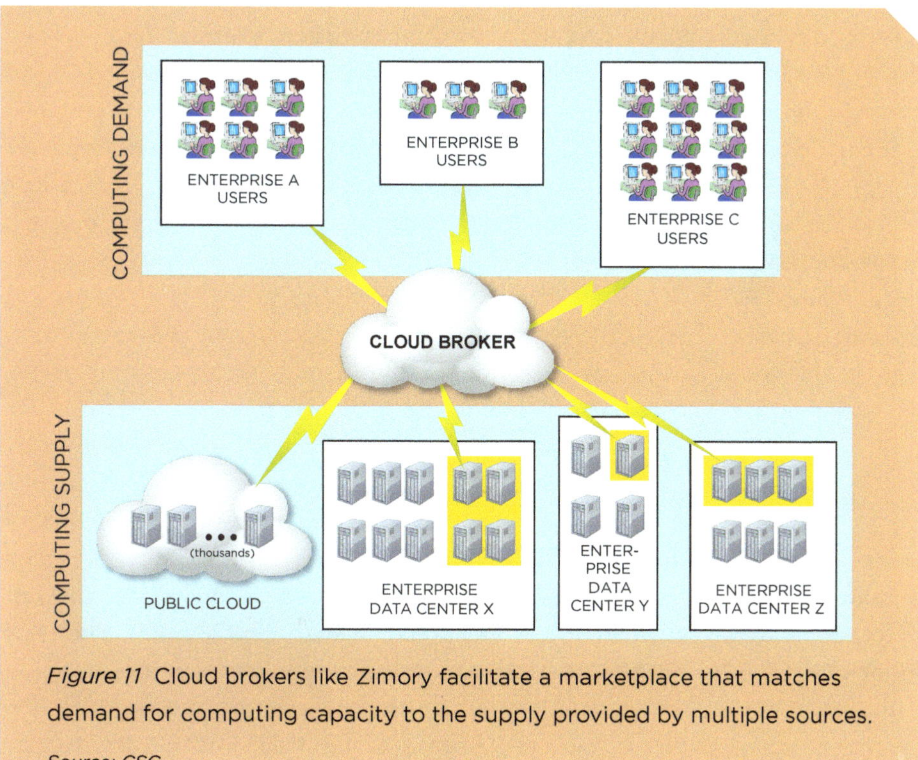

Figure 11 Cloud brokers like Zimory facilitate a marketplace that matches demand for computing capacity to the supply provided by multiple sources.

Source: CSC

An even more complete broker scenario is provided by the Zimory Public Cloud, also in the start-up phase. Zimory creates an open marketplace for computing capacity and acts as a broker between the supply and demand sides of the market (see Figure 11).

On the supply side, Zimory contracts with different public or private organizations that want to sell their unused compute capacity. These organizations are certified by Zimory and given a software agent to install that connects their capacity to the Zimory cloud. Zimory sets prices, makes contracts, sets up and maintains security, and bills customers for services rendered. On the demand side, the common Zimory API (application programming interface) makes all capacity seem homogeneous to the user. Users can search for various forms of capacity; select specific resources based on quantity and quality of performance, security or resource location; set the usage period; and specify the desired level of SLA. Zimory can migrate virtual machines and their software stacks around the clouds as needed to maintain the best positioning of resources according to user constraints.

Other providers looking at the cloud broker function include Kaavo, enStratus and CloudSwitch (reportedly developing a broker software appliance that would be installed in the data center and provide "an enterprise gateway to the cloud"[42]).

Perhaps most telling is the case of Elastra, which has reoriented its product in a new version. As illustrated in Figure 12, Elastra Server Cloud 2.0 is positioned to be the broker between public compute clouds, such as those created using Amazon's EC2 platform, and private cloud environments built on virtualization technology from vendors such as VMware and Eucalyptus Systems.

The Elastra approach is unique and has several parts. First, it starts by modeling an application to capture the infrastructure requirements that would be needed to support the application. This is a comprehensive view of an application that includes not just the software but a multi-vendor system of components that might include various types of servers, SANs, load balancers and other needed infrastructure.

Second, Elastra registers resources (including compute, storage and network resources) available from various cloud providers and captures the characteristics (down to such things as chip

Figure 12 ELASTRA SERVER CLOUD 2.0 FUNCTIONS AS AN AUTOMATED CLOUD BROKER

ELASTRA SERVER CLOUD 2.0
APPLICATION MODEL
APP COMPONENT 1
APP COMPONENT 2
APP COMPONENT 3
APP COMPONENT 4
PROVIDER RESOURCE PROFILES
APPLICATION DEPLOYMENT/ MANAGEMENT POLICIES
AUTOMATED BROKERING
PUBLIC CLOUD
APP COMPONENT 1
APP COMPONENT 4
APP COMPONENT 2
APP COMPONENT 3
PRIVATE CLOUD

Source: CSC

architecture, CPU speed, cores per socket, memory, attached storage and cost) of those resources. Third, policies, including preferences and constraints, are captured that govern how the application is to be deployed and scaled and under what conditions.

Last comes automated brokering. Based on the application requirements, policies and available resources both in public and private clouds, Server Cloud 2.0 (which is installed software) determines the best way to deploy the application. The result might be a hybrid cloud, with some application components running in public clouds and some internally.[43]

CREATING CONFIDENCE IN CLOUD SERVICES

In spite of the many potential benefits of cloud, the fact remains that enterprises are often reluctant to do business in the cloud. They fear such things as cloud lock-in, loss of control, unpredictable cloud availability and insufficient security (perceived or real). Assuring cloud services involves putting mechanisms in place to help alleviate these concerns so that enterprises feel safe conducting business in the cloud. Three important assurance mechanisms are: cloud monitoring, liquid security and cloud standards.

Monitoring. One of the problems with clouds is that users in the enterprise lack visibility into what is happening on the provider side. The enterprise may be using a large number of cloud nodes and virtual machines. How do you know their status, performance and problems? Do you even need to know? If you are using a high-level cloud service such as a SaaS or PraaS service, you may rely on the provider to worry about such things. But if you are using a low-level IaaS service, you need to know what is going on with your machines so you can be in control. In any case, you probably always want to know objectively whether or not SLAs are being met. Cloud monitoring addresses this need, as shown in Figure 13. (Also see "SLAs: A Shared Responsibility" on page 97.)

Monitoring is a common function in most data centers today. Data center personnel routinely use various tools to monitor networks and individual machines. Monitoring physical devices is one thing, but adequate tools to monitor virtual devices are often lacking. Put those virtual resources off-premise in a cloud and the problem is even worse.

Many cloud vendors and products have emerged to fill this gap. Tap-In Systems' Cloud Management Service, Coradiant (formerly Symphoniq) TrueView, Hyperic HQ, Hyperic CloudStatus, Vizioncore vFoglight, Amazon CloudWatch, Cloudkick and Zenoss are examples of products that monitor and report on virtualized assets in the cloud or the on-premise data center. Typically, both real-time and historical data may be presented covering asset status, availability, performance, alerts, bottlenecks and SLA conformance. Some of these products are meant to be installed in the enterprise data center and some in the cloud. Tap In Systems' Cloud Management Service, for example, is a cloud-hosted, on-demand, pay-as-you-go service that monitors both your public cloud and on-premise systems.

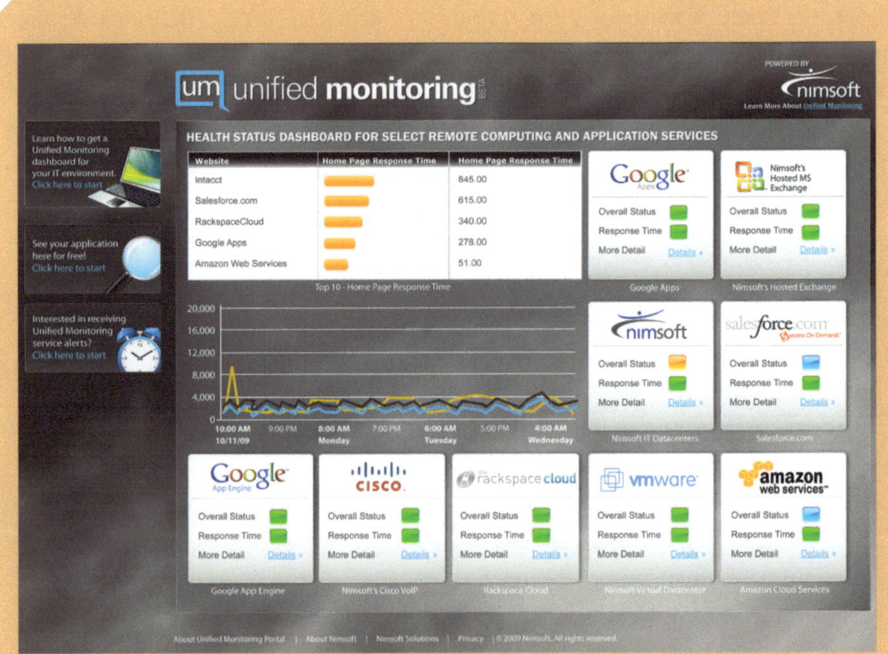

Figure 13 Nimsoft Unified Monitoring provides detailed performance metrics for all components of a business service, regardless of whether it is located internally in the data center or externally in the cloud.

Source: Nimsoft

SLAs: A SHARED RESPONSIBILITY

Cloud computing is all about services, but a service that is not available does not serve anyone and can actually harm a business's reputation and sales. Often, if a service goes down, your business goes down.

There are many reasons a service may be unavailable, including:

- An Internet path is down.
- The provider is down.
- The provider is out of business.
- The service is experiencing heavy volume.
- The service is under cyber attack.

To help protect against these situations, many organizations use well-defined service level agreements (SLAs). Whether for an outsourcer or an on-premise data center, SLAs establish stringent performance measures along with penalties for non-compliance. However, SLAs for the cloud tend to be minimal at present, and not easy to influence. Basically, it's take it or leave it.

SHORTCOMINGS

Many cloud SLAs are not extremely rigorous. For example, the Amazon EC2 SLA promises 99.95 percent availability (about four hours of downtime per year). That said, this may be satisfactory; not every application requires extreme availability, and most internal data centers probably don't achieve "five nines" (99.999 percent availability).

If a system does require high levels of availability, it may be possible to achieve that in a cloud, but don't expect many providers to guarantee it. There are, of course, exceptions. For example, 3Tera recently announced 99.999 percent availability.

Other providers, such as Rackspace, advertise 100 percent availability of network and HVAC systems (excluding scheduled maintenance).[44] This is great, but what is important is end-to-end service availability. A service comprises many different elements including the Internet, the provider network, HVAC, power, servers and software. All of these elements must be available simultaneously for the overall service to be available.

Cloud SLAs are also very minimal in terms of what they cover. Most address some measure of uptime. However, coverage of such things as mean time between failure, mean time to repair, time to recover data, and other more sophisticated measures you may be used to are not likely to be found.

Further, the uptime promised is meaningless unless you have some recourse when it falls short. Often, however, there is no recourse. Penalties associated with cloud SLAs are, in most cases, minimal. Suppose that Amazon is down for a day or more, violating its 99.95 percent availability SLA. Your recourse is 10 percent of what you paid that month. There are 720 hours in a month. Suppose you rent 10 servers from Amazon at the listed rate of $.10 per hour. Your bill for the month: $720. Your penalty payment from Amazon: $72. Did your business suffer more than $72 worth of damage due to the outage? Unless you are a lemonade stand, undoubtedly.

Even with no teeth, however, cloud SLAs serve a purpose. Essentially, they are a risk transfer mechanism. You may not get adequately compensated for losses, but at least there is someone on paper who is responsible.

SHARING RESPONSIBILITY

Having said that, cloud computing requires a shift in mindset regarding SLA responsibility. As opposed to placing the full burden of service availability solely on the provider, the current state of cloud computing dictates that responsibility for providing

(continued on the following page)

SLAS: A SHARED RESPONSIBILITY *(continued)*

adequate service be shared by both the provider and the enterprise. This involves two stages. First, the provider must strive to comply with its own stated SLA levels. Robust, flexible, autonomic architectures help to achieve this. For example, a design principle for Amazon S3 states: "The system considers the failure of components to be a normal mode of operation, and continues operation with no or minimal interruption."[45]

Second, the enterprise must implement measures to further guarantee service availability, by designing service usage scenarios that provide redundancy and the ability to receive uninterrupted service in case of provider failures.

This is a key point. In this new world of minimalist SLAs, enterprise IT departments need to take more responsibility for making sure their customers get the availability they need. Start by selecting providers that have good track records in actually meeting published SLAs. Then, be prepared to routinely deal with failure rather than act surprised and indignant about it.

There are different approaches for ensuring availability. It may be possible (for a price) for the enterprise to implement redundancy within a single provider's cloud. Amazon, for example, offers "availability zones" — completely redundant and physically isolated sets of infrastructure — for EC2, where replicated images and data can reside.[46] Additionally, IT has to take a close look at the architecture of applications, allowing for availability when realtime consistency is not needed.

An alternative approach is to have completely redundant installations running simultaneously in multiple clouds. Many are familiar with the concept of RAID — a redundant array of independent disks — in the storage world. CSC borrows this concept and proposes the cloud equivalent — RAIC, a redundant array of independent cloud providers. Simply put, RAIC addresses portability and reliability in the cloud through the use of multiple clouds simultaneously. As Mark Masterson of CSC, who coined the RAIC term,[47] puts it, "More providers equates to higher reliability. Moreover, distributing the pool of providers across a number of geographies could enable a design that is resistant to transient, localized problems with the Internet. An enterprise using a global RAIC could effectively achieve the same aggregate reliability as the global Internet itself."

In general, if you play in the cloud, you need to know where you can step. You need a backup plan that is well thought through for cases when an application or service goes down. Proceed, but have a plan, and actively share SLA responsibility with the provider. The risks of standing still are greater than the risks of moving forward.

Liquid Security. Because cloud services are delivered over a variety of networks from a variety of information and processing sources to a variety of user devices, security in the cloud needs to be "liquid" to cover the many operating environments in play. As discussed in the LEF Report *Liquid Security: Digital Trust When Time, Place and Platform Don't Matter,*[48] liquid security provides the digital trust needed to support enterprise value creation in an environment of multiple IT platforms (particularly mobile devices) and virtualized infrastructures. Digital trust is a technology strategy for enhancing business value while addressing information risk.[49]

Although the "weatherproofing" techniques[50] that are being applied to cloud computing today have provided enough digital trust in the cloud to bring palpable benefit to enterprises, they have also placed constraints on the types of applications, the amount of sharing, and the granularity of service and dynamic service adjustment that is possible with a fully formed cloud processing capability. Only a portion of the elastic power of cloud computing can be tapped by using these weatherproofing techniques: private clouds, safe applications and data (only moving applications and data with low security risk to the cloud), and presumptive security (believing that cloud vendors must have good security due to the nature of their business). For some enterprises and some needs, though, this will be enough.

Figure 14 DROPLETS OF LIQUID SECURITY DELIVER DIGITAL TRUST *IN* AND *FROM* THE CLOUD

Source: CSC

For others, however, these techniques represent only interim relief. Capturing the full benefit (business value) of cloud computing requires new digital trust technologies and techniques. These new digital trust technologies and techniques represent the needed liquid security that:

- delivers the evidence-backed confidence that is lost or hidden when platforms, applications and business processes move to a cloud
- creates and sustains a digital trust environment that liberates important enterprise functions so they can be pursued in the cloud without hesitation

These new liquid security technologies and techniques are beginning to emerge. They represent the first "droplets" of liquid security that can help deliver the trust evidence that is needed without destroying the elasticity of cloud processing. As illustrated in Figure 14, the first droplets of liquid security technology are evolving into two categories:

Capturing the full benefit (business value) of cloud computing requires new digital trust technologies and techniques.

1. technologies that help generate digital trust *in the cloud* itself (shown with boxes)
2. technologies that help deliver digital trust *from the cloud* (shown without boxes)

Those in the first category are most evident in the pursuit and delivery of PaaS and IaaS services. These are the digital trust technologies and techniques that measure, monitor, collect and report on the security and privacy configuration and the operating characteristics of the cloud itself.

For example, such characteristics as vulnerability discovery, data location and encryption status, patch status, operating condition, access control lists and audit records would be included in this cloud collection of trust evidence. These characteristics constitute elements of transparency that are needed to provide the evidence-based confidence that leads to digital trust and, ultimately, enterprise value. In order to receive the digital trust (liquid security) benefits, the outcomes of these technologies — i.e., the evidence that restores transparency — must also be made available to cloud consumers as shown with the gray arrow in Figure 14.

Figure 15 VPN-CUBED EXTENDS YOUR OWN INTERNAL SECURITY TO THE CLOUD

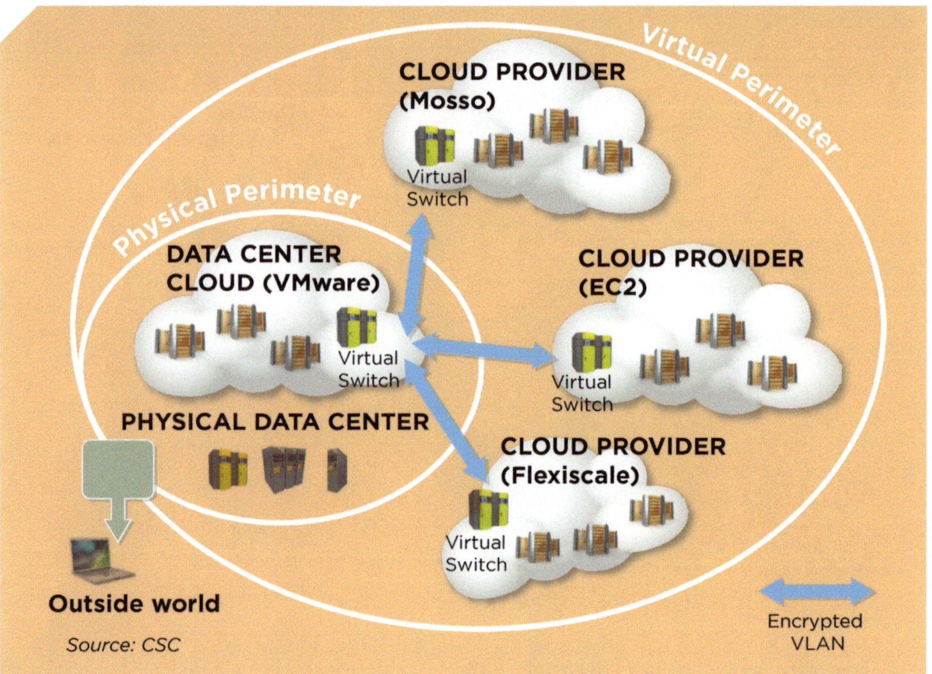

Source: CSC

The liquid security technologies in the second category are most evident in the pursuit and delivery of SaaS and BPaaS services. Examples include anti-virus as a service, anti-spam as a service, key management as a service, electronic signatures as a service, registered e-mail as a service and trusted time-stamping as a service. Liquid security delivered in this manner offers digital trust (and value) to the enterprise by providing security features as a service directly to enterprise work needs and workflow.

Some liquid security technologies can satisfy both categories. For instance, a security as a service vulnerability scanner served to clients through a cloud can also be used within the cloud to discover internal vulnerabilities. Although there is no precise equation for how to balance the two categories of liquid security technologies, it would seem illogical to serve up a liquid security service from a cloud which itself cannot claim digital trust.

One way to ensure that a public cloud has the opportunity to create digital trust is to extend the time-tested traditional technique of virtual private networking (VPN) to create the notion of a virtual private cloud (VPC). As enabled by products such as CohesiveFT's VPN-Cubed and the Amazon Virtual Private Cloud, a VPC stretches a dedicated set of cloud-provided resources to include some critical security resources that are client-owned and managed.

For example, VPN-Cubed places a virtual switch in your data center and another virtual switch on a virtual machine in your public cloud implementation. These switches are connected via encrypted VLAN. The net result is that your internal firewall is extended virtually to include your infrastructure in the public cloud. In essence, the public cloud is brought within your data center and receives the same internal security as your on-premise resources. The same method can be used to enclose multiple clouds within your secure, virtual perimeter. (See Figure 15.)

This extension of cloud computing to include user-owned security mechanisms can qualify more sensitive applications and processes for cloud computing, and thereby offer the opportunity for digital trust in the cloud to occur. New enterprise payoffs become possible with the liquid security potential of such technologies.

The Role of Standards. As with any major new wave of technology, there is an increasing call for industry standards for cloud computing. Many companies are waiting for clear standards to emerge for interoperability, security, transparency, quality-of-service (QoS), and cloud services in general before committing to move to the cloud. Several promises of the cloud, such as cross-cloud orchestration, will only be completely realized once some standards are

> **Many companies are waiting for clear standards to emerge for interoperability, security, transparency, quality-of-service (QoS), and cloud services in general before committing to move to the cloud.**

in place. Even with the cloud still in its infancy, the demand for standards is thundering louder every day.

This demand is being driven primarily by the need for cloud interoperability. Because moving applications and systems between clouds requires two clouds to use the same APIs and support the same services, cloud interoperability depends highly on standards — formal or informal — that cloud providers can agree on and implement consistently. Additionally, standards are seen by many to be the key to avoiding the lock-in of proprietary clouds.

The demand for standards is being driven primarily by the need for cloud interoperability.

As of fall 2009, at least 10 new organizations, a plethora of existing standards bodies, numerous companies and several government institutions were actively pursuing the creation and potential adoption of cloud standards. Many of these groups are collaborating and becoming more interwoven as the cloud covers a large swath of the IT field. For example, the Cloud Standards Coordination Working Group (cloud-standards.org) is beginning to tie together the standards efforts of multiple groups, including the Cloud Security Alliance, Distributed Management Task Force (DMTF), Open Cloud Consortium (OCC), OASIS and the Object Management Group (OMG).

Although there are several new players, such as Enomaly, a good number of the individual groups or companies working on cloud standards have been deeply involved in setting standards in many of the technologies underlying the cloud. OASIS is an existing organization that sets standards for Service Oriented Architecture and Web services, which themselves are foundational standards for the cloud. The Open Group has been defining standards for over a decade and has recently established a cloud-specific working group. Nearly all of these organizations are sponsored by vendors, both large and small. IBM, Sun (Oracle) and many of the established vendors are often hedging their bets by getting involved with several standards groups simultaneously.

Government organizations, including the U.S. General Services Administration (GSA) and the U.S. National Institute of Standards and Technology (NIST), are increasingly driving the discussion on cloud standards, particularly given the potential benefits governments could gain from cloud computing.[51] In September 2009, the GSA set up the Apps.Gov portal to provide other government agencies access to cloud-based services. (See "Self-Service Is the Order of the Day" on page 87.) Earlier that summer, the UK government announced plans for a "G-Cloud," a shared set of cloud capabilities for official agencies.[52] And in November 2009, the International Standards Organization (ISO) was said to be setting up a standards Study Group for cloud computing.[53]

Figure 16 SAMPLE OF PROPOSED CLOUD STANDARDS

STANDARD	PROPOSED BY
vCloud	VMware
Amazon Web Services (EC2, S3)	Eucalyptus Systems, Canonical
Unified Cloud Interface	Cloud Computing Interoperability Forum
CMDBf	Distributed Management Task Force (DMTF)
Open Cloud Computing Interface (OCCI)	Open Grid Forum (OGF)
Open Virtualization Format (OVF)	DMTF
Cloud Data Management Interface (CDMI)	Storage and Network Industry Association
Trusted Cloud Protocol	CSC

Source: CSC

With this maelstrom of organizations attempting to set standards for the cloud, the potential standards emerging are mostly focused on setting common APIs and definitions for infrastructure cloud services (IaaS). Examples include the Open Virtualization Format (OVF), which supports virtual machine interoperability, and Cloud Data Management Interface (CDMI), which aims to standardize interfaces for cloud-based storage. Many proposed standards, however, have yet to be fully explored or widely implemented and remain, for now, unproven. A sample of proposed standards is shown in Figure 16. Most of the standards efforts are focused on IaaS, including setting standards for virtualization, storage, security and networking.

For security, some cloud providers are using existing standards to raise the level of trust that potential customers haven't yet put into cloud offerings. Recently, some companies, including Microsoft, have been seeking SAS 70 or ISO 27001 security certification for their cloud services;[54] however, many potential cloud users are looking for cloud-specific security standards and certifications.

Christofer Hoff, director of cloud and virtualization solutions at Cisco, points out that the many existing security and network standards, upon which cloud computing depends, are themselves not adequate to meet the emerging security needs and concerns. "The protocols that provide the glue for our fragile Internet are showing their age; BGP, DNS and SSL are good examples," says Hoff. He adds, "Ultimately the most serious cloud computing concern is presented by way of the 'stacked turtles' analogy: layer upon layer of complex interdependencies predicated upon fragile trust models, framed upon nothing more than politeness, and with complexities and issues abstracted away with additional layers of indirection."[55]

Interestingly, the current giants in the cloud space — Google, Amazon and Microsoft — have little to no real involvement with these cloud standards efforts.[56] It seems they are more focused on increasing their foothold in this new market using more proprietary approaches. Even though these companies are building a track record (good and bad) of providing cloud services, they remain under criticism for not actively opening their interfaces and supporting official standards. The counter-argument to this is the need for innovation, as standards that are set too early may limit the ability of the industry to advance the cloud rapidly.

As Amazon Web Services (AWS) has become the mindshare leader, if not market leader, in the area of IaaS, other organizations have begun to use open source to copy Amazon's existing but proprietary APIs, hoping that with numerous and free implementations, the AWS interfaces will become de facto standards. Three open source efforts are now driving to make it possible to create interoperable clouds using Amazon as the model: Eucalyptus, Nimbus and OpenNebula. As Simon Wardley, software services manager at Canonical, which is packaging Eucalyptus with the Ubuntu operating system as Ubuntu Enterprise Cloud, puts it, "... the fastest way to achieve a standard is not through committee, conversation or whitepapers but through the release and adoption of not only a standard but also an operational means of achieving a standard."[57] (See "Open Sourcing the Private Cloud" on page 107.)

The cloud community will likely spawn many more often competing, sometimes messy, possible standards and several potential de facto standards before true standards start becoming real.[58] However, as history shows us, that's the way it always works.

All told, the cloud orchestration functionality needed to bolster, coordinate and assure cloud services will continue to emerge in the coming years. The result will be clouds that are easier to use, manage and trust. Of more importance, as portrayed in the remaining cloud effects, will be the accelerated transformation of both IT and the enterprise.

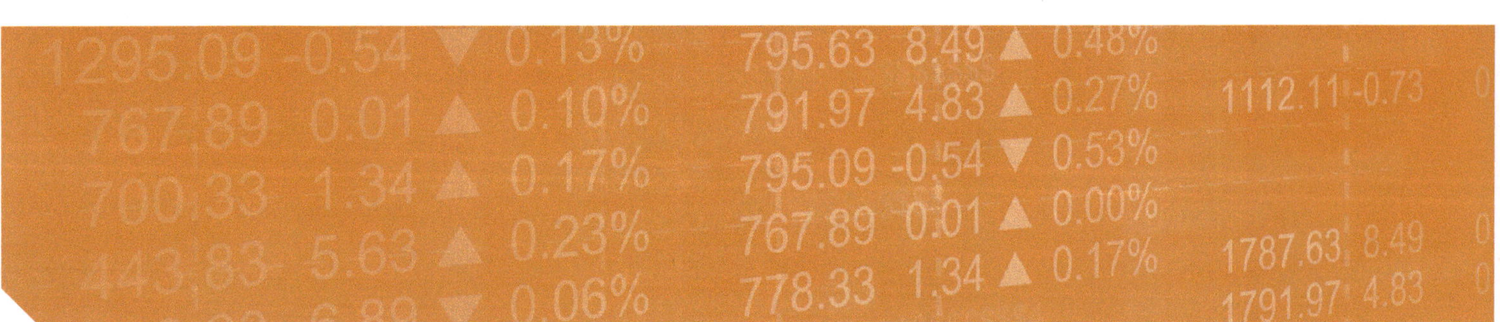

Cloud Effect 3

CLOUD ENABLES NEW IT OPTIONS

All enterprises have the opportunity to tap the benefits of cloud computing. The lure of lower capital expenditures, lower operating costs, green computing and scalable assets is strong, especially in today's economy. However, worries over security and privacy, loss of control, and availability of service (especially in light of highly publicized outages by major providers) may quickly throw a wet blanket on unbridled cloud enthusiasm.

These concerns, whether real or imagined, have led to a number of increasing choices as to how to realize the benefits of the cloud. What if cloud benefits could be obtained in-house, right in your own data center, while avoiding some of the concerns? Or what if there was a cloud that was restricted to a known, trusted community of businesses, with higher levels of transparency and security? Today there is a spectrum of cloud choices, from private clouds to semi-private clouds to public clouds, as well as the ability to mix these together into hybrid clouds. With a range of clouds, plus capabilities delivered as services up and down the stack, IT will have wide latitude to mold all these parts together to reinvent IT in many ways.

PRIVATE VS. PUBLIC CLOUDS

Although a private cloud often starts with virtualized resources, virtual machines or virtualized infrastructure alone do not a cloud make. Traditional IT resource configurations and usage, including co-location and even outsourcing, are not private clouds. There is much more to it.

Key pieces of the puzzle include core cloud elements such as an in-house grid, resource pools or fabrics (in contrast to individually managed machines), automated monitoring, dynamic provisioning, user-based resource allocation, metering and billing. In short, a private cloud behaves in many respects like a public cloud, providing a flexible set of resources. A private cloud may even employ the same APIs as a public cloud (which is an important element of enabling hybrid clouds.) What makes it private is that it is only shared within the confines of the enterprise network.

Private clouds show up primarily as two types: an on-premise (or in-house) cloud and a shared enterprise cloud. With an on-premise cloud, all or some of the IT resources in a data center are enabled to be shared. Emerging cloud platforms, such as the open source Ubuntu Enterprise Cloud,[59] give organizations the tools to build their own internal IaaS cloud capabilities, essentially creating a miniature version of Amazon's AWS in-house. (See "Open Sourcing the Private Cloud" on page 107.)

There are two major differences between private and public clouds:

- *Ownership of underlying IT resources.* In a public cloud, the provider owns the resources. In a private cloud, the enterprise continues to own the resources; thus, the headaches attendant to procuring, operating and managing these physical resources do not go away. Conversely, by controlling the underlying IT resources in a private cloud, an organization will have much higher transparency into what is happening in the cloud, and will avoid any potential issues that come with sharing resources with other organizations in public clouds (e.g., security and allocation).

- *Economics.* Enterprises that use public cloud services avoid capital expenditure for new IT resources; those implementing private clouds do not. Further, many public cloud providers have a scale of operations, operating efficiencies and price points that cannot be duplicated in an enterprise data center. Enterprises turning to the private cloud option should not expect to duplicate the short-term cost advantages of major public cloud providers. (See "Cloudonomics Provide Financial Incentive" on page 121.)

How you weigh these alternatives depends on your particular circumstances. One approach is to look purely at the cost-

Enterprises turning to the private cloud option should not expect to duplicate the short-term cost advantages of major public cloud providers.

benefit tradeoff between establishing your own private cloud versus moving to a public cloud. For example, by adopting the processes and systems for cloud computing internally, along with their scale, Bechtel envisions a shared enterprise cloud, a private cloud that is shared across the entire global enterprise. (See "Dialing Up and Down" on page 124.)

In comparison, ETS is going the public cloud route for one of its easier applications. The application, the speech recognition portion of the SpeechRater application, has spiky demand. ETS is moving it to the cloud for economic reasons and to learn. "We are proceeding with moving SpeechRater to Amazon because of the favorable economics, a successful proof of concept, and the opportunity to learn," explains John Taylor, Technology Evangelist at ETS.

Most companies looking at creating a private cloud are considering enabling an IaaS cloud approach, as it seems to be a logical evolution from the increasingly virtualized data centers that have been emerging over the last few years. Even if companies can never realize the same economies of scale as the large public cloud providers, many are looking at bringing some of the cloud in-house to benefit from at least some of the operational efficiencies of cloud computing, such as dynamic resource allocation and increased automation of IT.

The private cloud scenario offers numerous advantages and is often the preferred method of initial cloud adoption for many enterprises, particularly given the concerns with security and lack of clear standards today.

SEMI-PRIVATE CLOUDS

Clouds are not limited to private and public only. In addition, several intermediate types of clouds are emerging. Figure 17 shows the resulting spectrum of cloud types, ranging from private to semi-private to public clouds.

A semi-private cloud is not limited to a single enterprise nor is it open for general use. Rather, a semi-private cloud restricts its use to a defined community. For example, an enterprise could extend its private clouds to partners or collaborating enterprises.

The U.S. federal government, which has been an advocate of cloud computing despite serious concerns about privacy,

Figure 17 SPECTRUM OF CLOUD TYPES

On-Premise/ Internal	Shared Enterprise	Limited Membership	Community	Public	
				Cordys	PROCESS SERVICES
				Google Apps, SalesForce.com	APPLICATION SERVICES
				Windows Azure	PLATFORM SERVICES
Eucalyptus	Eucalyptus Bechtel	RACE (U.S. Department of Defense)	Nebula	Amazon EC2	INFRA-STRUCTURE SERVICES

Internal clouds do not yet typically offer cloud services at these stack levels.

Private | Semi-Private | Public

SPECTRUM OF CLOUD TYPES

Source: CSC

Figure 18 RACE PROVIDES CLOUD SERVICES TO MILLIONS OF USERS ACROSS THE U.S. ARMED FORCES

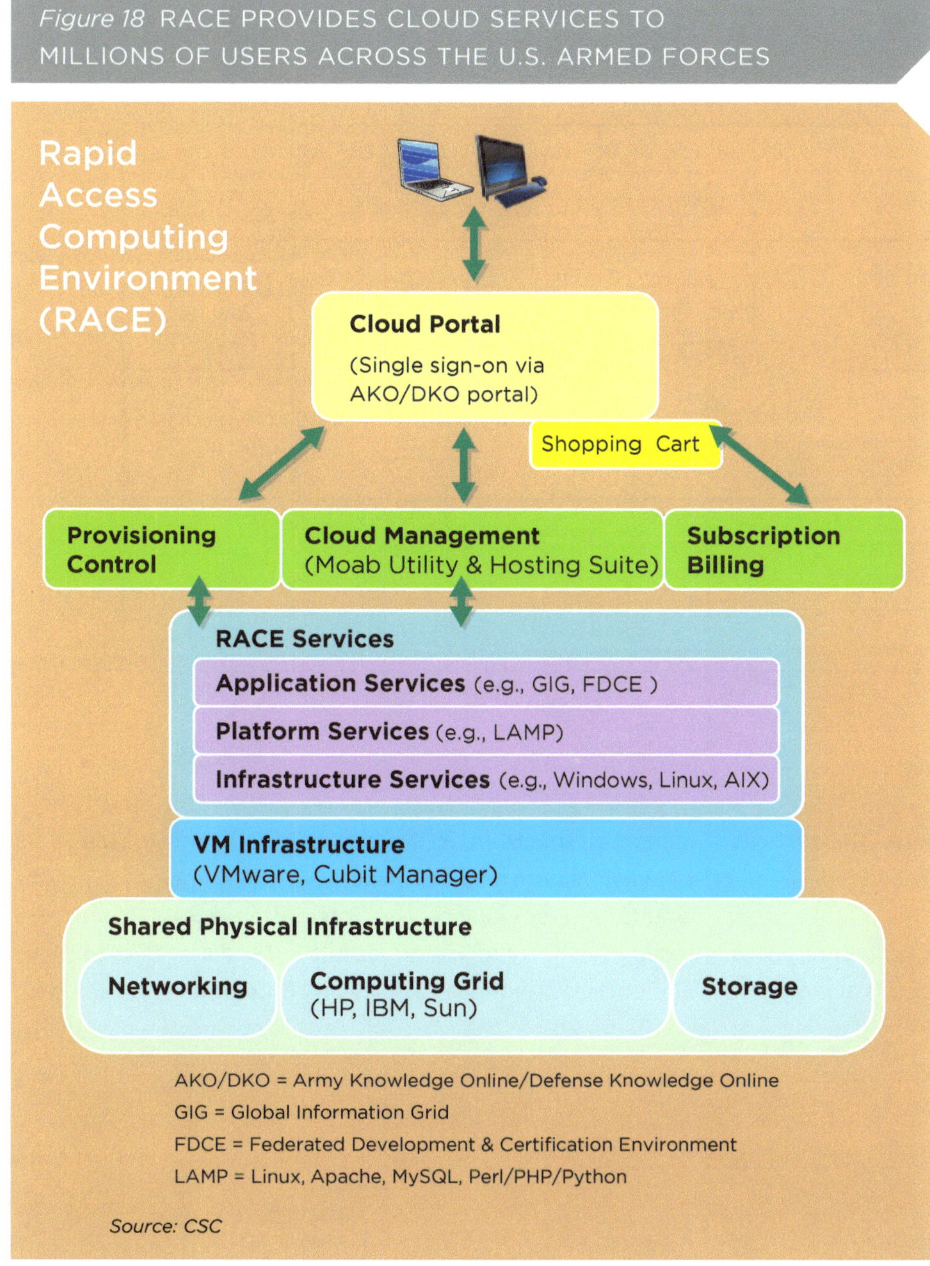

Source: CSC

offers an example. The U.S. Department of Defense operates its own cloud for all of its agencies. Run by the Defense Information Systems Agency (DISA), the Rapid Access Computing Environment (RACE) provides cloud-based computing for use by all of the armed services. (See Figure 18.) RACE now supports production environments for existing applications as well as development and testing of new applications. The Pentagon even boasts that its cloud is better than Google.[60]

In contrast to RACE, another option for the federal government is to use a third-party cloud specially architected to have restricted use. For example, the Trusted Cloud offered by CSC and Terremark (described on pages 115 and 116) is a highly secure cloud that provides services to security-conscious government organizations. In this semi-private cloud, a third-party provider (CSC and Terremark) delivers cloud services to a specifically defined government community.

Community clouds in the public sector are another example of semi-private clouds. Community clouds are clouds that are shared across similar and interrelated organizations, enabling them to gain some of the economic benefits of public clouds, but with increased focus on sharing specialized applications needed within that community. A case in point is Penguin Systems, which has recently launched Penguin on Demand, a pay-as-you-go service that provides access to high performance computing. This cloud targets a specific type of computing needed to support certain businesses. See "Cloud Drives Business Value" on page 125 for more on community clouds.

Even as the different cloud types vary in ownership, scale and services, there are common characteristics to all clouds across the spectrum, such as management of resource pools or fabrics instead of management of individual pieces of equipment; self-management, scheduling and load balancing of resources; dynamic provisioning; and automatic, demand-driven scaling of services.

Determining which type of cloud is appropriate requires analysis as well as consideration of how specific needs, costs and concerns need to be addressed. All these will vary not just based on your organization, but also on the specific layer of cloud services being sought. At the most basic level, choosing a point along the spectrum is a tradeoff between control and economics.

As clouds appear at different stack layers and along different parts of the cloud spectrum, it is unlikely that a single cloud will fulfill all IT and application needs of an organization. As

Figure 19 ENTERPRISES WILL USE MULTIPLE CLOUD SERVICES ACROSS THE SPECTRUM OF CLOUD TYPES

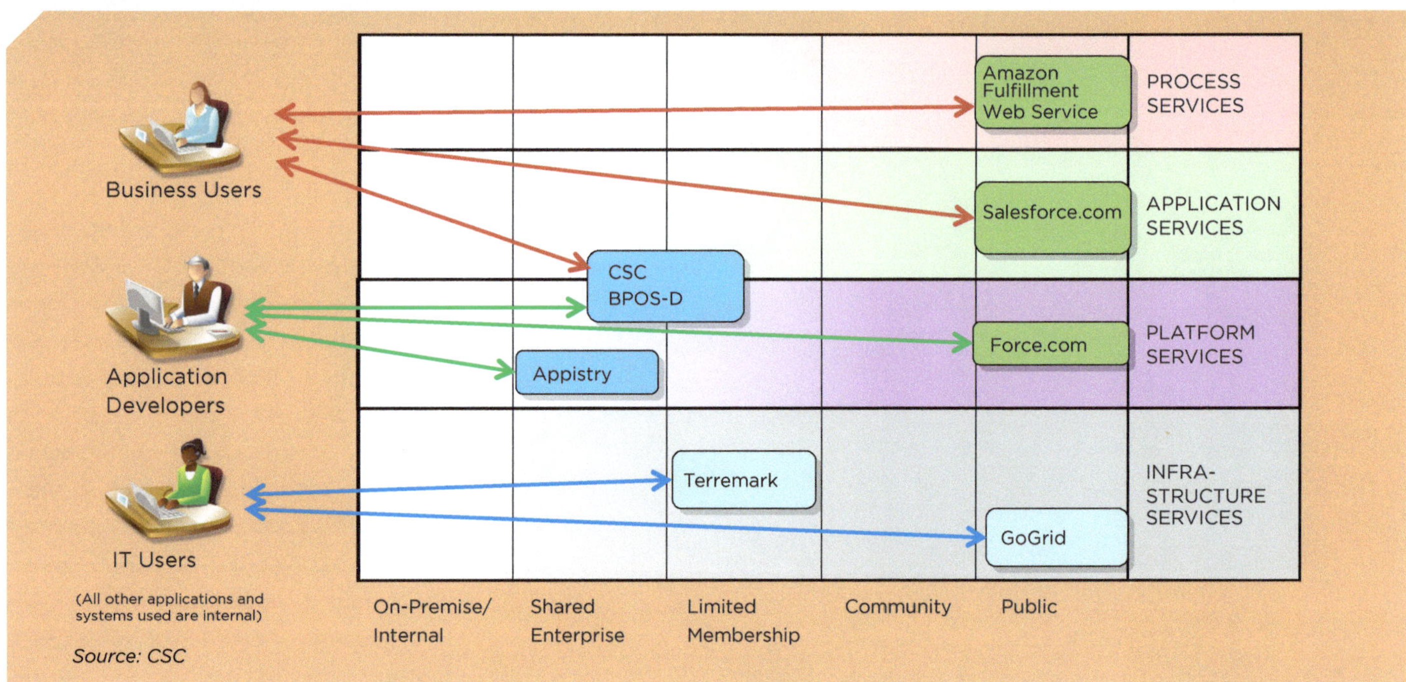

Business Users
Application Developers
IT Users
(All other applications and systems used are internal)
Amazon Fulfillment Web Service
PROCESS SERVICES
Salesforce.com
APPLICATION SERVICES
CSC BPOS-D
Force.com
Appistry
PLATFORM SERVICES
Terremark
GoGrid
INFRA-STRUCTURE SERVICES
On-Premise/ Internal
Shared Enterprise
Limited Membership
Community
Public

Source: CSC

shown in Figure 19, organizations will likely tap the services of multiple clouds from different providers.

Just using individual clouds, then, is only the start. Enterprises need the ability to connect services between clouds at any point along the spectrum, as well as be able to move seamlessly between cloud service providers, including their own private clouds. Interoperability and integration across clouds are required not only to use clouds but to build new IT capabilities and business solutions out of them. Enter the hybrid cloud.

Figure 20 HYBRID CLOUD SCENARIOS

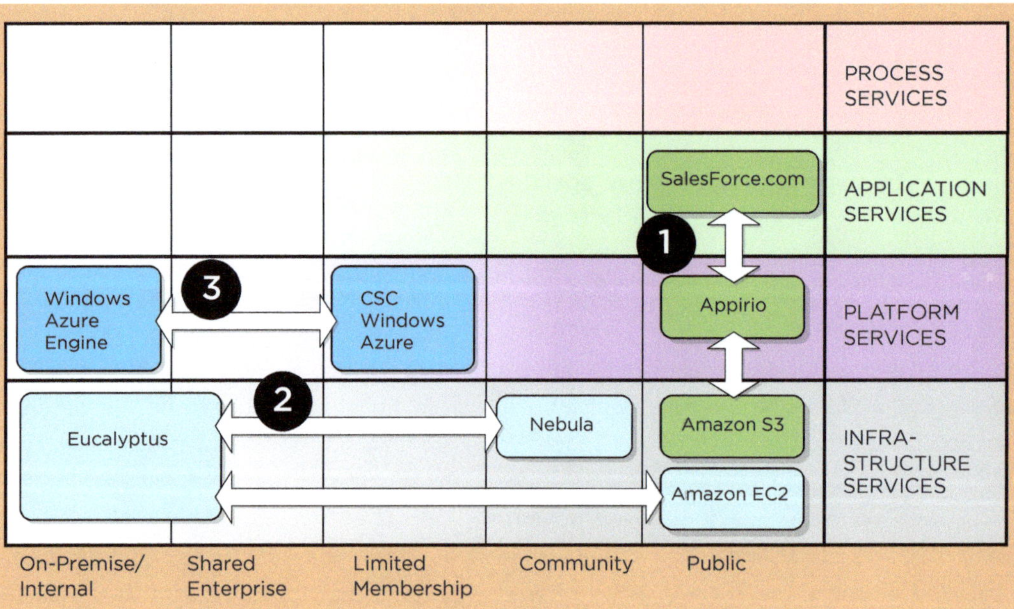

PROCESS SERVICES
SalesForce.com
APPLICATION SERVICES
1
Windows Azure Engine
3
CSC Windows Azure
Appirio
PLATFORM SERVICES
2
Eucalyptus
Nebula
Amazon S3
Amazon EC2
INFRA-STRUCTURE SERVICES
On-Premise/ Internal
Shared Enterprise
Limited Membership
Community
Public

Source: CSC

HYBRID CLOUDS

Hybrid clouds are about finding the right mix of clouds, regardless of where they fall on the spectrum of types. In some cases, the mix is found by combining and integrating the capabilities across different clouds. Scenario 1 in Figure 20 shows an example in which a customer of Salesforce.com uses Appirio's new storage service to extend its Salesforce application storage into Amazon's S3.[61] In this example, the hybrid cloud consists of connecting two public clouds through a third party service. What enables this scenario (connecting two clouds for additional functionality) is the availability of easily accessible and usable APIs to connect clouds in new ways.

The most common use of the hybrid cloud, however, is to describe the transparent and seamless connection between a private cloud and a public (or semi-private) cloud. This connection is key to making it easy to switch between clouds.

"Easy switching between providers is essential for a fully functioning cloud marketplace," asserts Simon Wardley, software services manager at Canonical and noted cloud computing expert. "This requires choice in providers, access to data and interoperability of the services provided. Just like the electricity grid, when you switch providers you want the service to work in the same way, and you don't want to rewire your house." An important step in this direction is Canonical's Ubuntu-Eucalyptus initiative to provide portability between public and private clouds through an open source EC2-style system. (See "Open Sourcing the Private Cloud" below.)

Scenario 2 in Figure 20 shows an example of how a hybrid cloud, using the capabilities of Eucalyptus, enables an organization to run the same system or applications in any of three clouds, as they all operate using the same API and enable the transfer of standardized resource types. Two common goals of such a hybrid cloud are 1) to enable "cloudbursting," where additional application capacity is automatically provisioned and used in the public cloud (usually on a temporary basis) in response to increased user demand; and 2) to enable organizations to run integrated applications in a cloud that meets specific requirements, such as running applications using sensitive data in a private cloud, while using cheaper public cloud resources for applications with less sensitive data.

As the previous scenario involves IaaS clouds, the same type of interoperability is required to enable PaaS hybrid clouds. In scenario 3, an organization may build Windows Azure-based applications and choose, based on multiple factors, to run them either locally or, in this case, in a CSC-hosted Windows Azure cloud.[62] As Windows Azure provides a common platform for building and running applications, in the end businesses won't really care which cloud their applications run in, as long as they perform adequately.

OPEN SOURCING THE PRIVATE CLOUD

What do you get when you cross a Koala with a eucalyptus tree? An Australian nature hike, for one thing, but also a readily available private cloud. Koala is an operating system distribution and Eucalyptus is cloud software. Both are open source and, when combined, they give enterprises a powerful way to create private clouds that can interoperate with public clouds.

Eucalyptus enables enterprises to set up private clouds that emulate the look and feel of Amazon's Elastic Compute Cloud (EC2), because Eucalyptus uses the same APIs as EC2. This provides important portability and flexibility, since work in the private cloud can be easily shifted to the Amazon cloud, and vice versa. Born as a research project at the University of California,

(continued on the following page)

OPEN SOURCING THE PRIVATE CLOUD *(continued)*

Santa Barbara, Eucalyptus went commercial in 2009 with the formation of Eucalyptus Systems.

In a related commercial move, the Eucalyptus software was incorporated into the latest version of the Ubuntu operating system, code named Karmic Koala. (Ubuntu is a popular Linux distribution.) In October 2009, Canonical released Ubuntu 9.10, which embeds Eucalyptus in its server version to deliver the Ubuntu Enterprise Cloud (UEC) environment. The Ubuntu 9.10 release gives anyone the ability to create their own Amazon Machine Images (AMIs) using EC2 APIs. Thus enterprises using Ubuntu 9.10 have ready access to tools to create virtual machines deployed either on a private cloud (UEC) or on EC2.

Eucalyptus addresses the creation of private clouds from a different level than products such as AppLogic, CloudIQ, XAP or Enterprise Cloud Server. These products address deployment and scaling of applications on clouds. Eucalyptus, on the other hand, creates a cloud architecture from existing infrastructure and automates the life cycle of virtual machines within that infrastructure, but does not deal with the creation, deployment, scaling or management of applications on the infrastructure.

Ubuntu, however, is poised to fill this gap by making it easier to deploy applications on the cloud infrastructure and, according to founder Mark Shuttleworth, "make those clouds dance, with dynamically growing and shrinking resource allocations depending on your needs."[63] Furthermore, since Eucalyptus is API-compatible with EC2, it can take advantage of the growing ecosystem of AWS tools and expertise, such as RightScale's ability to register and manage Eucalyptus-based private clouds along with other clouds.[64]

Eucalyptus is also a key component of the Nebula cloud being created by NASA Ames Research Center. Eucalyptus gives NASA researchers a simple approach to on-demand computing and enables virtual servers in the Nebula environment to be run on EC2 (or other Xen-based virtualization environments) by outside partners, collaborators or independent researchers.[65] That flexibility was essential for Nebula, which is being built on the principles of transparency and public collaboration.[66] (For more on Nebula, see page 127.)

Cloud Interoperability. To be able to seamlessly move applications (whether built on IaaS or PaaS) between clouds, interoperability is required — or, specifically, a set of standards, interconnectivity, and a common architectural framework that enables interoperability. Formal cloud interoperability standards will take time to be worked out by the industry.

As stated earlier in "The Role of Standards," most standardization efforts are focused around IaaS and cloud interoperability. Examples include vCloud and the Open Cloud Computing Interface (OCCI) specifications, which both aim to define an accepted standard API for managing IaaS resources and capabilities.

Cloud platforms like Eucalyptus provide a foundation for building your own IaaS cloud, giving you internal cloud capabilities while enabling future interoperability with compatible clouds. With Eucalyptus at the core, organizations like Canonical, OpenNebula (based on the NASA effort) and VMOps[67] are instead counting on the de facto standardization of Amazon's cloud API. Adding to the confusion is the growing number of clouds providers whose initial focus is on capabilities over wide-scale interoperability. Companies like Majitek, Joyent and Flexiscale aren't waiting around for standards but are instead bringing capabilities quickly to market, even if it involves their own APIs.

However, all companies — IaaS providers in particular — are promising different levels of interoperability based on APIs, hypervisors, operating systems and other components of their clouds.

An example of the importance of cloud interoperability comes from pharmaceutical giant Eli Lilly. Dave Powers, an IT specialist at Lilly, turned to Eucalyptus after having initial success with EC2. Powers created quite a stir when he was able to help a Lilly researcher accomplish in one afternoon on EC2 what would have taken 90 days if Lilly had gone the typical route of procuring and installing the hardware needed for a complex drug discovery analysis. However, Amazon's EC2 was not a complete replacement for all of Lilly's analytic computing tasks. Lilly was not ready to place its most sensitive data in the public cloud.

The question was: What could Lilly use that was compatible with its work on Amazon's EC2, but that could be deployed behind Lilly's firewall in a secured area? The answer turned out to be open source software that was compatible with the EC2 APIs — namely, Eucalyptus running on top of the CentOS operating system and Xen hypervisor. Working with Eucalyptus Systems, Lilly was able to help guide the birth of a commercially supported, open source cloud that is compatible with Amazon APIs but deployable in private. Lilly now has the best of both worlds: cloud services and the safety of the corporate firewall. Going forward, Lilly is working to make Eucalyptus run on top of VMware's vSphere cloud operating system.

Hybrid clouds are likely to become the norm.

For PaaS clouds, interoperability options are either based on use of common stacks (e.g., LAMP) or else seem even farther in the future. Despite some common approaches that are emerging, like those based on JavaSpaces, Tuple Space or other distributed computing patterns, much of what's available is still very proprietary. Although some companies may be large enough to gain acceptance even with proprietary approaches, such as Microsoft with Windows Azure, the PaaS space has yet to emerge with possible de facto standards the way Amazon's AWS has emerged in the IaaS space.

As cloud interoperability standards (de facto or formal) are increasingly adopted, hybrid clouds are likely to become the norm, particularly as companies choose to not just move IT capabilities to the cloud but weave them together — across private, semi-private and public types — into entirely new solutions.

ARCHITECTING FOR THE CLOUD

Even as cloud services mature, interoperability becomes easier, and the economic advantages of IT shift to the cloud, it will not always be simple to use the cloud effectively. Just as enterprise IT enabled even more complex, highly integrated solutions within the traditional data center, cloud computing will bring new arrangements of technology — all of which will require many existing and new architectural approaches, patterns and examples to make these arrangements work. Two important practices, one common and one emerging, are Service Oriented Architecture (SOA) and Service Oriented Enterprise (SOE).

SOA and SOE as a Foundation. Even before the notion of cloud computing started taking shape, IT organizations wanted to interconnect and integrate application services and exchange data over the Internet. The rise of Web-based services (using such technologies as SOAP and REST), combined with the architectural patterns of modularity and loose coupling, led to the increased adoption of SOA, where IT and business services could be built to be accessed and consumed in a modular fashion over the enterprise network (for reusability) and over the Internet (for cross-organizational process and data integration). With SOA driving the design of new applications and IT capabilities, enterprise IT and external service providers began turning any application, data or resource into a Web-accessible service, which could then be assembled into new solutions. This too was Amazon's journey, as it created AWS initially to service Amazon's affiliates in a more efficient manner.

For many organizations, the adoption of SOA inside the company led to a natural next step: becoming a Service Oriented Enterprise or SOE. In 2004, Intel defined SOE as "an enterprise that implements and exposes its business processes through an SOA and that provides frameworks for managing its business processes across an SOA landscape."[68] Whereas SOE was largely focused on a single enterprise, the cloud takes this definition a step further, where the SOA landscape is no longer provided internally (with a few external integration points) but has moved to clouds that could reside anywhere out on the Internet. Any organization that has already taken steps to become an SOE is well positioned to use and even start moving to the cloud. In such an SOE, business applications and consumption of IT services are already based on assembling services and service-enabled processes over the network.

As Scott Dowell, enterprise technologist in CSC's Navy Marine Corps Technology Center, puts it, "The SOE brings interoperability and agility to the forefront of system design. A major theme for the SOE is to assume that the system will have integration requirements from the beginning, rather than adding them on later as an afterthought." In the SOE, the future of business is collaboration, which requires integration across systems and organizational boundaries. The future of this collaboration is in the cloud.

> **"The SOE [Service Oriented Enterprise] brings interoperability and agility to the forefront of system design."** — *Scott Dowell*

New Development and Runtime Platforms. Several PaaS cloud providers are looking higher up the stack to enable private clouds and a seamless path to public clouds. Instead of just using the same traditional application and information architectures already in place within the enterprise, these PaaS providers are instead providing new development and runtime platforms that take advantage of the distributed and scalable nature of the cloud, including using grid — both compute and data — approaches, incorporating unorthodox data management techniques (e.g., tuple-space, in-memory databases), and using dynamic parallelism (e.g., lock services, concurrent workflows) and distributed coordination algorithms (e.g., Paxos).

The outcome is a new breed of application frameworks that enterprises can use to transform existing applications and build new applications that automatically take advantage of the distributed, parallel, scalable capabilities of clouds. Two such frameworks come from Appistry and GigaSpaces.

Fabric Architecture: Applications as Dynamically Woven Components. Appistry's product, CloudIQ, is a scalable platform for enterprise applications that is agnostic to the underlying hardware, whether in a public or private data center. Appistry's platform is described as an application fabric — software that takes a large number of machines and weaves them together so they appear as one machine to the application.

The fabric provides a layer of abstraction between the infrastructure and the application, so the application is better able to leverage the infrastructure and be more flexible, scalable and reliable. The infrastructure is managed as a whole (not by individual machine) and provides application-level fault tolerance that protects the application from any hardware failure. Indeed, the fabric is almost an organic entity. It is self-organizing and self-managing. When a new node is added, it is automatically discovered by the fabric and provisioned with everything it needs to function as a member of the fabric. When a node leaves, others automatically take over.

Underneath the fabric is a grid of commodity machines. Reflecting the philosophy that the hardware should not matter and should be expected to fail, the grid can be built on inexpensive, commodity machines. One of Appistry's customers even successfully incorporated $300 computers from Wal-Mart into its fabric.[69] If a machine fails, it can simply be discarded without affecting the overall fabric.

Though based on a grid-like x86/Windows/Linux compute infrastructure, the fabric is very different from a grid. There is no central control node or scheduler — these functions are completely distributed. Each node in the fabric performs all necessary fabric functions. There is complete redundancy. As Michael Groner of Appistry says, "If the fabric contains 100 nodes, they all are capable of performing all necessary functions. If you kill 99 of those nodes, the remaining one node will still perform all necessary functions of the fabric."

In addition to this type of fault-tolerance, the fabric is designed for application scaling. This includes both scaling up within a single machine and scaling out across multiple machines.

Space-Based Architecture. Some vendors focus just beneath the application, at the platform level, and provide a cloud-ready platform that supports public clouds, private clouds and hybrids. GigaSpaces is a prime example.

GigaSpaces has long addressed how to build applications on multiple computers. Its eXtreme Application Platform (XAP), which functions like an application server, provides an abstraction that allows you to see your entire set of computers as a single runtime environment and enables linear scaling of applications as data volumes, transactions and users increase.

The problem inhibiting scalability of most applications is their traditional multi-tier architecture, which is siloed and does not scale well. The solution is not to improve the multi-tier approach but to go beyond it, to a SOA built on shared spaces in a grid computing framework. GigaSpaces' Space-Based Architecture (SBA) takes this approach, turning everything — i.e., the middleware and the application — into a service. This approach collapses the siloed tiers into a single, self-contained processing unit that includes all steps of the business process, all services, messaging, data and the Web container. The processing unit is run in-memory on a single machine. The processing unit is the fundamental component, usually deployed on a grid. It implements a share-nothing architecture and is, by definition, linearly scalable, allowing an application to scale up on a single server or out across multiple servers. These servers can be in the on-premise data center (private cloud) or a third-party data center (public cloud).

GigaSpaces' recent partnership with GoGrid strengthens the public cloud option.[70] While enterprises have been using XAP in production in the public cloud (e.g., Amazon EC2) for over a year, enterprises can now extend their infrastructure to GoGrid's infrastructure (an IaaS offering), taking advantage of GoGrid's enterprise experience, capabilities and SLA guarantees. Enterprises can also start with their own IT resources and "burst" to the GoGrid cloud as needed. In this way, XAP is a building block to not only the public cloud but the hybrid cloud. (See Figure 21.)

In sum, the cloud is forging a new type of enterprise IT, including a new type of data center, that is flexible, efficient and geared to handle the highly volatile requirements of many of today's applications (particularly those that run on x86-based hardware). With infrastructure that is architected and managed much differently than in a traditional client-server data center, the private cloud provides significant business benefit without many of the perceived cloud issues, and provides a stepping stone for ultimate migration to the public cloud. By mimicking the cloud in-house, the enterprise is poised to rally external cloud resources next.

REALITY CHECK: LEGACY SYSTEMS AND THE CLOUD

There's no doubt that enterprises are showing increasing interest in building private clouds as well as reaching out to public (or semi-private) clouds However, one fact of life will stay true for a very long time: many applications and their current traditional infrastructures — legacy systems — will continue to exist, remaining in place for many years before they are turned off. For clouds to be of use in the real world, they have to co-exist with, if not work with, the legacy systems and legacy infrastructures that remain. For example, while in the past many legacy COBOL applications have seemed destined to be stuck on premise, organizations are now successfully using MicroFocus COBOL to migrate even these to the cloud.

In some cases, paths between internal legacy systems and cloud services are being provided. For example, Pervasive is a company whose DataIntegrator product creates an integration bridge between an internal SAP application and Salesforce.com.[71] As clouds — particularly at the PaaS and SaaS layers — become mature, many more legacy-to-cloud integration tools will appear. However, until then, many cases of "cloud integration" will involve transferring files from the enterprise data center to and from a cloud, in a traditional bulk file copy

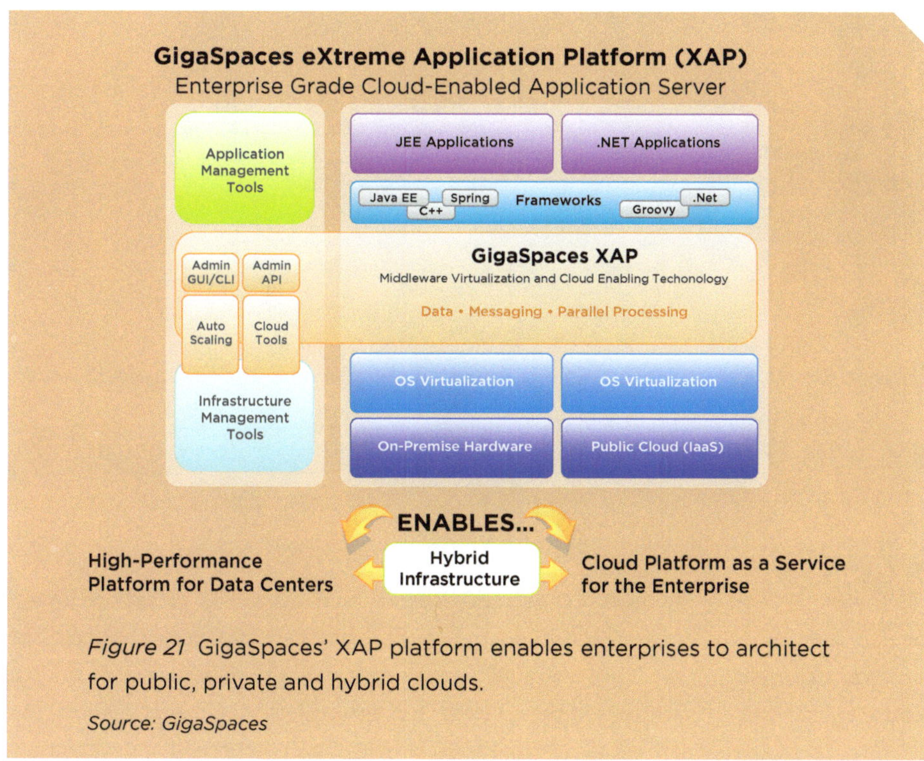

Figure 21 GigaSpaces' XAP platform enables enterprises to architect for public, private and hybrid clouds.

Source: GigaSpaces

approach (which can actually be more efficient than using an API, but does not represent tight application integration.)

Still, many enterprises can move more of their applications and systems into clouds, particularly external ones, only if there's a clear path to establish close co-existence, often replacing a tight coupling that previously existed within a single data center. One solution is to service-enable the legacy systems left behind, allowing them to be more easily connected via Web services or another SOA mechanism. (See Figure 22.)

"If you are thinking about modernizing your applications towards the cloud, use SOA as a style of architecture and stand up a services 'hub,' rather than relying on old point-to-point connections to service-enable all your legacy systems. This gives you the flexibility to modernize your applications incrementally, including moving them piecemeal to cloud services," says Jim Fenner, senior SOA architect at CSC.

Another possibility is the availability of "legacy IaaS" clouds, where older systems can be moved and run in the cloud. For many x86-based systems, this is already possible, given most IaaS providers use x86-based virtualized platforms. However, for older or niche operating systems that operate on non-X86 system architectures, this depends on whether cloud providers see market possibilities. As described in Volume 1, some companies are considering building clouds based on non-x86 architectures, such as IBM's zSeries mainframes or AIX systems.[72] Yet other challenges remain in moving legacy applications to the cloud, as they are often not architected to be horizontally scalable and may be difficult to port into cloud environments.[73] This area of the cloud ecosystem has yet to be fully explored.

Given the plethora of architectural possibilities with the cloud, further guidance is being developed to help enterprises begin mapping their path to the cloud. Examples of such guidance are two architectural cube models: Jericho, from the Open Group, and Radeztsky, created by Sun engineer Scott Radeztsky.[74] Both of these reference models provide ways of identifying how application and system components can be laid out to work, even if they cross multiple cloud boundaries.

Figure 22 USE A SERVICES (SOA) BUS TO CONNECT LEGACY SYSTEMS AND CLOUD SERVICES

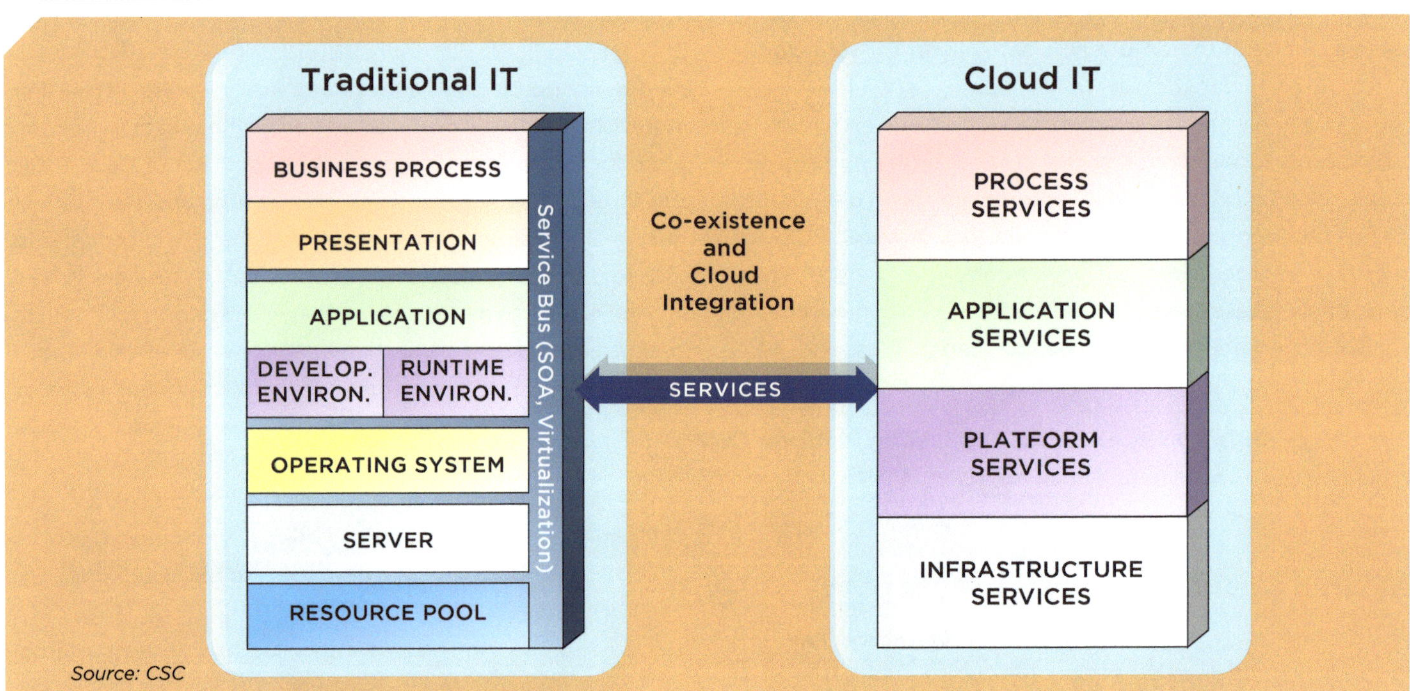

Source: CSC

FUTURE SHOCK: CLOUD AND TRADITIONAL DATA CENTERS SWITCH ROLES

For most IT organizations, the cloud will initially be seen as a way of extending IT, adding services and capacity incrementally from the cloud. Eventually, as the vast majority of applications and IT services are provisioned and served from the cloud, the internal data center will no longer be the primary source of IT capabilities.

Rather, the internal data center will likely become a secondary "backup" set of capabilities in the increasingly rare (yet still possible) situation where all network connectivity to the external world — the Internet — is lost temporarily. For the next few years, the local data center will continue to survive, supporting the most sensitive data and being able to send out the bills if the Internet goes dark. This local data center, however, may only consist of a single rack containing a highly integrated computing and storage stack, such as Cisco's Unified Computing System.

At some point in the future, the potential for a "no rack" IT environment may come about, where the only physical IT components remaining in the enterprise are network switches and the connection to the Internet, as well as client platforms such as PCs, netbooks and smartphones. (See figure 23.) If a company can rely entirely on public wireless sources, even those physical remnants of IT may disappear. Smaller companies are already looking into this possibility, such as Appirio and Capital SCF, whose CTO Chris Swan hopes to "never buy a server."[75] With over 200 employees, Appirio has been a "serverless enterprise" for several years, using a growing number of cloud-based office productivity applications, ERP components and application platforms for all its needs.[76]

Thus, over time, IT becomes the part of the organization that defines, connects and integrates solutions together first, if the business hasn't already taken on that role itself.[77] If security, performance and regulatory issues reach a point where nearly all business can trust the cloud completely, what we call IT today will be relegated to the history books.[78] In its wake will be a newly refreshed IT capability that is highly consultative in nature. Instead of "racking and stacking" and servicing desktops, IT will focus more on policy, strategic issues and creating value for the business. It will also focus on giving guidance and advice, and on assisting with platform creation that will allow end users to work independently. These "double deep" employees, who are both business and IT savvy, will do their own IT. Thus the IT department's role will change from engineer to advisor, a personal change if not a cultural change for IT personnel.

At some point in the future, the potential for a "no rack" IT environment may come about.

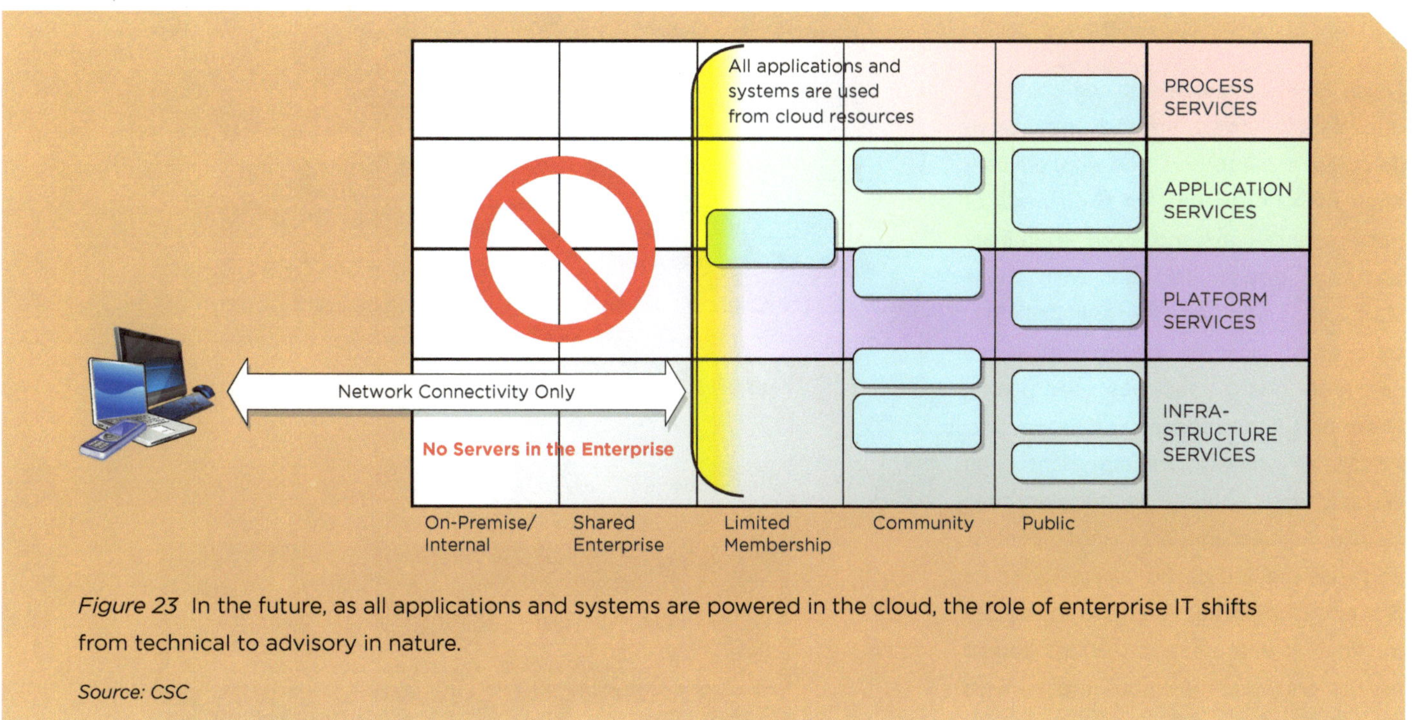

Figure 23 In the future, as all applications and systems are powered in the cloud, the role of enterprise IT shifts from technical to advisory in nature.

Source: CSC

As enterprise IT faces the prospects of hollowing out and shifting to an advisory role, the external mega data centers that are part of this transformation are already humming away.

Cloud Effect 4

MEGA DATA CENTERS POWER IT ALL

Gigantic data centers on a previously unheard-of scale are emerging around the world. These warehouse-size facilities may be up to 10 football fields in size and represent billions of dollars in investment. Intel says that by 2012, mega data centers run by the likes of Google, Microsoft, Amazon and Facebook will account for 20 to 25 percent of its server chip sales.[79]

These warehouse-size data centers, introduced in Volume 1, embody new technologies, architectures and economics.[80] They may house tens of thousands of servers and consume over 20 megawatts of power. To deal with these staggering numbers, these installations tend to be built in strategic locations near abundant supplies of power, water and fiber access. (See Figure 24.) Advanced power management and water-based cooling techniques help keep utility requirements under control, and spell the end of the raised-floor data center.[81] Google has even filed a patent for floating data centers that are cooled by the surrounding water and harness the power of wave energy.

Minimum processing units in these mega data centers are not individual servers or even racks, but often pods or "data centers in a box" — containers housing large numbers of densely packed servers. (See Figure 25.) Processors are often highly virtualized, allowing significant increases in average server utilization.

Figure 24 This Google data center is located in The Dalles, Oregon, along the Columbia River. The area provides abundant power, water and fiber access, making it attractive for mega data centers.

Source: Melanie Conner

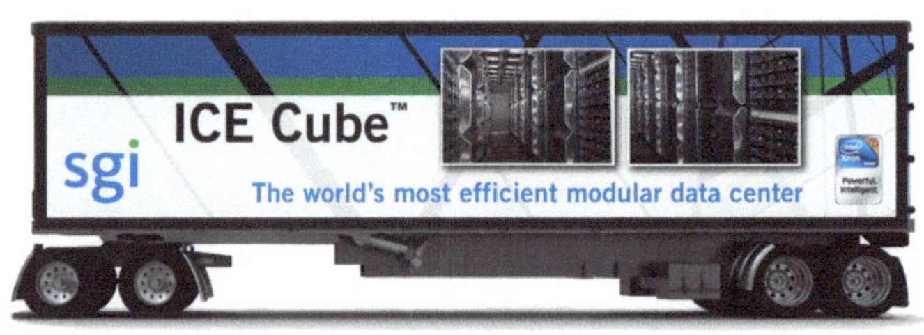

Figure 25 Data Center in a Box: In contrast to the traditional data center rack, the sealed shipping container housing servers, storage and networking equipment is quickly becoming a common approach for increasing the amount of computing power per cubic foot of space in the data center. The containers are portable and enable rapid set-up.

Source: SGI

Many of these data centers are implemented using commodity servers, with the expectation that individual pieces of equipment will fail. They are architected, however, to be immune to such failures. Extensive automation detects problems and immediately reconfigures the infrastructure on-the-fly to ensure that there is no noticeable impact due to a failure. Periodically, such failed equipment is simply ripped out and discarded or recycled. Some mega-centers are also remarkable for the variety of communication options they make available, serving as the nexus of scores of communication carriers.

PLAYERS

Who is building these behemoths and why? Three groups predominate. First are the pioneers of the cloud rEvolution: Google, Amazon and Yahoo. These companies had extensive infrastructures servicing their core consumer-driven businesses and have leveraged these assets into new lines of business by offering cloud services. Amazon, for example, is constructing a large, three-building data center with an adjacent 10-megawatt power substation in Boardman, Oregon. And, although exact numbers are proprietary, Google is thought to have over one million servers housed in dozens of large data centers around the world.[82]

The second group is the traditional IT vendors such as IBM, HP, Microsoft and Sun (Oracle). These vendors, although typically having large data centers, are escalating the rush towards mega-centers as they enter the cloud business. IBM's Computing On Demand (CoD) service provides access to 14,000 processors and 56 terabytes of storage spread across six global CoD centers.[83] For its part, Microsoft is planning to set up 20 new billion-dollar data centers during the next 20 years to support cloud computing, and has two cloud data centers already operating.[84] Microsoft's next (4th) generation data center is based on a new container design filled with over 2,000 servers and designed to operate outdoors with little to no water.[85]

The third major group is communications companies such as AT&T, Verizon, Terremark and Switch Networks. These companies have experience managing large facilities and can leverage their extensive communication networks. AT&T is planning to put a billion dollars into its global network this year, dedicating five so-called super-IDCs or Internet Data Centers in the United States, Europe and Asia to support its new Synaptic Hosting cloud services.[86] Sun, acquired by Oracle (ostensibly, at least in part, to obtain its cloud computing capability), runs its cloud business in a colossal facility called the SuperNAP (Network Access Point), operated by Switch Communications in the Nevada desert. This facility is just one of eight facilities operated by Switch within a six to seven mile radius in a no-fly zone south of Las Vegas. It sprawls over 407,000 square feet of data center floor space, requires 100 megawatts of power provisioned from two separate power grids, has enough cooling and power density to run at 1,500 watts per square foot (10 times the industry average of 150 watts), provides access to 27 national network carriers, and guarantees 100 percent uptime.[87]

On the other side of the country, Terremark is constructing what it calls the "NAP of the Capital Region" in Culpeper, Virginia.[88] This large, multi-center facility provides connectivity to over 170 telecommunication carriers, is highly secure, and is being used by CSC to offer Trusted Cloud Services to government clients.[89] Terremark's data centers, originally designed for telecommunication carriers, provide the unique connectivity you would expect from a cloud provider, and peering arrangements. VMware acquired a five percent share of Terremark in June 2009, underscoring Terremark's importance as a bridge to the cloud for the enterprise (Terremark uses VMware products in its data centers).[90]

Economies of Scale. The companies building mega-centers are making significant investments to capitalize on cloud strategies. By creating mega-centers to support cloud services, significant economies of scale can be gained that allow providers to make a profit while offering cloud services that are priced competitive with — or depending on the use case, significantly cheaper than — an enterprise data center. In "Internet-Scale Service Efficiency," James Hamilton, noted blogger and member of the Amazon Web Services team, observes that data centers serving very large populations can purchase hardware, network bandwidth and power for one-fifth to one-seventh the prices offered to data centers serving medium-sized populations.[91] Further, the fixed costs of software development and deployment can be amortized over many more users. These types of economies are illustrated in Figure 26.

Data centers serving very large populations can purchase hardware, network bandwidth and power for one-fifth to one-seventh the prices offered to data centers serving medium-sized populations.

Figure 26 SERVICES ECONOMIES OF SCALE (2008)

Technology	Medium-Sized Service (~1,000 Servers)	Very Large Service (~50,000 Servers)	Savings Ratio
NETWORK	$95/Mbps/month	$13/Mbps/month	7.1:1
STORAGE	$2.20/GByte/month	$0.40/GByte/month	5.7:1
ADMINISTRATION	~140 servers/system administrator	>1,000 servers/system administrator	7.1:1

Data Source: James Hamilton, http://mvdirona.com/jrh/TalksAndPapers/JamesRH_Ladis2008.pdf.
Also see James Hamilton's blog, Perspectives, at: http://perspectives.mvdirona.com/

The enterprise data centers of the future will be more about the procurement of services, not assets, that are elastic in nature and location independent — and thus can be satisfied by the mega-center. The luxury of fewer, larger data centers has been the tradition of high performance computing environments, and now that luxury is being made available to all organizations regardless of size. That said, the centralization and consolidation of computing power into a few massive data centers should be viewed as a trend but not necessarily an end state.

DESIGNED TO SHARE

The traditional data center is typically not designed for sharing; specific resources (e.g., servers) are dedicated to a specific application or use. Even when an outsourcer is used, specific resources are dedicated to a specific customer. Cloud computing, however, is rooted in sharing because it services a wide array of needs. The old world of IT didn't need to share, but the new world of IT — cloud — does.

Thus we see resource sharing — otherwise known as "multitenancy" — taking hold among cloud providers. Multitenancy is a form of abstraction that provides customers ("tenants") with the illusion that they are using dedicated resources when, in fact, those resources are simultaneously being used by others. This is one of the tricks of the trade that helps provide economies of scale in the cloud. Catering to many customers with the same infrastructure helps cloud providers maintain high utilization of their resources and helps spread fixed investment over a broader base. Many types of resources can be multitenant in the cloud, including facilities, servers, software and databases.

- *Shared facilities.* It should come as no surprise that cloud services may be provided from a facility that is simultaneously providing services to others. What may be surprising is that these facilities may be shared by hundreds if not thousands of other enterprises and possibly millions of individual consumers. Yet, there are degrees of exception. A case in point is the Trusted Cloud Services data center operated by Terremark and CSC. This highly secure facility, though still multitenant, has isolated sections (PODS) that cater only to government agencies as a strategy for limiting exposure and maintaining security.

- *Shared servers.* In traditional, on-premise data centers, servers are dedicated to specific uses. A virtualized server within the data center may host many virtual machines, each of which is doing something different, but it's still all your stuff. In the cloud, however, servers are usually multitenant, with virtual machine for several different companies isolated from each other but hosted on the same physical server. The ability to host and swap out any virtual machine regardless of customer helps keep a cloud provider's server utilization very high. Recently, even Savvis, which traditionally provided only high-end, dedicated infrastructure, took the leap into the cloud, offering the option for users to self-provision shared servers.[92]

- *Shared software.* When a cloud provider offers software as a service, the software may very well (though not always) be multitenant. This means that different users from different companies use a single copy of the software at the same time. To accommodate these different users, providers use metadata to deliver a limited degree of customization. This allows providers to use a standard edition of the software while catering to the individual needs of the different tenants. It also allows providers to deliver many new versions (sometimes weekly) to all customers with little effort. While this concept is very familiar to individual consumers who regularly use shared applications such as Gmail, the concept of shared software for enterprises is more radical.

- *Shared databases.* SaaS providers may also implement multitenant databases. In such a database, there is a common schema that is shared by all tenants. Further, one tenant's data may reside in one row of the database while another tenant's data occupies the very next row. Metadata is again used to identify and separate a comprehensive view of all data for a specific customer. General cloud databases (e.g., Amazon's SimpleDB and Google's Bigtable) that are not SaaS-related but may be used for any purpose are also multitenant, but do not have a common schema for each item (see "Scaling and Databases" on page 41).

Though more and more vendors are adopting a multitenant strategy, the poster child for multitenancy is Salesforce.com, which has pioneered a completely multitenant architecture at the hardware, software and database levels. (See Figure 27.) It should be noted that although Salesforce.com has remained true to multitenant principals, physical limitations have forced it to stray from the single instance ideal. Due to database size limitations, as of June 2008 Salesforce.com operated eight application instances to support over 43,000 customers.[93]

In the world of SaaS there is a raging debate on the use of multitenancy. Why have multitenant software and databases when virtualization makes it so easy to give customers their own resources? And, with virtualization, a SaaS application does not have to be specially architected for multitenancy. Many SaaS vendors, in fact, take the virtualization route, and may use individual virtual appliances as the means to scale their offerings across many customers.

But, something gets lost in the shuffle. For an application provider, there is benefit to having all users on a single software instance instead of spread across multiple instances. A multitenant architecture gives a comprehensive view that lets the provider analyze how the application is being used across all customers. This offers opportunities to improve customer service and retention, plan future enhancements, and ultimately gain competitive advantage.[94]

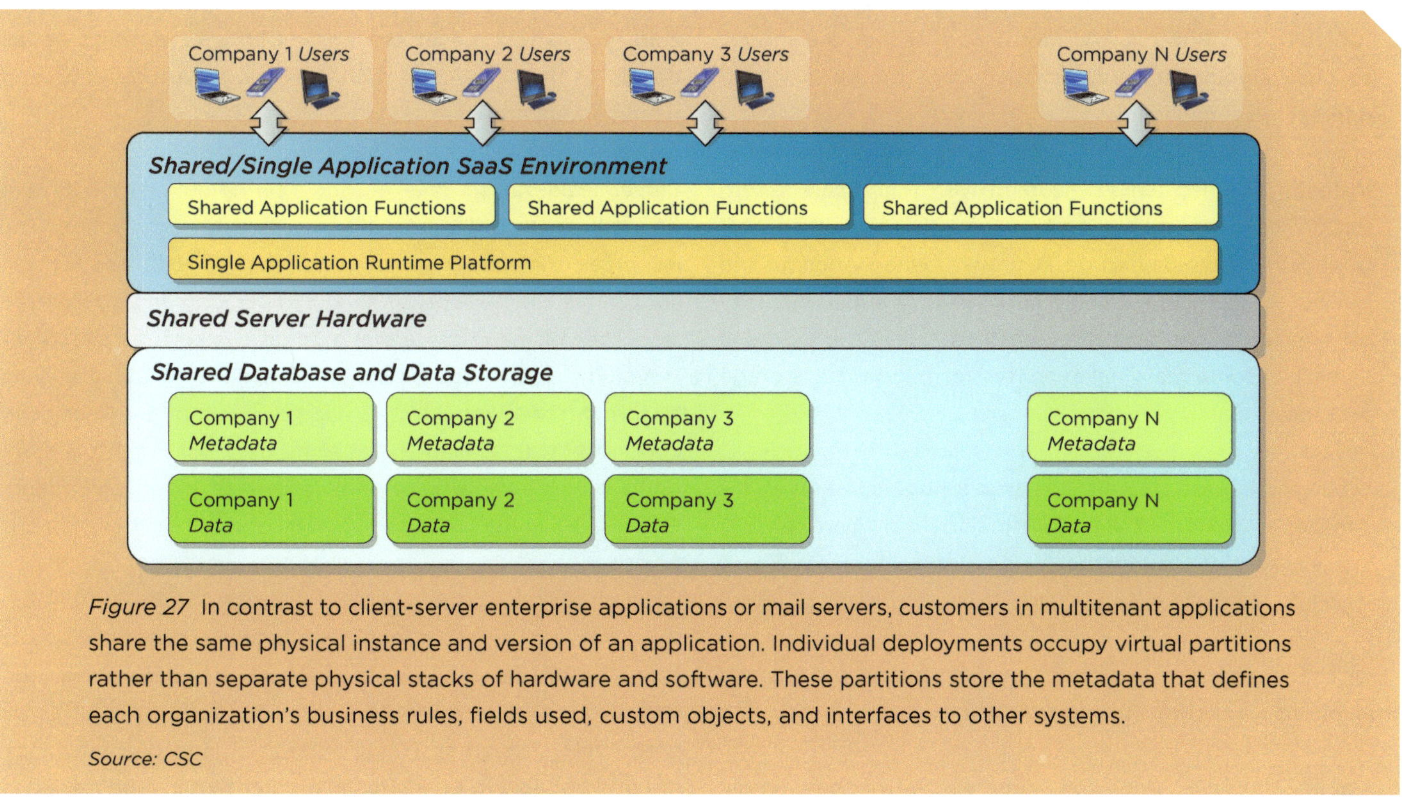

Figure 27 In contrast to client-server enterprise applications or mail servers, customers in multitenant applications share the same physical instance and version of an application. Individual deployments occupy virtual partitions rather than separate physical stacks of hardware and software. These partitions store the metadata that defines each organization's business rules, fields used, custom objects, and interfaces to other systems.

Source: CSC

DESIGNED TO SCALE

In addition to sharing, another characteristic of cloud data centers is scalability — the ability to grow and shrink resources as needed to meet performance and demand requirements. Further, this type of elastic change can occur relatively quickly: resources can be scaled *right away,* not in weeks or days.

The story of Animoto, as reported in The New York Times in May 2008, is a potent example:

> A vivid example of cloud power comes from Animoto, an 18-month-old start-up in New York that lets customers upload images and music and automatically creates customized Web-based video presentations from them; many people then share them with friends. Animoto gives a free video presentation to anyone who signs up for its service, and earlier this spring about 5,000 people a day were trying it.
>
> Then, in mid-April [2008], Facebook users went into a small frenzy over the application, and Animoto had nearly 750,000 people sign up in three days. At the peak, almost 25,000 people tried Animoto in a single hour.
>
> To satisfy that leap in demand with servers, the company would have needed to multiply its server capacity nearly 100-fold. . . . But . . . [Animoto] had neither the money to build significant server capacity nor the skills — and interest — to manage it.
>
> Instead, they had already worked with RightScale . . . to design their application for Amazon's cloud. That paid off during the three-day surge in growth, when Animoto did not buy or configure a single new server. It added capacity on Amazon, at the cost of about 10 cents a server per hour, as well as some marginal expenses for bandwidth, storage and some related services.
>
> While there were hiccups — it was a huge spike, even for Amazon — none of them were major. And when demand slowed, Animoto automatically lowered its server use, and its bill.[95]

Over the course of a few days, Animoto dialed way up and then dialed way down. That's scalability in action.

Scalability, however, does not automatically happen simply by adding resources. Scalability must be architected into the overall system, as was the case with Animoto. Amazon, for one, understands that scalability is not easy and that if it is an after-thought, adding resources will not necessarily result in improved performance.[96] For effective scalability, attention must be given to hardware, multi-purpose grids and databases.

Scaling and Hardware. The ability to scale IT resources starts with hardware. The infrastructure supporting applications and processes must be able to easily and quickly expand and contract, as needed, without disruption or downtime. At the most basic level, the ability for a provider to scale up physical hardware gets down to how quickly new computers can be procured and installed. This has led some providers to take the route of deploying cheap commodity servers. Google, for example, assembles its own servers quickly, using Velcro to attach bulk-purchased, commodity boards together.[97]

Few cloud providers, however, dedicate physical machines to customers. In most cases, it is virtual hardware that is made available, and hardware scaling is primarily a matter of launching and shutting down virtual machines. Scaling up the hardware then becomes the ability to allocate and allow virtual machines to make use of all resources, including all cores, of a physical machine. Other than the fact that some physical servers may employ hardware-assisted virtualization at the chip level, this type of scaling has little to do with actual design of the server and more to do with virtualization and management software.

Server scale-out is similar. Scaling a server out beyond its own boundaries is an illusion delivered through abstraction. The resources of many servers must be made to appear as a single entity. This can be accomplished by liberating and pooling the resources of many servers à la 3Leaf Systems, as described in Volume 2,[98] or coordinating the actions of those servers by forming them into clusters and grids. Although IT has been concerned with scaling up for some time, scaling out is more difficult and a more important feature of cloud computing. Figure 28 summarizes the characteristics of scale up versus scale out.

Multi-Purpose Grids. Clouds are usually based on grids comprised of large numbers of loosely-coupled, distributed virtual or physical computers. A grid manifests itself as an abstraction. Instead of a large number of individual machines, the grid appears to be a large computer that can be managed as a single entity.

Figure 28 SCALE UP VS. SCALE OUT

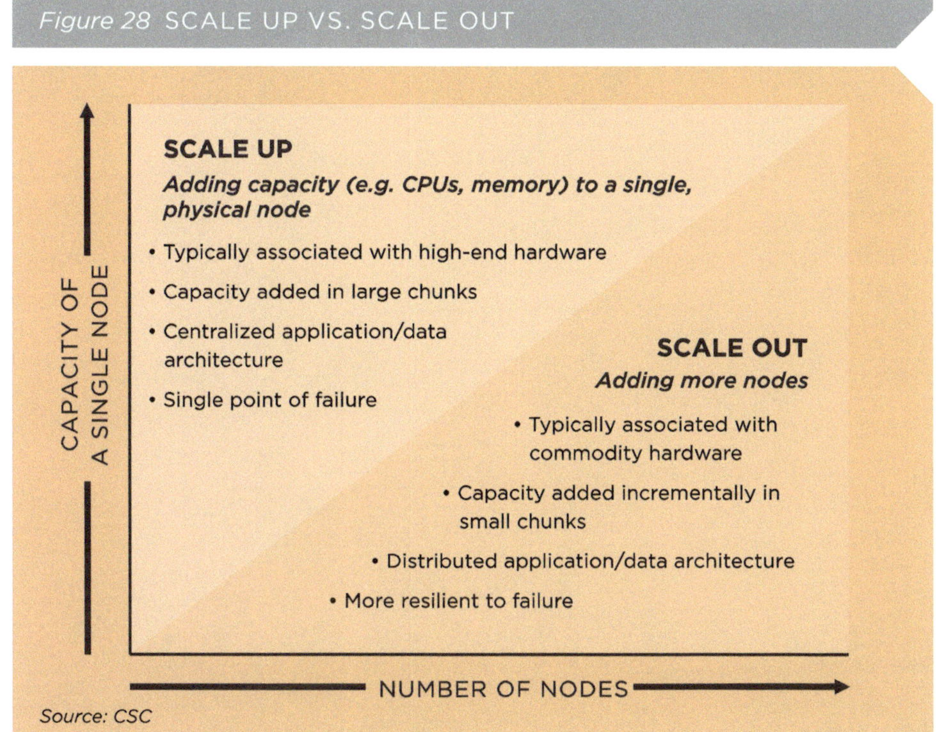

Source: CSC

running across multiple nodes, some grid architectures make use of very large In Memory Data Grids (IMDGs) that can accommodate terabytes of data.

Scaling and Databases. Scaling also has significant implications for data and databases in the cloud, as noted in Volume 1.[99] Often used in the enterprise, the relational database — though very robust and flexible in its capabilities — is limited in its ability to scale easily across many servers. This constraint poses problems in the cloud, where potentially massive and elastic scaling comes with the territory and is often an overriding consideration. As a result, cloud providers such as Google, Amazon and others have tended to adopt other database models that are simple and easily scalable.

With proper orchestration and management, clouds can use grids to address a wide variety of computing applications. Grids can coordinate many small commodity servers to provide the processing power of a virtual supercomputer. This makes clouds able to support computationally intensive processing tasks in areas such as business intelligence and complex financial and scientific simulations.

But it is not just the number crunching prowess of grids that is important. They are also ideal to enable and scale future cloud demands. The flexibility and distributed nature of grids is important for support of the growing number of applications based on Service Oriented Architectures and Event Driven Architectures, as well as the demand placed by the growing number of applications requiring the very high concurrent transaction volumes and low response times typical with extreme transaction processing. (Note that while most infrastructure clouds are grid-based, some purely SaaS clouds may not be. A case-in-point is Salesforce.com, which uses a "Big Iron" approach.)

In addition to processing grids, storage grids are used to coordinate data needs across the many nodes of the compute grid. This is often handled with technology such as iSCSI Storage Area Networks. However, to minimize latency and accommodate any statefullness that may persist in processes

Of particular note is the key-value data store, which is the basis for Google BigTable, Amazon SimpleDB and Microsoft SQL Data Services. Shown in Figure 29, the key-value store provides a hierarchical partitioning that is easily distributed across many nodes as volume grows, and it supports multitenancy to boot.

Key-value stores have domains that are roughly equivalent to tables in a relational system. Domains contain items identified by unique keys. Unlike tables, however, there is no defined schema for a domain. The domain is simply a bucket to hold items, and each item may have its own schema. All data associated with an item is included with the item. In this sense, the key-value store is somewhat akin to an object store and, indeed, can eliminate the need for object-to-relational mapping (ORM) that is sometimes used with object-oriented systems. Key-value stores are simple and do not provide many of the features, such as integrity constraints, provided by most relational database management systems. Rather, they reflect closely the needs of a specific application and must rely on the application to provide these functions.[100]

Key-value data stores are finding increased use particularly in situations requiring a high degree of database scalability. For example, online storage provider ElephantDrive incorporated Amazon's S3 into its regular business operations, and now uses S3 to store the majority of its client data. Scalability of the database

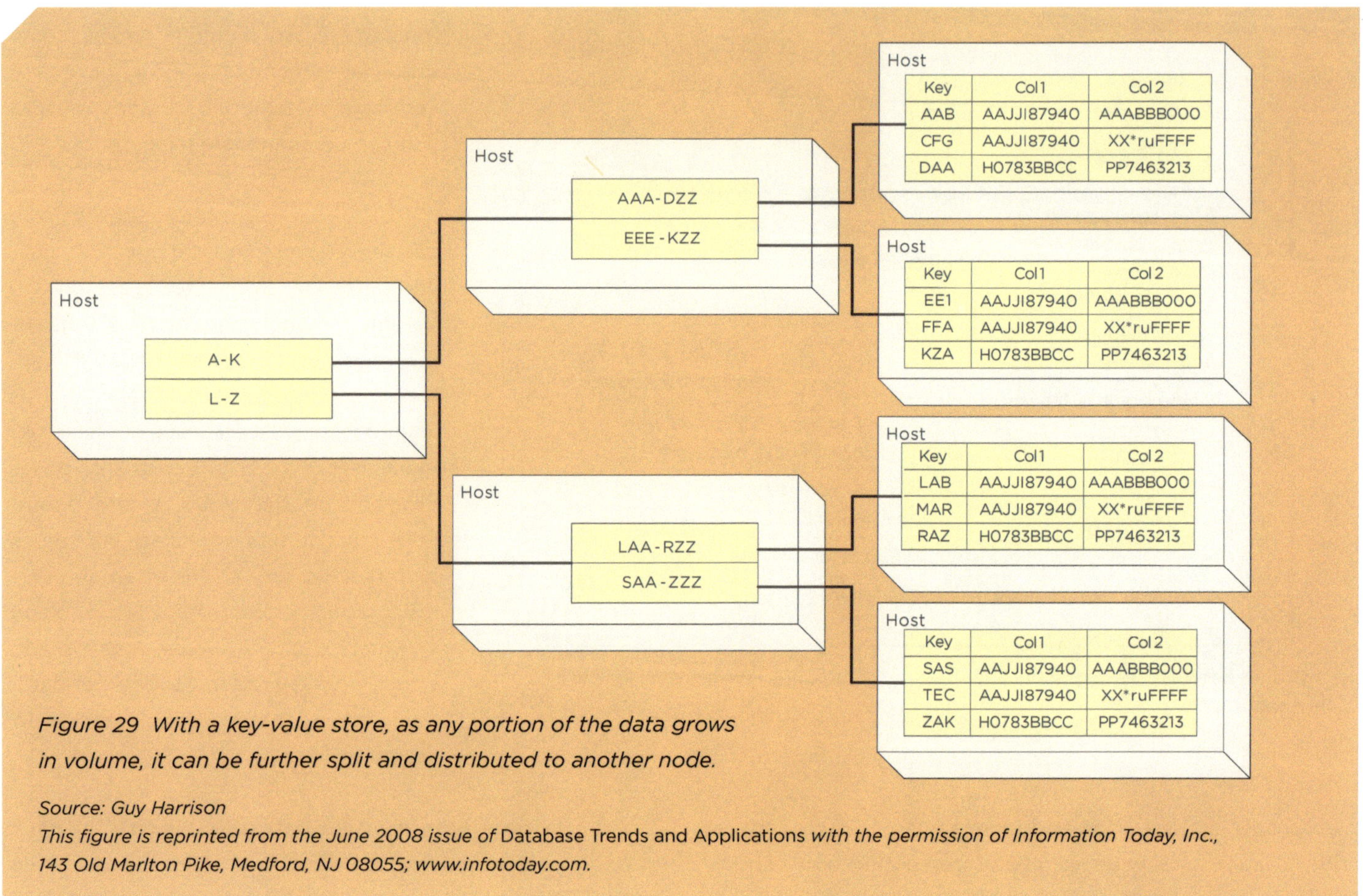

Figure 29 With a key-value store, as any portion of the data grows in volume, it can be further split and distributed to another node.

Source: Guy Harrison

This figure is reprinted from the June 2008 issue of Database Trends and Applications *with the permission of Information Today, Inc., 143 Old Marlton Pike, Medford, NJ 08055; www.infotoday.com.*

has been excellent, handling a doubling of the company's user base and a quadrupling of its stored digital assets. According to Amazon, "ElephantDrive has expanded the total amount of storage it transfers and manages by almost 20 percent each week without increasing capital costs."[101]

Another example of high database scalability can be found beneath your Web searches. Did you ever wonder how search engines like Google can take a search request, search the entire Internet, and deliver results in a fraction of a second? The answer is a programming approach called MapReduce, developed specifically to address this type of problem. Now assuming increasing importance is Hadoop and the Hadoop File System (HDFS), which is an open source implementation of the MapReduce programming model.

Hadoop provides a highly scalable approach to the storage and processing of very large datasets on the order of tens of petabytes (Big Data). Hadoop can take in multiple sources of structured and unstructured data and process it in arbitrary ways at a later time. Subsets of the data are stored in distributed fashion across large numbers of commodity processors. Processing of the data is done in parallel by bringing the processing to the data on each machine, as opposed to bringing the data to the processing.[102] With new Hadoop distributions by Cloudera and Yahoo, this approach to very large-scale data storage and processing is becoming a de facto standard.

Hadoop provides a highly scalable approach to the storage and processing of very large datasets on the order of tens of petabytes.

Cloud Effect 5

CLOUDONOMICS PROVIDE FINANCIAL INCENTIVE

With cloud computing potentially affecting all enterprises, whether large or small, commercial or public sector, the impact on the global economy will be significant. Cloud presents a new economic proposition which, as noted in Volume 1, economist Brian Arthur says will usher in a whole new economy.[103] The first economic shifts to emerge are in the costs and prices of cloud services. This section examines the factors underpinning these new "cloudonomics," the much-debated Capex vs. Opex benefits of cloud computing, and how one company, Bechtel, is putting cloudonomics to work.

CLOUDONOMICS UNDERPINNINGS

The fact that major cloud providers such as Google, Amazon and Yahoo can achieve IT cost levels that are an order of magnitude less than for a traditional enterprise data center is astounding — until it is realized that the operations of these providers bear little resemblance to typical data center operations. They are not just enterprise data centers deployed over the Internet. The cloudonomics that the cloud providers enjoy are driven by several factors described below. (See Figure 30.)

Economies of Scale. A number of major cloud providers (but not all) benefit from economies of scale due to consumerization. The massive consumer markets served by cloud pioneers such as Google, Amazon and Yahoo have led to IT infrastructures on a previously unheard-of scale. Yahoo successfully supports over 250 million e-mail accounts, dwarfing by orders of magnitude the e-mail accounts of any one enterprise. This type of scale helps cloud providers keep acquisition costs down.

Figure 30 FACTORS THAT OFTEN GIVE CLOUD PROVIDERS AN OPERATING COST ADVANTAGE OVER ON-PREMISE DATA CENTERS

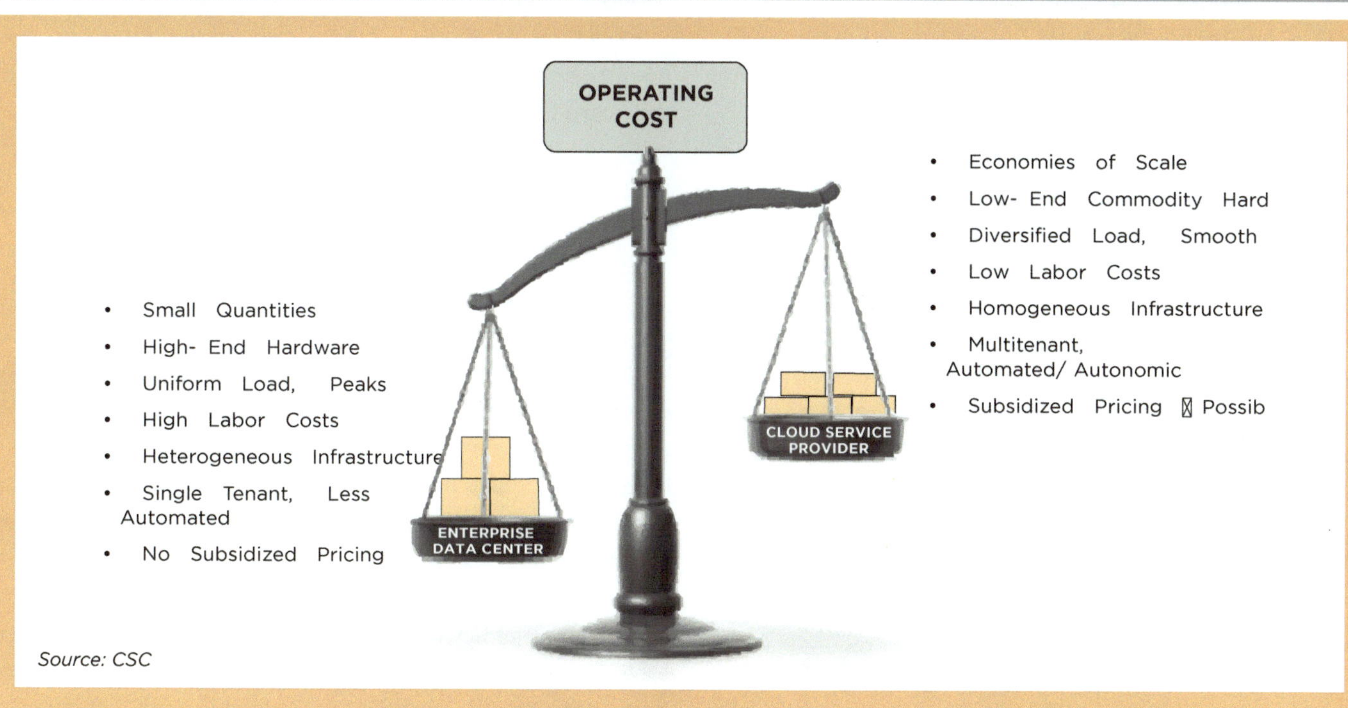

Source: CSC

The massive consumer markets served by cloud pioneers such as Google, Amazon and Yahoo have led to IT infrastructures on a previously unheard-of scale.

Fine China vs. Paper Plates. In addition to economies of scale, cloud providers benefit from infrastructures that are different from those in most enterprise data centers. These infrastructures are usually based on commodity hardware (discussed in Volume 1[104]). The difference between typical enterprise hardware versus cloud provider hardware can be referred to metaphorically as "fine china" versus "paper plates." Many enterprises seem to take delight in acquiring sophisticated, high-end hardware — i.e., fine china. Cloud providers, on the other hand, take delight in acquiring the cheapest hardware possible — i.e., paper plates. It is even rumored that Google uses treated cardboard mother boards (environmentally friendly, of course!).

In addition, instead of buying complete, assembled hardware, some of these providers may purchase mass quantities of raw components in bulk from low-cost suppliers, eliminating the middleman that enterprise data centers must go through. They then self-assemble these components into customized infrastructure. All of these factors lead to infrastructure acquisition costs for cloud providers that are one-seventh to one-tenth those of a typical enterprise.

Load Diversification. Another factor is load diversification. Clouds service large numbers of customers, each of which has a different demand profile (load requirement). The net result is that overall load on the cloud infrastructure is relatively stable and predictable (the diversification levels out the load), allowing cloud providers to service the load with less hardware than would otherwise be needed. This benefit is not enjoyed by enterprise data centers, which service only one organization. Although there may be many different applications running, total demand for the data center reflects the overall business cycle for the organization. Infrastructure must be purchased to meet peak loads since there are no counterbalancing sources of demand.

Lower Labor Costs. As noted in Figure 26 using data from James Hamilton, a single cloud provider system administrator can typically handle on the order of thousands of servers as opposed to hundreds for an enterprise data center. Labor costs for large cloud providers are consequently lower than in most enterprise data centers. According to Hamilton, "In the enterprise, most studies report that the cost of people dominates the cost of servers and data center infrastructure. In the cloud services world, we see a very different trend. Here we find that the costs of servers dominate, followed by mechanical systems, and then power distribution. As an example, looking at all aspects of operational costs in a mid-sized service led years ago, the human administrative costs were under 10% of the overall operational costs. I've seen very large, extremely well run services where the people costs have been driven below 4%."[105]

Homogeneous, Multitenant, Automated. Infrastructure in many enterprise data centers has grown like Topsy, resulting in a heterogeneous mix of hardware. Cloud infrastructure, on the other hand, is largely homogeneous. This makes management of cloud infrastructure easier, requires a smaller skill mix, and helps boost purchasing power. Cloud providers are also more likely than individual enterprises to incorporate infrastructures that are multitenant, highly automated and autonomic. These features all help reduce the cost of maintenance and management of hardware and software. Cloud providers can invest more heavily in automated management because the investment is amortized across many more servers.

Subsidized Pricing. Some of the leading cloud providers (Google, Amazon, Yahoo) have completely different business models than traditional IT service providers, with major revenue streams that are separate from their cloud offerings. While the impact of this on cloud pricing is not clear, the potential exists for these providers to under-price cloud services, using their other revenue sources to subsidize the cloud offerings.

CLOUDONOMICS DRIVE THE BIG SWITCH IN CAPEX VS. OPEX

While many talk about the benefits of cloud strictly in terms of converting capital expenditure (Capex) to operational expenditure (Opex), the real benefit is more fully explained in terms of closely matching computing supply to computing demand — the ability to turn on, dial up, dial down, and then turn off computing resources as needed. This is a continuation of the long-standing Capex-to-Opex, fixed-costs-to-variable-costs trend that has been a core driver of the IT service model evolution (think time sharing, outsourcing, and now cloud). The difference with cloud computing is that services are on-demand, more refined (granular), delivered more quickly, can be individually controlled (self-provisioned), and do not require a long-term contract.

One much-publicized example[106] is the project manager at The New York Times who converted 11 million scanned articles (four terabytes of data) into PDF files for on-line distribution in 24 hours using Amazon S3 and 100 EC2 instances, and simply expensed it (no formal budgeting was needed for the Amazon bill that was reported to be $240[107]). Another example is Norwegian-based Eventseer.net, which required seven days to regenerate over 750,000 highly interconnected Web pages on a single server but now uses 25 Amazon EC2 instances to accomplish the job in five hours every night, for about the cost of a pint of beer in Norway. In both examples, the companies were able to avoid expensive and time-consuming hardware procurement (whether in the form of upgrades, new equipment or access to existing equipment) and were able to match computing supply to their computing demands.

The real benefit of cloud is more fully explained in terms of closely matching computing supply to computing demand.

But in spite of such anecdotes that tout the benefits of cloud computing, the truth is that the economic benefit is not straightforward and must be carefully evaluated on a case-by-case basis using the same types of analysis typically applied to any outsourcing or leasing decision.[108] A decision on whether or not to use cloud computing should be made based on a total business case that is right given the unique goals and strategies of the organization.

When making an economic decision regarding cloud computing, be sure to factor in total cost, including all pertinent capital and operational expenditures. Analyze these costs as you would for any outsourcing or lease decision. Keep in mind the following points.

Capex. Elimination of up-front capital expenditure for IT resources is the key to unlocking many cloud benefits. Instead of buying computer hardware and software, organizations can "rent" what is needed from a cloud provider. Not only is the cash needed to make large capital outlays reduced, so is the financial risk of committing to such acquisitions. Because enterprises can turn resources on in the cloud with no capital outlay, IT resources can be obtained more quickly and easily, without the need for deep pockets or advance commitment. And because resources can be turned off at a moment's notice, organizations can try before they buy. If for any reason the product doesn't work out as hoped, the service can be terminated with minimal financial loss.

Even though there are no up-front acquisition costs with cloud, however, cloud is not always a better deal. Perhaps there is excess capacity already available in-house that can be tapped. Even if new capacity must be acquired, other factors come into play. For example, if maintaining internal control is a strong enough issue, the decision to spend $2,000 in Capex to buy and own a server may be justified. What if, however, you need 50 servers? The same arguments apply, but coming up with $100,000 is an entirely different matter and may very well swing the decision toward the cloud. Urgency is also an issue. If a single server is needed immediately, there may be no alternative but to use the cloud if in-house IT can't get the machine for a month or more. A final consideration is duration of need. If you will only need the server for a few months, why buy it? Better to turn one on, use it, and then turn it off in the cloud.

Opex. Reduction in Capex does not come for free but is shifted, in part, to Opex — the "rent" that is paid to the service provider. The traditional up-front acquisition model is replaced by a subscription- or utility-type pay-per-use model based on operational expenditure. This Opex may or may not be less than the corresponding expense that would be incurred if the assets were purchased and maintained internally.

Many factors come into play here. For example, the enterprise does not directly pay software licensing costs in those cases where the software is owned by the provider and made available via SaaS. Similarly, maintenance agreements for hardware or software are no longer directly paid by the enterprise if the assets are obtained in the cloud, and personnel expenses for operating and maintaining these assets are no longer incurred.

Rather, these costs are incurred by the cloud provider and passed on as part of the rent. The provider, however, has the advantage of being able to amortize these costs across many different organizations using the service.

Finally, internal power, cooling, and other facility expenses for the infrastructure may sometimes be reduced if physical resources are permanently shifted from the on-premise data center to the cloud.

Total Economic Picture. Economic decisions regarding cloud computing must be based on total cost including all pertinent capital and operational costs. For instance, the cost of a virtual machine in the cloud is simple to determine and understand. For example, current rates for Amazon EC2 are $.10 per hour for a single, small Linux/Unix machine image. This equates to $876 per year or $73 per month — seemingly pretty inexpensive. Don't think, however, that this is the only expense involved. Someone needs to monitor and manage all of those virtual machines in the cloud.

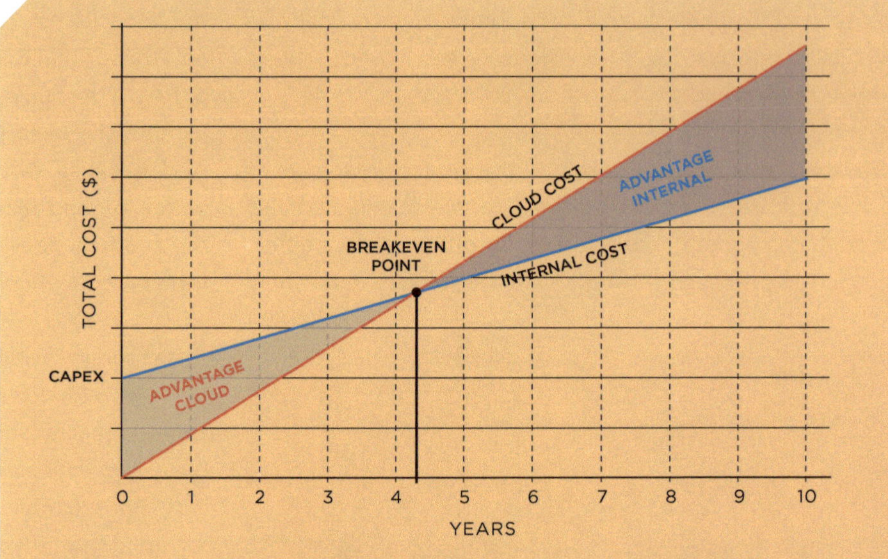

Figure 31 If internal operational costs are less than cloud rent (upper right), the total cost of a cloud solution will be best only in the short-term, until a breakeven point is exceeded.

Source: CSC

Compare this to the operational costs of a server that is maintained internally. This includes costs for any licensing or maintenance agreements, power, air, facility space, personnel, etc. Most organizations don't have a handle on what the true operational cost of a single piece of equipment is.

If the internal operational cost is higher than the rental cost in the cloud, then it is always better cost-wise to use the cloud. The decision is not as straightforward, however, if the internal operating cost is less than cloud rent. Total expense over time, including both Capex and Opex, must be taken into account, and the best decision must be determined by breakeven analysis (see Figure 31). This analysis would show a total cost advantage for the cloud only for a period of time. Beyond that period, the advantage switches to internal ownership. This has implications for the potential permanent use of cloud resources for a specific purpose, but only if the breakeven period falls within corporate guidelines (if any) for a capital investment.

Dialing Up and Down. One of the biggest cost advantages of the cloud comes from the ability to turn capacity on and off as needed. Suppose you need servers for nine months to service the load illustrated in Figure 32. Suppose the cost of these server instances on EC2 is $73 per month. Total cost for the needed capacity for 9 months is 23 server-months or $1,679 in the cloud. To service the same load internally would require the purchase of five servers. At $2,000 per server, total internal cost for the servers would be $10,000 plus internal operational costs for all five servers to service the same load.

The cloud economic model gives enterprises more options due to its flexibility and potential for IT savings. These savings

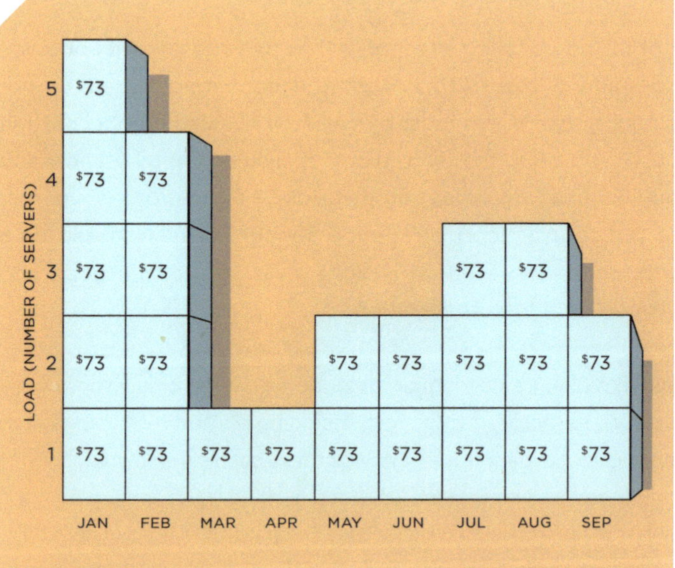

Figure 32 Match what you rent from the cloud to your actual demand, shown in this hypothetical server load.

Source: CSC

can allow the business to operate on a reduced budget, be used for IT expenditures that may not have been affordable in the past, or be invested in the core business.

Construction giant Bechtel learned this after extensively researching the major cloud providers. As reported in Network World[109] and summarized in Figure 33, this research uncovered differences between the operational and cost models of the cloud providers and Bechtel's own internal operations. Armed with this information, Bechtel began to revamp its internal IT to emulate the operating models of these major cloud providers. Among other changes in its philosophy, Bechtel is adopting the networking practices of YouTube, the standardized server approach of Google, the extreme virtualization of Amazon, and the multitenant application support strategy of Salesforce.com.

The cost shifts Bechtel found between the cloud providers and itself are reflective of Brian Arthur's assertion that "the arrival of a new technology causes the web of prices and production in the economy to stretch and reshape itself across all industries."[110] We are beginning to see this dynamic play out as a new era of cloudonomics unfolds.

	Bechtel Internal Statistics	Cloud Provider Statistics
BANDWIDTH COST	$500/megabit	$10-15
STORAGE COST	$3.75/gigabyte	$0.10
SERVER UTILIZATION (average)	2.3%	70-75%*
DATA CENTER SPACE	N	one-tenth N

Figure 33 New cloud operating models can result in significant cost advantages.

* Bechtel's estimated average after virtualization.

Data Source: http://www.networkworld.com/news/2008/102908-bechtel.html

"The arrival of a new technology causes the web of prices and production in the economy to stretch and reshape itself across all industries." *– Brian Arthur*

Cloud Effect 6

CLOUD DRIVES BUSINESS VALUE

As IT begins to reap some of the rewards of cloudonomics, the real payoff will be the business value cloud drives. As stated in the introduction to this volume, cloud enables the enterprise to do entirely new things. Cloud represents new business opportunities for all, especially in the areas of agility, collaboration, innovation, evaluation (business analytics), and new venues for conducting business.

AGILITY: BEING FAST AND FLEXIBLE

More and more, the ability for a business to thrive and survive is dependent on business agility — the ability for a business to respond to changing market conditions, be quick to market, and capitalize on shifting windows of opportunity.

Business agility, however, is not easy to achieve. It requires both flexibility and speed. The business must be organized in a manner that allows it to respond quickly to new situations; it must have roles, responsibilities and decision rights that are conducive to rapid decision making; and it must have processes established that support agile response.

In contrast, traditional IT departments have invested large amounts of time, effort and money in building, tuning and running highly stable systems. Quick change and rapid response do not fit well with this model. Further, resources may not be available when needed, since all requests must contend with all others for a finite and relatively small pool of IT resources.

Cloud computing provides the ability to enable and support business agility in a manner not previously possible. This can be game changing for the enterprise. Need an application to support 100,000 users on 20 new servers by the end of the week? No problem. You can have it by the end of the day using IaaS or SaaS services in the cloud. You don't even have to buy anything up-front. And, when the opportunity has run its course, simply release the resources and stop paying. Need to spin up an entirely new business process? Do it quickly in the cloud. Even if a new application must be developed from scratch, accelerated development and testing life cycles can be accomplished in the cloud. The result is faster time-to-launch, time-to-market and time-to-value.

People tend to talk almost exclusively about the Capex and Opex advantages of cloud as if nothing else matters. However, as described in "Cloudonomics Provide Financial Incentive," although these savings can sometimes be substantial, this view misses the mark. The truth is that Capex and Opex savings pale in comparison to the potential agility benefits enabled by the cloud. The impact that improved agility can have in terms of reduced cycle times, better customer service, or faster time-to-market is significant. Which is likely to be greater: cost savings for a few servers or a new business opportunity? Consider the spate of interest in the United States over the success of the U.S. soccer team when it reached the semifinals of the Confederations Cup in June 2009. The marketing opportunity presented by this fleeting window of opportunity could best be capitalized on by an agile company with systems capable of rapid response.[111] Use of cloud services enables both the rapid response needed to make it operationally feasible, as well as the reasonable cost needed to make it financially feasible, to capitalize on such opportunities.

The truth is that Capex and Opex savings pale in comparison to the potential agility benefits enabled by the cloud. The impact that improved agility can have in terms of reduced cycle times, better customer service, or faster time-to-market is significant.

Another example of agility is provided by California-based Eduify, which turned to Microsoft and the cloud to help with a new product launch. Eduify was founded to provide students with educational technology that can assist them in researching topics faster and writing better. To create its solution, Eduify received assistance from Microsoft technologies and services such as Windows Azure platform services, the Microsoft BizSpark ecosystem, and Windows Mobile 6. Eduify took advantage of these technological and business resources to create a solution that delivers online writing help to students anywhere, anytime, with functionality and a user experience not possible from the Web alone. At the same time, Eduify gained a 40 percent faster time-to-market, $500,000 in development and other savings, and easier access to the largest market of mobile device users. According to Dan Merritts, vice president of marketing at Eduify, "The faster time-to-market that we got with BizSpark and Azure are crucial to our success. It gives us an important competitive advantage, and it helps prove our business strategy with investors."[112]

The cloud enables a new business mindset. "Your mind really changes quickly when you can solve problems using IT resources but you don't need a long-term commitment and you don't have to wait a long time to get them," says Michael Crandell, CEO of RightScale. "Cloud computing changes the whole pattern of agility at a much lower cost."[113]

COLLABORATION: WORKING WITHOUT BOUNDARIES

Today many organizations have employees spread across the globe. Even at a single site, workers are increasingly mobile and may conduct a significant portion of work away from the office. Frequently, workers from different companies must coordinate to complete a transaction.

The ability to collaborate — to share information and work together to achieve common goals — is increasingly critical. Collaboration requires common access to a single source of trusted data and the ability to transcend time, space and technology with virtual teams. Figure 34 illustrates this by showing the broad scope of collaboration for a large pharmaceutical company.

Everyone is familiar with traditional collaboration tools and approaches. These include such things as e-mail, calendars, instant messaging, chatting, file sharing, project management, workflow, audio conferencing, video conferencing, event scheduling, webinars, screen sharing, work grouping and mind mapping. Many of these collaboration tools have been around for years and are implemented internally in most organizations today. More recent in the business world is the adoption of consumer collaboration techniques such as blogs, wikis and virtual worlds.

Figure 34 LARGE-SCALE COLLABORATION AT A PHARMACEUTICAL COMPANY

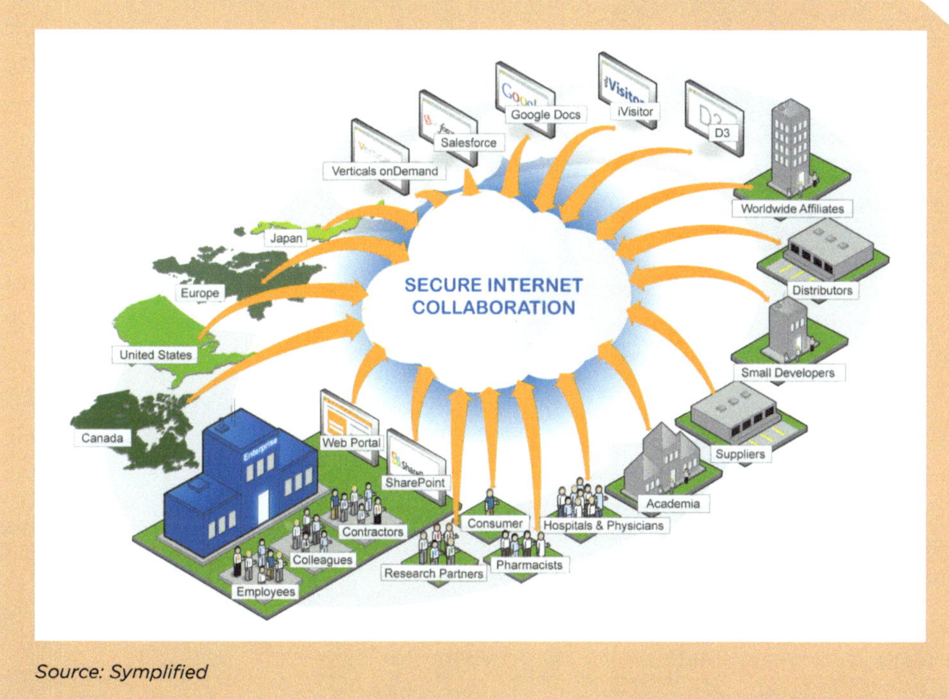

Source: Symplified

While these tools provide undeniable benefit, they still are costly and difficult to administer, do not easily accommodate external collaboration in an effective way, and are not core to the business. As a result, many organizations are increasingly looking to the cloud as the most efficient and effective venue for collaboration. The cloud provides a centralized information repository that can scale to large proportions, is easily shared, requires no internal infrastructure investment, and can be used as needed. Previously we noted how GE and the cities of Washington, D.C. and Los Angeles are taking advantage of cloud-based collaboration and productivity tools, replacing their traditional desktop equivalents.

Elsewhere, Resilient Technologies tapped the cloud to solve a distance problem and at the same time improve the efficiency of document sharing, as reported in AJAXWorld Magazine:

> Resilient Technologies of Wausau, Wisconsin, was working with Frank Rath of the University of Wisconsin to develop a special airless tire for Humvees in Iraq. By collaborating with the university, Resilient was able to tap into leading polymer scientists and mechanical engineers to conduct cutting-edge R&D.
>
> The problem was that Resilient Technologies is about 120 miles and a two-hour drive from the university's campus in Madison. To make matters worse, one of the key members of the Resilience team was based in West Virginia, nearly 1,000 miles away.
>
> The team tried out a cloud-based solution from PBwiki, and soon the entire project team was on it, including 12 people from Resilient, five polymer scientists, and three mechanical engineers. This allowed the team to cut down on time-consuming and costly travel.[114]

Then there is NASA, which usually operates above the clouds and now, with its Nebula project, is operating in the cloud. Nebula is a cloud computing pilot under development at the NASA Ames Research Center. Built around principles of transparency and public collaboration, Nebula will ultimately provide infrastructure, platform and software services. As described on the Nebula Web site:

> As a hybrid cloud, Nebula enhances NASA's ability to collaborate with external researchers by providing consistent tool sets and high-speed data connections.
>
> Nebula is currently being used for education and public outreach, for collaboration and public input, and also for mission support. Nebula's capabilities, for example, are already being realized as amateur astronomers upload high resolution photographs. Astronomy enthusiasts are informally working with NASA scientists to get a better view of the Moon using the LCROSS participation site built on the Nebula platform. Nebula is helping drive the creation of what NASA terms "citizen science," where real people can track this significant event and share critical data with our organization.[115]

BT is another organization that is serious about collaboration and innovation, embracing open innovation ecosystems and numerous other approaches. BT makes extensive use of cloud-based virtual worlds, including the popular Second Life, to spur innovation. BT believes Second Life is not just for technology enthusiasts: "Many leading organisations already have a presence in Second Life and you can see why. Imagine sharing a new product in 3D with your customers worldwide and receiving immediate feedback during its development process. Or what if you could build a space where your customers could interact with your products in an immersive virtual world, such as Second Life."[116]

BT uses this capability in several ways. One is called Capability Island. According to BT, "Within BT's Capability Island, we illustrate how we develop solutions using reusable product and service components known as 21CN Capabilities, which are illustrated in the 3D environment as colourful building blocks. Avatars can physically interact with them, and view how these capabilities are 'mashed-up' to create products and services such as BT Vision. This brings technology to life and stimulates innovation by demonstrating how 21CN Capabilities, such as 'session management and control' and 'content processing' can fit together to create new services."[117]

Another application is the BT Dragon's Den: "We have created a virtual 'Dragon's Den', where employees pitch new business ideas to senior management virtually rather than in person. Discussions with senior managers in a virtual world are more relaxed and candidates feel more at ease and innovation is stimulated as there are no geographical boundaries, meaning that employees can collaborate across the globe."[118]

A unique vision of collaboration has to do with scalable objects in the cloud, proposed by HP as "content spaces." HP believes that communities or ecosystems of future workers and developers will build spaces in the cloud around content and mold them to fit the job at hand. According to HP Laboratories, ". . . we see an inversion of the traditional application-content hierarchy through a move to content-centered working — applications are brought to content rather than content to applications. . . . The ability of users and groups to adapt content spaces to their immediate requirements allows shared working environments to be created in a fraction of the time required today, as needed; used; then destroyed, cheaply and simply, fundamentally changing the mechanics of collaborative work."[119]

Cloud-based collaboration, however, is not without issues. Organizations must develop a new culture of collaboration and sharing. Decision rights must be rethought, and issues around data security and intellectual property resolved. Other security issues such as identity and claims-based authorization must be resolved as well. Who will be the broker and manager of these things between the collaborating parties? These issues are real but not insurmountable.

Indeed, solutions are starting to appear. One example is Symplified, whose SinglePoint product is described as a security integration as a service platform. Symplified essentially provides a "security cloud" that sits between users and various SaaS providers, providing single-sign-on capability along with authentication and audit trails. (See Figure 34.) This type of model helps to enable secure collaboration for cloud-based ecosystems.

Products like this will be crucial, for as stated earlier, the future of business is collaboration, and the future of collaboration is in the cloud.

The future of business is collaboration, and the future of collaboration is in the cloud.

INNOVATION: STAYING A STEP AHEAD

Innovation is a key to competitive advantage. Particularly in a poor economy with strong competition, a company's continued survival can be dependent on staying a step ahead with new products, services, business processes and operating efficiencies sparked by creative ideas. Many companies have established offices of innovation to infuse innovation into the corporate culture. Now, the cloud is becoming a key enabler of innovation. This viewpoint is echoed by Yahoo's contention: "Cloud is not about cost cutting. It is about value creation enabling innovation."[120]

Although innovation is often serendipitous, it is most effective when approached as a process. This process involves forming many new ideas, "quick testing" ideas to find the few nuggets with real potential value, incubating the promising ideas, and ultimately bringing them into operation or to market. Cloud computing effectively supports all aspects of this process.

Many Heads are Better Than One. Recall the important role played by collaboration in the innovation process. A systematic approach to innovation is dependent on idea formation, which in turn requires the ability to collect and share data, information and ideas. These abilities are supported by collaboration. Further, according to Lynda Gratton, author of *Hot Spots*, breakthrough innovation comes from boundary spanning that leverages weak ties to people outside the immediate organization.[121] This concept is spawning innovation ecosystems consisting of customers, suppliers, academic institutions and other external organizations that can contribute ideas and provide unique insights to solving problems and creating business value. Cloud computing is beginning to provide the cauldron for this type of activity. Data from many sources can be combined and made available in the cloud for access by many people, providing a creative stew of information and minds.

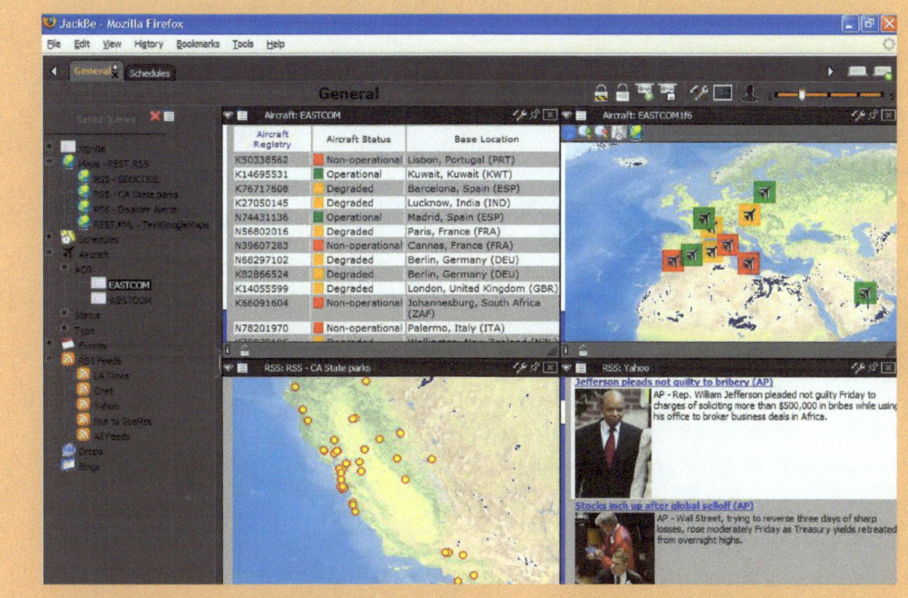

Figure 35 This mashup, called Overwatch, gives U.S. Defense Intelligence Agency staffers the ability to create an informational view of a situation on-the-fly, right from the browser.

Source: JackBe Corporation

New Arrangements. Innovation is often the result of new arrangements — that is, the combination of existing components in new or unexpected ways.[122] The entire concept of cloud-based services that can be combined into new services illustrates this. For example, mashups are applications created through the combination and consumption of cloud-based services. The ability to creatively combine existing capabilities and data to provide new value is powerful.

The concept of boundary spanning is spawning innovation ecosystems consisting of customers, suppliers, academic institutions and other external organizations that can contribute ideas and provide unique insights to solving problems and creating business value.

There are many examples of consumer mashups on the Web, from crime reporting to speed trap identifiers to shopping helpers to international cab fare finders.

On the enterprise front, mashups are being used in a variety of areas, from government to e-commerce to telephony. The U.S. Defense Intelligence Agency uses an internal mashup called Overwatch to make intelligence gathering and analysis more timely. (See Figure 35.) The U.S. Environmental Protection Agency provides a Web mashup called Window to My Environment that lets citizens enter a zip code and see its air quality, ultraviolet index, water quality, nearby hazardous waste sites and more.[123] In early 2009 Google Australia engineers used government data to plot deadly bushfires ravaging southeastern Australia on a map that was updated in realtime and accessible to all.[124]

Mashups are a vehicle for innovation because they combine disparate data sources and functionality to yield new insights. Enterprises are always looking for ways to leverage their data, and mashups, emboldened by the cloud, are a key contemporary tool for doing that.

Failing to Succeed. When it comes to innovation, you often have to fail in order to succeed. Every fifth grader knows that Thomas Edison made thousands of unsuccessful attempts before finally creating a light bulb that worked. When it comes to trying out ideas requiring some degree of IT support, cloud computing can speed up this discovery process. As reported in The Wall Street Journal: "Technology is transforming innovation at its core, allowing companies to test new ideas at speeds and prices that were unimaginable even a decade ago. . . . The result? Innovation initiatives that used to take months and megabucks to coordinate and launch can often be started in seconds for cents."[125]

Figure 36 CORDYS BUSINESS OPERATIONS PLATFORM

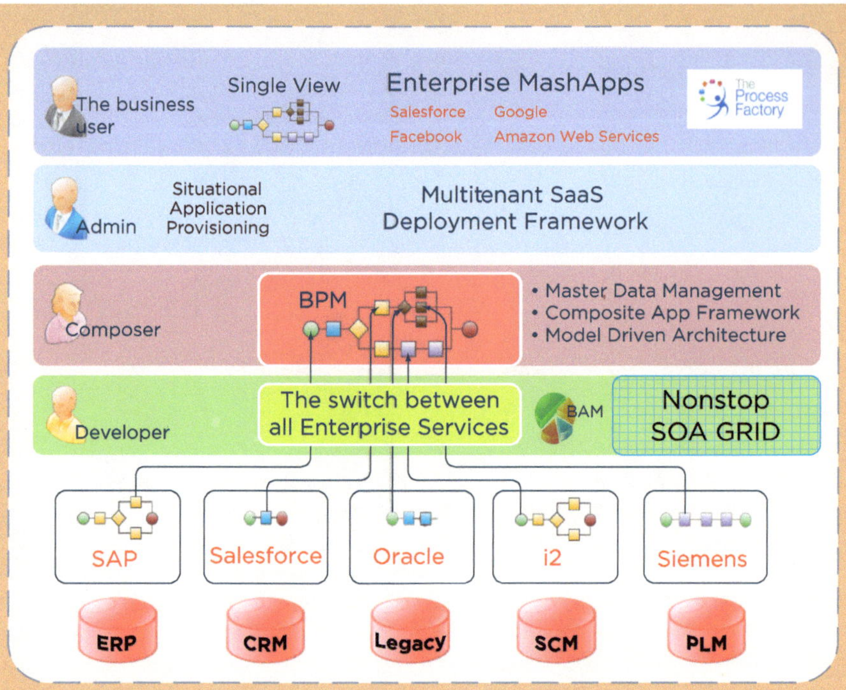

Source: Cordys

In the cloud, many ideas and scenarios can be tried out quickly and in parallel for reasonable cost, and without having to commit internal IT resources. Because trial costs may be relatively inexpensive, financial justification of innovations is easier, and the pool of innovations brought to the table tends to be larger. When the price of failure is low, companies are more willing to take the risk. The pool of potential innovations also tends to grow due to a lowering of the psychological barrier against innovation. When ideas are continually shot down for lack of funds, lack of equipment, or inability to respond, people naturally stop trying. The cloud alleviates this condition.

Cloud computing also allows the use of "fail fast"[126] approaches that can quickly sift through many potential ideas and focus in on those that are most promising. This subset of ideas can then be prototyped in a cloud sandbox that can be established without capital expenditure and shut off when no longer needed. Analytics and simulations that might be needed to evaluate and fine tune ideas can also be performed efficiently and cost-effectively in the cloud. Finally, those ideas that prove worthy can be launched as new processes or products rapidly by establishing the needed IT infrastructure in the cloud.

Cloud computing also allows the use of "fail fast" approaches that can quickly sift through many potential ideas and focus in on those that are most promising.

The promise of cloud in supporting innovation has attracted supporters in both the public and private sectors. U.S. Federal CIO Vivek Kundra is a champion of innovation and wants to use the cloud to accelerate the speed of innovation in government.[127] As Peter Fingar, author of *Dot.Cloud: The 21st Century Business Platform* and former CIO, declares, "Cloud computing isn't just about on-demand IT; *it's about on-demand business innovation.*"[128]

A Platform for Innovation. Cordys provides a versatile approach to innovation. Although we could have mentioned Cordys as an example of an application at the application service level or as a development platform at the platform service level, we have chosen to highlight its contributions towards business innovation. In fact, Cordys describes itself as a global provider of software for business process innovation and enterprise cloud orchestration.

The vision of the Cordys platform is to empower customers to dramatically improve the speed of change and fundamentally alter the way they innovate business operations.[129] Several key capabilities come into play here, all enabled by the Cordys Business Operations Platform. (See Figure 36.) Using these capabilities, businesses can quickly design, develop, deploy and improve working processes along with supporting applications.

Innovation to systematically improve processes begins with understanding current levels of performance. Business Activity Monitoring (BAM) provides the needed information to analyze and understand processes across the business. Business Process Management (BPM) capability provided by the Cordys Process Factory then provides the means to create or modify business processes on-the-fly. Processes are modeled using Business Process Modeling Notation (BPMN), and the resulting model is immediately executable as an actual working process without the need for programming.

"Cloud computing isn't just about on-demand IT; *it's about on-demand business innovation.*" — *Peter Fingar*

Processes that have been developed usually need to be supported by various software applications, some of which may already exist in-house as legacy systems, some of which may need to be created, and some of which may exist somewhere on the Web. The Cordys platform enables all of these scenarios. Using a SOA-based approach, existing applications including SAP, Oracle, IBM Websphere, Microsoft.NET and others can be harnessed non-invasively to support business processes. New, Web-based mashup applications (MashApps) can be developed quickly at low cost and executed immediately.

In support of the MashApps concept, Cordys is also establishing an open, online community for mashup development, creating an ecosystem of providers and applications that can be mixed and matched as needed to create new applications to support processes. And, using cloudsourcing, Cordys enables software in its cloud to be integrated with public clouds, on-premise legacy systems and private clouds.

The Cordys platform is based on a completely multitenant architecture and is powered by a highly scalable, non-stop SOA grid. "In the transition of an organization towards processes, availability of the processes is as important as the dial tone of your phone. We have achieved that with this platform approach," says Cordys Chief Technology Officer Theodoor van Donge.

All of this results in an ecosystem of a different kind — the Cordys Enterprise Cloud Orchestration System (ECOSystem). ECOSystem brings it all together, creating complete end-to-end processes supported by manual activities, on-premise legacy systems and cloud-based applications as needed, all from the cloud.

EVALUATION: BRINGING BUSINESS INTELLIGENCE TO THE MASSES

Organizations are awash in data but struggle to harness it for decision-making. Being able to use business intelligence (BI) tools to convert data into meaningful information can significantly improve the organization's ability to make effective decisions. Across industries, BI is assuming increased importance in many areas including complex sales and marketing analyses, financial analyses and supply chain analyses.

Unfortunately, because BI analyses require special software and often a very significant amount of processing power, relatively few organizations have been able to take advantage of this potentially important tool in the business arsenal. Cloud computing, however, helps bring the benefits of BI to the masses. At the same time, cloud introduces new data never before available for analysis — what we'll call cloud data — that can provide a fresh look at previously unmeasureable, or difficult to measure, trends.

Turning Internal Information Into Insights. With the cloud, companies no longer have to have the large-scale internal processing capability needed for BI analyses. The required computing power can be obtained when needed without up-front investment from the cloud, paid for as-used, and turned off when the analysis is complete. This brings BI techniques into play for even small companies. It also means that analyses can be run more frequently. Analyses can be run just-in-time and therefore can be more timely for supporting decisions. Also, more scenarios or simulations can be tried out each time (even in parallel), which helps improve the quality and accuracy of business decisions.

And, deploying BI has never been easier. For example, RightScale, Jaspersoft (provider of open source BI software), Talend (provider of open source data integration software) and Vertica (provider of high-performance analytic database management systems) have come together to offer an integrated BI solutions stack. The result: It is now possible to deploy low-cost, integrated BI capability "with a push of the button from [the] RightScale management dashboard."[130]

BI in the cloud is an emergent concept, and while some analysts have pointed out that it has not yet fully caught on, the 2009 BI technology poll conducted by BeyeNETWORK found that the technologies most likely to impact BI are SaaS and cloud.[131] Some major players would seem to agree. IBM, for example, has recently started implementing analytics clouds. And SAS, the largest independent BI software company, sees a healthy market developing and is planning its own $70 million cloud computing facility.[132]

Crane Pumps & Systems (CP&S) is one company that has tapped cloud power to support BI.[133] Since 1948, CP&S has manufactured a diverse range of pumps, accessories and services to provide successful solutions for water, wastewater, military and engineered pump market segments. To ensure continued market success, CP&S enhanced its focus on managing vendor supply chains, assembly, and delivery, and resolved to be a leader in on-time delivery. "It was towards this specific goal that CP&S realized that an effective grasp of their data through reporting and analysis would be essential. In addition, the company understood that giving transparent and company-wide access to this data, 'for everyone to see,' would be the ideal way forward."[134]

But in the down economy of 2008, CP&S had difficulty justifying an in-house BI solution and began looking towards the cloud. CP&S had three primary requirements:

1. Give a wider pool of decision-makers the tools to see, understand and act upon their data, without waiting for IT to do this for them.

2. Provide good value for the company in terms of having powerful and interactive BI tools without adding burden to the IT team or end users.

3. Allow themselves the flexibility to deploy as much BI as they required without wasteful overhead.

This quest led them to BI SaaS provider Logi XML and the Logi Info (managed reporting, analysis and dashboards) and Logi Ad Hoc (reporting, analysis and dashboards for end users) products. CP&S BI project lead Scott Brooks reflects on their experience: "During these economic times all departments, including IT, must operate on maximum efficiency. Having someone solely dedicated to supporting a BI solution is not realistic. With Logi, we were able to implement at our own pace (no outside expert contractors needed) and weren't committed to many hours of user admin. Logi enabled us to simply and easily make as much or as little use of our BI tool as we needed."[135]

Analyzing Cloud Data. Another aspect of BI is the ability to take advantage of very large pools of information — collective intelligence — that are accumulated in, and only available from, the cloud. An example is the extensive amount of data maintained by search engines such as Google and Yahoo. The collective data regarding what people are searching for, at what times, in what locations, results in a rich and useful source of information. In 2008, Google used a tool called Google Flu Trends to track the spread of flu in the United States. By analyzing keyword searches for flu-related terms, Google created a surprisingly accurate early warning system for the spread of infectious disease.[136] Ten years ago, cloud data like this did not exist.

By analyzing keyword searches for flu-related terms, Google created a surprisingly accurate early warning system for the spread of infectious disease.

Similar analyses can be used in business. Tools such as Google Trends and Google Insights provide the means to harness search data to support business marketing efforts. Anita Campbell, editor of Small Business Trends, provides the following examples.[137] Using Google Trends, she was able to track the growth of the term "cloud computing" from October 2007 to September 2008. (See Figure 37). Note the sharp spike around August 2008. Such knowledge can help marketers shape the direction of marketing efforts.

She also made use of Google Insights to gain unique knowledge about a specific product. (See Figure 38.) Campbell writes: ". . . over at The App Gap, I wrote about using Google Insights to test a competitor's foothold within different states. For instance, there

I used it to create this state map showing search volume for 'WordPress.' As you can see, WordPress is a more popular search term in Western states such as California, Utah, Oregon and Washington. Of course, the data is limited because it relates only to search volume. But it could give you valuable insight into the relative consumer awareness that competing products have in a particular state. Or it might tell you whether it is worthwhile to spend the money to exhibit at a seminar or tradeshow in that location."[138]

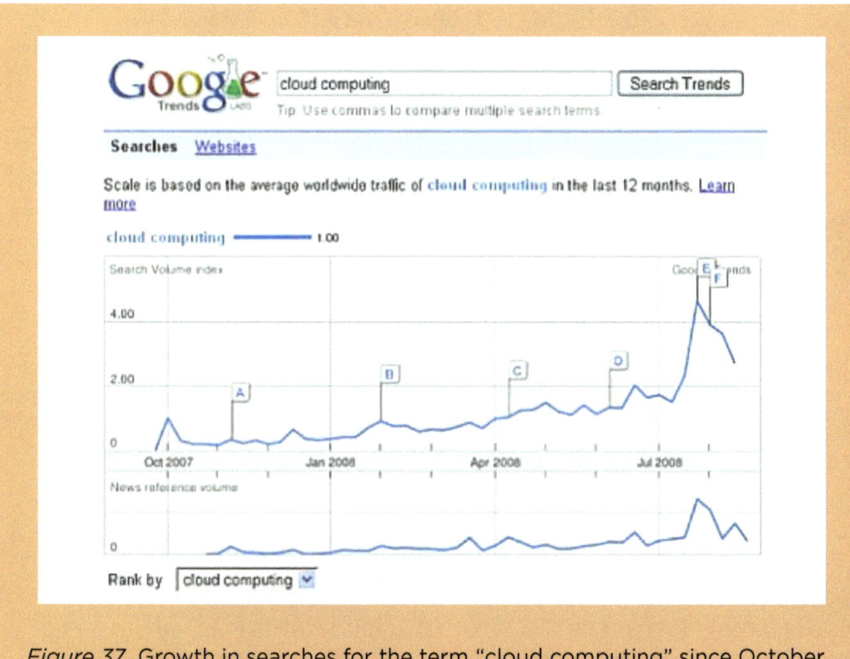

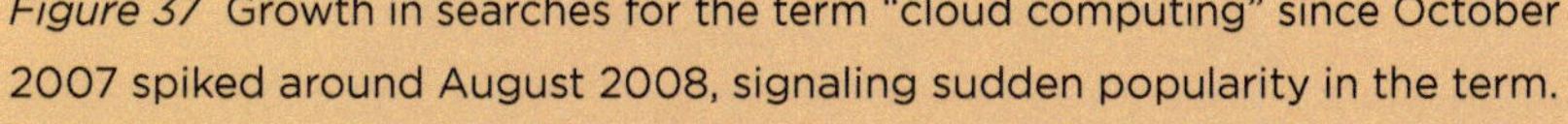

Figure 37 Growth in searches for the term "cloud computing" since October 2007 spiked around August 2008, signaling sudden popularity in the term.

Source: Small Business Trends

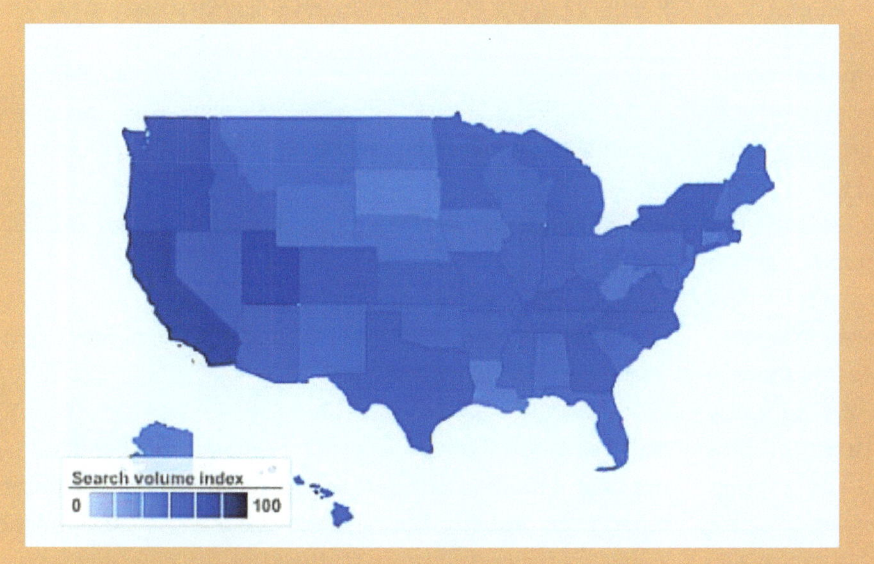

Figure 38 Search volume for "WordPress" from 2004-2008, by state, indicates the term's relative popularity in Western states, offering potential market insights.

Source: Small Business Trends

NEW VENUES FOR BUSINESS

Earlier we explored how cloud computing can enable more effective collaboration. Although collaboration primarily involves multiple individuals or organizations simultaneously working together on a task or problem, the cloud may also support broader cooperation and specific business conditions needed by entire communities of users. Such communities have flourished in the consumer world for some time now. Whether social communities formed around Facebook or MySpace or special interest groups focused on music (LastFM), photos (Flickr) or videos (YouTube), online communities are by now commonplace. Similar cloud-based communities are beginning to form in the commercial world. Examples include industry-focused clouds and clouds supporting an extended supply chain.

General purpose public clouds such as Amazon, Rackspace and GoGrid are versatile in that anyone may use them for any purpose. However, the flip side of this versatility is that potential users requiring specific conditions such as regulatory compliance may not be willing or able to use these clouds. Consider, though, a cloud that caters to the needs of a specific group or industry, such as the healthcare industry. Such a cloud could be architected to be HIPAA-compliant and provide specific tools and capabilities needed by healthcare professionals and organizations. In fact, Amazon has provided guidelines for HIPAA compliance using AWS,[139] and there are several examples of HIPAA-compliant applications built on AWS.[140]

Figure 39 AMITIVE COORDINATES THE SUPPLY CHAIN ECOSYSTEM

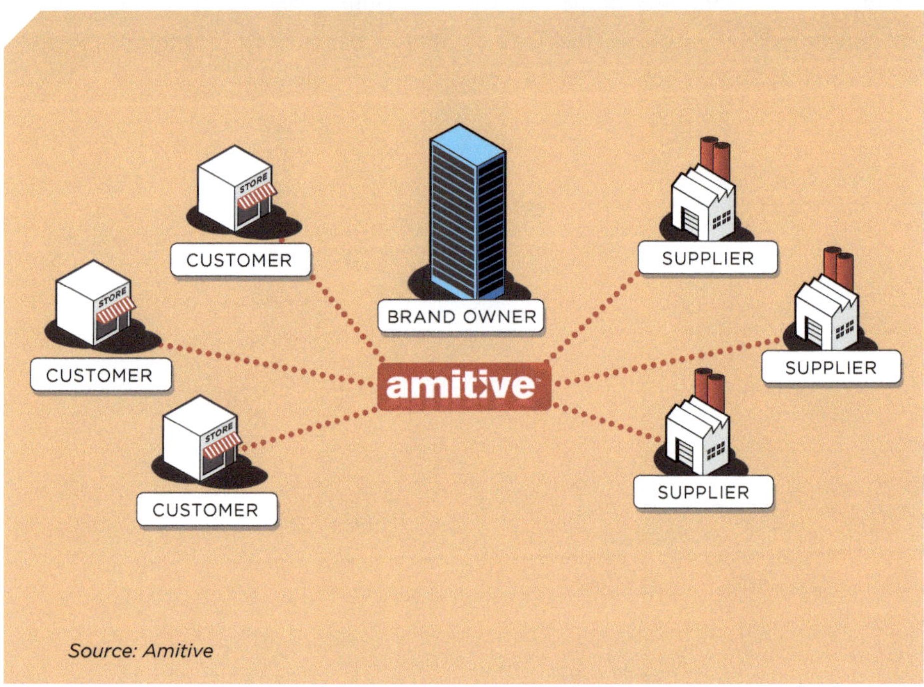

Source: Amitive

While a single healthcare cloud does not exist, small examples are beginning to pop up that exhibit at least some cloud characteristics. One such cloud has been implemented by the Beth Israel Deaconess Medical Center (BIDMC) together with its Beth Israel Deaconess Physicians Organization (BIDPO) and service provider Concordant.[141] This implementation provides services to small doctor offices in the Boston area. Using a SaaS-type service model, doctors are able to pay a subscription fee and use centrally provided software to manage their offices and medical records over the Internet. While the efficacy of the healthcare cloud concept is still hotly debated, such models are becoming more prevalent in large healthcare networks throughout the country.

Manufacturing is another industry ripe with opportunity for cloud computing. Particularly when entire supply chains are considered, the need for inter-organization cooperation and coordination is significant.

Clouds are beginning to form to support supply chain communities. An example is SaaS provider Amitive, whose Unity 5.0 product is aimed at enabling "Community SCM [Supply Chain Management] for both large and small companies that outsource manufacturing."[142] As shown in Figure 39, Amitive creates supply chain ecosystems consisting of brand owners, suppliers, customers, carriers and other organizations that can all interact via the cloud to globally manage forecasts, orders, purchasing, inventory, fulfillment and logistics. Amitive's approach to multitenant applications provides "each Amitive community with the ability to create its own set of customized business processes. This is quite different than earlier SaaS applications, in which companies could only modify pre-existing business processes. . . . This advanced architecture is essential to handling the complexities of the supply chain world, in which processes such as 'sales order creation' or 'fulfillment' vary dramatically from company to company."[143]

Another cloud to serve these types of needs has been developed and is operated by HP: the HP Cloud Computing Ecosystem for Manufacturing Industries. This scalable, on-demand, multitenant, pay-as-you-go cloud consists of:

- technology-enabled services that are used by manufacturing, distribution and retail companies to track, trace, recall and authenticate manufacturing products

- a development and run-time environment that provides data, analytic, management and security services

- a scalable infrastructure that automates resource provisioning and system management.[144]

It makes sense that in a world of multiple clouds and myriad business demands, specialized clouds will emerge. Whether tuned to an industry, business activity or technical workload, specialized clouds will open the door to new innovations and signal a maturing of the cloud ecosystem.

THE FUTURE OF BUSINESS IN THE CLOUD

The cloud phenomenon will continue to gain momentum and evolve in new and surprising directions. In the coming years the impact on business will become even more profound as barriers fall, the nature of business changes, competition heats up, the digital domain revolutionizes the economy, and a new economy enhanced with biological properties emerges.

BARRIERS FALL

In spite of the many potential benefits of cloud computing, not to mention the popularity of such enterprise cloud pioneers as Salesforce.com, the cloud is still primarily being used to support niche areas such as system development and testing, business intelligence, data backup, disaster recovery, e-mail, personal productivity and other ancillary applications. Although there are exceptions, cloud is not a ubiquitous venue for conducting business yet.

There are numerous reasons. Suspect security, lack of trust, fear of lock-in, reticence to relinquish control, unsuitability of legacy applications, integration complexity, and poor SLAs are just some of the barriers that often prevent enterprise business from moving to the cloud.

This situation, however, is changing and will continue to improve. Solutions are emerging in the market to address all of these barriers, and cloud standards are being developed. It is likely in the next several years that many of these barriers to cloud adoption will be eliminated, or at least mitigated, to the point that use of cloud computing for enterprise business purposes will be a more feasible and acceptable option than it is today. Many businesses will also just become more comfortable with — or at least accepting of — any remaining cloud computing issues given the passage of time, just as people have come to accept if not embrace the Internet, making it part of everyday life even as its dangers have increased.

THE NATURE OF BUSINESS CHANGES

The very nature of business itself is also likely to change in response to the cloud. As the concept of cloud-based services becomes more entrenched, businesses will have less of a need or desire to do everything internally. Core competencies and functions providing competitive advantage will form the basis of business, while ancillary or support functions will be jettisoned and obtained from providers in the cloud. This will lead to a simultaneous increase in the number of providers offering specialized but common business functions, and a decrease in the size of individual businesses. These smaller businesses entailing high-value functions will rely on end-to-end business processes orchestrated in the cloud and will consume specialized support services as needed.

As forecast in William Davidow and Michael Malone's 1992 book *The Virtual Corporation*,[145] the cloud will also give rise to conducting business in a more virtual way. The use of cloud-based simulations and massive analyses of both structured and unstructured data will become the norm for trying out business concepts and decisions before they are actually enacted. And, as the community of people with whom we regularly interact becomes more global, virtual worlds will become a common venue for conducting business.

All of these changes will require new business skills and methods of operation. The abilities to cooperate and collaborate, to innovate, to redefine and share decisions rights, and to spread responsibilities across diverse organizations will assume increasing importance. "Double-deep" personnel will thrive. The very structure of business organizations will need to morph into forms more conducive to agile, flexible and collaborative operating models.

COMPETITION HEATS UP

The cloud will strengthen business competition by lowering barriers to entry, improving corporate agility, and helping open up third world economies. Lower Capex requirements, global availability of cloud-based workers, and reduced transaction costs will make it easier to start new businesses. These small businesses will be active players in the cloud, where they can use the most powerful and sophisticated IT infrastructures in the world for minimal cost. This levels the playing field, giving small businesses access to IT resources once only available to (and affordable by) large enterprises.

On the flip side, large companies will be able to match small company agility because they will be able to test new ideas quickly in the cloud, ultimately leading to faster time-to-market for new products, processes and campaigns. Cycle times will be significantly reduced using cloud computing.

Provider businesses will face increasing competition as well. As the cloud phenomenon continues to gather steam, more and more new vendors will emerge to fill expanding niches. At the same time, a general shakeout of providers will occur due to business failure or what will likely be an increasing number of cloud acquisitions.

On a macro level, cloud will help make competition more global by enabling faster development of third world economies, which no longer have to put in place complex and expensive IT infrastructure.

FROM TECHNOLOGY EVOLUTION TO ECONOMIC REVOLUTION

As described in Volume 1, the domain of digital technology has been evolving over many decades, bringing with it several waves of technology that have morphed computation from automated calculations to an entire industry of information technology, telecommunications, and digital content that interconnects the world.[146] This change of the digital domain has been a series of slow evolutions, whereby a large hierarchy of hard and soft technologies have been combined and recombined into new assemblies and components. The latest of these evolutions is cloud.

But there is a revolutionary side to cloud as well. At the LEF Client Forum in November 2009, Brian Arthur described collections of technologies, be it railroads or electronics, as big toolboxes of functionalities. Whereas innovation has traditionally been seen as adding new pieces to these toolboxes, Arthur argued that true innovation happens as the economy encounters changes in technology — in this case, as the economy encounters cloud computing.

"History shows that technology drives innovation in the economy. That's where cloud is going to make a huge difference. As the global economy continues to encounter and integrate with the digital domain — the entire body of computational and communication technology — the whole economy changes," said Arthur. "As the resulting change sweeps across the economy, you get what economist Joseph Schumpeter called 'gales of creative destruction.' Every business changes, and that's what we call a *revolution*.

"As to the current hype, cloud has been somewhat oversold today. Technologically, it's only an evolution, but I believe that with the cloud and other digital technologies, a new economic world is emerging."

THE DIGITAL BIOLOGY OF THE NEW ECONOMY

According to Arthur, in the past, technology has given the economy its muscle. But with cloud computing, digital technology is emerging as the economy's nervous system. "With the cloud plus sensors and actuators, an expanded economy is emerging that is giving the economy the ability to have intelligence. This is a revolution in the economy," Arthur declares. "In the 1800s, technology provided a muscular system for the economy; today technology is providing a *neural system* for the economy — a system that can sense and act appropriately."

As a result, not only is cloud computing changing existing industries, but it is also giving rise to new economic structures

"In the 1800s, technology provided a muscular system for the economy; today technology is providing a *neural system* for the economy — a system that can sense and act appropriately." — *Brian Arthur*

and markets. Already, for computer gaming and entertainment media, we are seeing a shift to an entirely digital economy, with no physical artifacts created or traded — only bits.

This highly integrated system of systems, where everything is managed as bits, is leading to a parallel economic structure that Arthur refers to as "the unseen economy." It is self-organizing, self-directing, self-configuring and ephemeral (certain transactions may last only fractions of a second) — becoming, collectively, a more intelligent platform that integrates and controls all other traditional economies. Cloud computing, along with other technologies that are increasingly intertwined with the digital world, is driving technology from its traditional mechanistic "clockwork" structure to something more analogous to biology, acquiring properties associated with living organisms.

And it all makes sense, says Arthur: "This unseen digital economy is doing something very appropriate and very biological in nature. It is an adaptive, complex and progressively intelligent system — not a dumb economy, and not just data processing. This virtual economy senses and reacts in increasingly sophisticated ways."

Cloud computing will greatly advance the on-going quest for more intelligent systems that will make businesses and people work and play smarter. Clouds are in the forecast, to be sure; the overall outlook for business in the cloud is bright.

NOTES

1. "Cloud rEvolution: Laying the Foundation," CSC Leading Edge Forum, Volume 1, *Cloud rEvolution* series, September 2009, http://assets1.csc.com/lef/downloads/LEF_2009CloudRev_Vol1_Foundations.pdf; and "Cloud rEvolution: The Art of Abstraction," CSC Leading Edge Forum, Volume 2, *Cloud rEvolution* series, October 2009, http://assets1.csc.com/lef/downloads/LEF_2009CloudRev_Vol2_Abstraction.pdf

2. "Architecture rEvolution: Exploring the Network Effect on Infrastructure, Applications and Business Process," CSC Leading Edge Forum, 2003. http://assets1.csc.com/lef/downloads/1143_1.pdf

3. NIST Computer Security Division — Computer Security Resource Center, http://csrc.nist.gov/groups/SNS/cloud-computing/

4. "Cloud rEvolution: The Art of Abstraction," CSC Leading Edge Forum, Volume 2, *Cloud rEvolution* series, October 2009, pp. 70-71. http://assets1.csc.com/lef/downloads/LEF_2009CloudRev_Vol2_Abstraction.pdf

5. "The Next Wave: Everything as a Service," Hewlett-Packard, Shane Robison Executive Viewpoint, February 2008, http://www.hp.com/hpinfo/execteam/articles/robison/08eaas.html. Also see HP's Everything as a Service site, http://www.hp.com/hpinfo/initiatives/eaas/index.html.

6. BlueLock Virtual Cloud Computing, http://www.bluelock.com/solutions/hosting/virtualcloud.html

7. Nirvanix uses Raid 6, which stripes one copy of data to three disks (for Nirvanix's one location/copy policy). So if a user chooses five locations, that would be an effective 15 copies on 15 disks. The majority of enterprises choose two copies, resulting in two Raid 6 copies in separate locations in the Nirvanix network. In other words, it is one RAID 6 protected copy in one location. If a user sets a policy for more than one location, then each location has a RAID 6 protected copy. RAID 6 stripes the data to three disks for protection purposes, but to Nirvanix's file system it looks like one copy.

8. "NASA to send lunar data to Nirvanix's cloud for disaster recovery," SearchDisasterRecovery.com, 12 March 2009. http://searchdisasterrecovery.techtarget.com/news/article/0,289142,sid190_gci1350630,00.html

9. "U.S. government sets up online 'app store,'" CNN.com, 16 September 2009. http://www.cnn.com/2009/TECH/09/16/government.app.store/index.html

10. Rollbase company profile, CrunchBase, http://www.crunchbase.com/company/rollbase

NOTES

11. Intacct company overview, http://us.intacct.com/corporate/index.php

12. "Google Apps Unseats Incumbent Microsoft Office in Washington, DC," ReadWriteWeb, 13 October 2008. http://www.readwriteweb.com/archives/google_apps_microsoft_dc.php

13. "Los Angeles OKs plan to use Google Web services," MSN Money, 27 October 2009, http://news.moneycentral.msn.com/ticker/article.aspx?Feed=AP&Date=20091027&ID=10606469&Symbol=CSC; and "City of Los Angeles and CSC Kick Off Implementation of Google Apps Cloud Computing Solution," press release, 14 December 2009, http://www.csc.com/newsroom/press_releases/38422

14. "Cloud Sourcing: The rise of on-demand BPO," *Outsourcing,* Insights, Issue 13, August 2009. http://www.the-outsourcing.com/Insights/Issue13/cloud.html

15. Amazon Fulfillment Web Service, http://aws.amazon.com/fws/

16. "Eight ways that cloud computing will change business," Dion Hinchcliffe's Enterprise Web 2.0 blog, ZDNet.com, 5 June 2009, http://blogs.zdnet.com/Hinchcliffe/?p=488 (Self-service is #6.)

17. "Cloud rEvolution: The Art of Abstraction," CSC Leading Edge Forum, Volume 2, *Cloud rEvolution* series, October 2009, p. 62. http://assets1.csc.com/lef/downloads/LEF_2009CloudRev_Vol2_Abstraction.pdf

18. Citrix Dazzle — Technology Preview, http://www.citrix.com/English/ps2/products/feature.asp?contentID=1690066

19. "Now, Even the Government Has an App Store," Bits Blog, *The New York Times,* 15 September 2009. http://bits.blogs.nytimes.com/2009/09/15/now-even-the-government-has-an-app-store/

20. "CSC Selected as the Provider for the Windows Azure Platform," press release, 14 July 2009. http://www.csc.com/newsroom/press_releases/29509-csc_selected_as_a_provider_for_the_windows_azure_platform

21. "CSC to Resell Cloud-Based Microsoft Online Services," press release, 1 July 2009. http://www.csc.com/cloud/press_releases/29146-csc_to_resell_cloud_based_microsoft_online_services

NOTES

22. "Oracle Plans Utah Data Center To Support SaaS Business," *InformationWeek*, 19 May 2008. http://www.informationweek.com/news/services/hosted_apps/showArticle.jhtml?articleID=207801092

23. "Larry Ellison's Brilliant Anti-Cloud Computing Rant," *The Wall Street Journal,* 25 September 2008. (Article is offline.) See video http://www.youtube.com/watch?v=0FacYAI6DY0

24. "Hooray! Oracle acquisition of Sun makes perfect sense," Dana Gardner's BriefingsDirect blog, ZDNet.com, 20 April 2009. http://blogs.zdnet.com/Gardner/?p=2903

25. "Oracle Set To Take The Lead on Cloud Computing," Gerson Lehrman Group, 4 May 2009. http://www.glgroup.com/News/Oracle-Set-To-Take-The-Lead-on-Cloud-Computing-38269.html

26. "IBM challenges Google Apps with Lotus Cloud E-Mail," eChannelLine, 6 October 2009. http://www.echannelline.com/usa/story.cfm?item=25044

27. "I.B.M. to Help Clients Fight Cost and Complexity," *The New York Times,* 15 June 2009. http://www.nytimes.com/2009/06/15/technology/business-computing/15blue.html?_r=2

28. "IBM Research and SAP Demonstrate New Cloud Technology: Real-Time Application Mobility," IBM press release, 2 March 2009. http://www-03.ibm.com/press/us/en/pressrelease/26824.wss

29. "HP, Intel, Yahoo join forces on cloud computing research," CNET News, 29 July 2008. http://news.cnet.com/8301-1001_3-10001390-92.html

30. "SAP confirms Business ByDesign delay," Between the Lines blog, ZDNet.com, 30 April 2008. http://blogs.zdnet.com/BTL/?p=8658

31. "SAP's Business ByDesign coming to mobile devices," Reuters, 21 May 2009. http://www.reuters.com/article/technologyNews/idUSTRE54K4SR20090521?feedType=RSS&feedName=technologyNews

32. "SAP executive: Business ByDesign ramp up not imminent," ITworld, 30 April 2009. http://www.itworld.com/saas/67266/sap-executive-business-bydesign-ramp-not-imminent

NOTES

33. W. Brian Arthur, *The Nature of Technology: What It Is and How It Evolves* (New York: Free Press, August 2009), p. 135.

34. Ibid., p. 134.

35. FastScale Stack Manager, http://www.fastscale.com/technology/stackmanager.shtml

36. "Cloud rEvolution: The Art of Abstraction," CSC Leading Edge Forum, Volume 2, *Cloud rEvolution* series, October 2009, "Virtual Appliances: Software Stack to Go," pp. 65-66. http://assets1.csc.com/lef/downloads/LEF_2009CloudRev_Vol2_Abstraction.pdf

37. Ibid., "Portable, Disposable Infrastructure," pp. 11-12.

38. "Navigating the Fog — Billing, Metering & Measuring the Cloud," Reuven Cohen's ElasticVapor: Life in the Cloud blog, 1 March 2009. http://www.elasticvapor.com/2009/03/navigating-fog-billing-metering.html

39. "Cloud Brokers: The Next Big Opportunity?," Data Center Knowledge, 27 July 2009. http://www.datacenterknowledge.com/archives/2009/07/27/cloud-brokers-the-next-big-opportunity/

40. "Consoles, Management Tools and Brokers," OnDemand Beat blog, 15 September 2009. http://www.ondemandbeat.com/2009/09/15/consoles-management-tools-and-brokers/

41. "Red Hat builds one API for many clouds," ZDNet UK, 4 September 2009. http://news.zdnet.co.uk/software/0,1000000121,39739505,00.htm

42. "CloudSwitch Raises $8 Million," Data Center Knowledge, 1 July 2009. http://www.datacenterknowledge.com/archives/2009/07/01/cloudswitch-raises-8-million/

43. Interview with Stuart Charlton, Chief Software Architect, Elastra, 14 August 2009. http://www.johnmwillis.com/cloudcafe/cloud-cafe-37-elastra-with-stu-charlton/

44. Rackspace Managed Service Level Agreement, http://dealer.webmanagement.us/pdf/Managed_SLA.pdf

45. Amazon S3 Design Principles, http://aws.amazon.com/s3/#principles

NOTES

46. "Announcing Elastic IP Addresses and Availability Zones for Amazon EC2," http://aws.amazon.com/about-aws/whats-new/2008/03/26/announcing-elastic-ip-addresses-and-availability-zones-for-amazon-ec2/

47. "RAIC — pronounce it 'rake,' please," Mark Masterson's Process Perfection blog, 28 January 2009. http://www.jroller.com/MasterMark/entry/raic_pronounce_it_rake_please

48. "Liquid Security: Digital Trust When Time, Place and Platform Don't Matter," CSC Leading Edge Forum, Volume 5, *Digital Trust* series, September 2007. http://assets1.csc.com/lef/downloads/LEF_2007DigitalTrustVol5.pdf

49. "Digital Trust: Shaking Hands with the Digital Enterprise," CSC Leading Edge Forum, Volume 1, *Digital Trust* series, June 2007, p. 7. http://assets1.csc.com/lef/downloads/LEFReports2007_DigitalTrustVol1.pdf. See the entire eight-volume Digital Trust series at www.csc.com/lefreports.

50. Ronald B. Knode, "Digital Trust in the Cloud: Liquid Security in Cloudy Places," CSC, August 2009, "Weatherproofing the Cloud to Provide Some Digital Trust," pp. 21-23. http://assets1.csc.com/lef/downloads/Digital_Trust_in_the_Cloud.pdf

51. "Federal Budget Hastens Cloud Adoption," BNET, 14 May 2009. http://industry.bnet.com/technology/10001732/federal-budget-hastens-cloud-adoption/ Click "Blog Post."

52. "UK Government CIO sheds light on 'G-Cloud' plans," Reuven Cohen's ElasticVapor: Life in the Cloud blog, 18 June 2009. http://www.elasticvapor.com/2009/06/uk-government-cio-sheds-light-on-g.html

53. "ISO Forms Group for Cloud Computing Standards," 9 November 2009. http://linux.sys-con.com/node/1176795

54. "Microsoft Azure: Security in the Cloud," WindowSecurity.com, 11 November 2009. http://www.windowsecurity.com/articles/Microsoft-Azure-Security-Cloud.html

55. "Can We Secure Cloud Computing? Can We Afford Not To?" Christofer Hoff's Rational Survivability blog, 22 October 2009. http://www.rationalsurvivability.com/blog/?p=1491

56. "VMware vs. Amazon...ROUND ONE...FIGHT!" Cloudscaling.com, 15 September 2009. http://cloudscaling.com/blog/cloud-computing/vmware-vs-amazon-round-one-fight

NOTES

57. "Open Standards are not enough...," Simon Wardley blog, 1 December 2007, http://blog.gardeviance.org/2007/12/open-standards-are-not-enough.html. See a related blog post, "The cloud computing standards war," 3 September 2009, http://blog.gardeviance.org/2009/09/cloud-computing-standards-war.html

58. "Cloud Standards are Misunderstood," Cloudscaling.com, 29 September 2009. http://cloudscaling.com/blog/cloud-computing/cloud-standards-are-misunderstood

59. Ubuntu Enterprise Cloud, http://www.ubuntu.com/products/whatisubuntu/serveredition/cloud/UEC

60. "Pentagon claims its cloud is better than Google's," The Cloud Clinic, 6 October 2009. http://thecloudclinic.com/2009/10/pentagon-claims-its-cloud-is-better-than-googles/

61. "Early users find savings in cloud storage," *Computerworld*, 13 July 2009. http://www.computerworld.com/s/article/print/340460/Cash_in_the_Cloud?taxonomyName=Storage&taxonomyId=19

62. "CSC to Resell Microsoft Cloud Services," DevSource, 5 July 2009. http://www.devsource.com/c/a/Architecture/CSC-to-Resell-Microsoft-Cloud-Services/

63. "Ubuntu's Karmic Koala will make 'cloud dance,'" silicon.com, 23 February 2009. http://software.silicon.com/os/0,39024651,39398331,00.htm

64. "RightScale to Extend Cloud Management to Private & Hybrid Clouds," Open Source Magazine, 20 April 2009. http://opensource.sys-con.com/node/927453

65. NASA Nebula Virtalization, http://nebula.nasa.gov/services/virtualization/

66. About the Nebula Platform, http://nebula.nasa.gov/about/

67. "The 'DIY cloud' market heats up," The 451 Group, IT-tude.com, 2008. http://www.gridipedia.eu/diycloud-vmops.html

68. George Brown and Robert Carpenter, "Successful Application of Service-Oriented Architecture Across the Enterprise and Beyond," *Intel Technology Journal,* Volume 8, Issue 4, 17 November 2004, p. 347. http://download.intel.com/technology/itj/2004/volume08issue04/art09_successful/vol8_art09.pdf

NOTES

69. "Appistry: Why buy Xeons when Wal-Mart Pentium 4's will do?," Between the Lines blog, ZDNet.com, 16 May 2005. http://blogs.zdnet.com/BTL/?p=1385

70. "GigaSpaces & GoGrid Join Forces to Create an Enterprise-grade PaaS Offering for Java and .NET," press release, 7 October 2009. http://www.gigaspaces.com/node/1366

71. "Pervasive Updates Tools For Growing SaaS Market," IntelligentEnterprise.com, April 2007. http://www.intelligententerprise.com/showArticle.jhtml?articleID=198702295 http://intelligent-enterprise.informationweek.com/channels/enterprise_applications/erp/showArticle.jhtml?articleID=198702295

72. "Cloud rEvolution: Laying the Foundation," CSC Leading Edge Forum, Volume 1, *Cloud rEvolution* series, September 2009, pp. 19-20. http://assets1.csc.com/lef/downloads/LEF_2009CloudRev_Vol1_Foundations.pdf

73. "Five Problems Keeping Legacy Apps Out of the Cloud," *Computerworld*, 15 October 2009. http://news.idg.no/cw/art.cfm?id=58EAB41D-1A64-6A71-CE11847B191CB22D

74. "Cloud Cube Model: Selecting Cloud Formations for Secure Collaboration," Jericho Forum position paper, Version 1.0, April 2009, http://www.opengroup.org/jericho/cloud_cube_model_v1.0.pdf (the Jericho Forum is a consortium in The Open Group); and "Radeztsky's Cube & The Interoperability Metaverse," Reuven Cohen's ElasticVapor: Life in the Cloud blog, 14 February 2009, http://www.elasticvapor.com/2009/02/radeztskys-cube-interoperability.html

75. "Capital SCF Hopes To Never Buy a Server," NoMoreServers.com, 10 November 2009. http://nomoreservers.com/andys-daily-ace/capitalscf/

76. "Tour of a Serverless Enterprise," 14 August 2008. http://office20.com/docs/DOC-1125

77. "The Future of IT: Doing Business in the Cloud," CSC, 26 August 2009. http://www.csc.com/features/stories/31506-the_future_of_it_doing_business_in_the_cloud#

78. "Preparing for the End of IT as We Know It," Sun Microsystems, May 2007. http://www.sun.com/emrkt/innercircle/newsletter/0507sponsor.html

NOTES

79. "Intel sees future in Mega Data Center," Channel Register, 18 February 2009. http://www.channelregister.co.uk/2009/02/18/the_intel_cloud

80. "Cloud rEvolution: Laying the Foundation," CSC Leading Edge Forum, Volume 1, *Cloud rEvolution* series, September 2009, "The New Data Center: Denser, Modular and Greener," pp. 21-23. http://assets1.csc.com/lef/downloads/LEF_2009CloudRev_Vol1_Foundations.pdf

81. "Tech Titans Building Boom," *IEEE Spectrum,* February 2009. http://spectrum.ieee.org/green-tech/buildings/tech-titans-building-boom/0

82. Ibid.

83. "IBM Computing On Demand Uses Clouds to Increase Business Productivity," IBM case study, 30 March 2009. http://www-01.ibm.com/software/success/cssdb.nsf/CS/ARBN-7QJRWV?OpenDocument&Site=default&cty=en_us

84. "Microsoft invests massively in data centers for cloud computing," The H: Security News and Open Source Developments, 26 November 2008. http://www.h-online.com/newsticker/news/item/Microsoft-invests-massively-in-data-centres-for-cloud-computing-739015.html.
Also see "Microsoft Aggressively Investing in Supersize Cloud Data Centers," CircleID, 27 November 2008. http://www.circleid.com/posts/microsoft_supersize_cloud_data_centers

85. "Microsoft's Windows Azure Cloud Container," Data Center Knowledge, 18 November 2009. http://www.datacenterknowledge.com/archives/2009/11/18/microsofts-windows-azure-cloud-container

86. "Cloud Computing — AT&T Takes to the Cloud," SYS-CON.TV, 8 August 2008. http://tv.sys-con.com/node/633745

87. "Mega Data Center: Seeing is Believing," Scott Mattoon's What Happens Downstream blog, 17 March 2009, http://blogs.sun.com/downstream/entry/mega_data_center_seeing_is; and "Vegas data center bets on 100& uptime," *Network World,* 22 January 2009, http://www.networkworld.com/news/2009/012209-supernap-data-center.html

88. NAP of the Capital Region, Terremark, http://www.terremark.com/technology-platform/nap-of-the-capital-region.aspx

NOTES

89. CSC Trusted Cloud Services, http://www.trustedcloudservices.com/

90. "VMware's Terremark investment signals deeper foray into public cloud," SearchCloudComputing.com, 10 June 2009. http://searchcloudcomputing.techtarget.com/news/article/0,289142,sid201_gci1358890,00.html

91. "Internet-Scale Service Efficiency," James Hamilton presentation, 16 September 2008. http://mvdirona.com/jrh/TalksAndPapers/JamesRH_Ladis2008.pdf

92. "Savvis bursts into cloud computing," *Network World*, 12 February 2009. http://www.networkworld.com/news/2009/021209-savvis-cloud.html

93. "Many degrees of multi-tenancy," Software as Services blog, ZDNet, 16 June 2008. http://blogs.zdnet.com/SAAS/?p=533

94. "The SaaS Single-Tenancy vs. Multi-Tenancy Debate," Sixteen Ventures, 14 April 2009. http://sixteenventures.com/blog/saas-single-tenancy-vs-multi-tenancy.html

95. "Cloud Computing: So You Don't Have to Stand Still," *The New York Times,* 25 May 2008. http://www.nytimes.com/2008/05/25/technology/25proto.html?_r=1&scp=1&sq=animoto&st=nyt

96. "A Word on Scalability," Werner Vogels' All Things Distributed blog, 30 March 2006. http://www.allthingsdistributed.com/2006/03/a_word_on_scalability.html

97. Nicholas Carr, *The Big Switch, Rewiring the World, from Edison to Google* (New York: W.W. Norton & Company, 2008), p. 65. Also mentioned in "Cloud rEvolution: Laying the Foundation," CSC Leading Edge Forum, Volume 1, *Cloud rEvolution* series, September 2009, p. 19, http://assets1.csc.com/lef/downloads/LEF_2009CloudRev_Vol1_Foundations.pdf

98. "Cloud rEvolution: The Art of Abstraction," CSC Leading Edge Forum, Volume 2, *Cloud rEvolution* series, October 2009, "Liberating Server Resources," pp.56-57. http://assets1.csc.com/lef/downloads/LEF_2009CloudRev_Vol2_Abstraction.pdf

NOTES

99. "Cloud rEvolution: Laying the Foundation," CSC Leading Edge Forum, Volume 1, *Cloud rEvolution* series, September 2009, "Database Advances," p. 28. http://assets1.csc.com/lef/downloads/LEF_2009CloudRev_Vol1_Foundations.pdf

100. "Is the Relational Database Doomed?," ReadWriteEnterprise, 12 February 2009. http://www.readwriteweb.com/enterprise/2009/02/is-the-relational-database-doomed.php

101. ElephantDrive Case Study, Amazon Web Services, http://aws.amazon.com/solutions/case-studies/elephantdrive/

102. "5 Common Questions About Hadoop," Cloudera's Hadoop & Big Data Blog, http://www.cloudera.com/blog/2009/05/14/5-common-questions-about-hadoop/

103. "Cloud rEvolution: Laying the Foundation," CSC Leading Edge Forum, Volume 1, *Cloud rEvolution* series, September 2009, pp. 10-11. http://assets1.csc.com/lef/downloads/LEF_2009CloudRev_Vol1_Foundations.pdf

104. Ibid., p. 4 and pp. 15-16.

105. "McKinsey Speculates that Cloud Computing May Be More Expensive than Internal IT," James Hamilton's Perspectives blog, 20 April 2009. http://perspectives.mvdirona.com/2009/04/21/McKinseySpeculatesThatCloudComputingMayBeMoreExpensiveThanInternalIT.aspx

106. "Self-service, Prorated Super Computing Fun!," NYTimes Open Blog, 1 November 2007. http://open.blogs.nytimes.com/2007/11/01/self-service-prorated-super-computing-fun/?scp=1-b&sq=prorated+supercomputing+fun&st=nyt

107. "The new economics of computing," Nicholas Carr's Rough Type blog, 5 November 2008. http://www.roughtype.com/archives/2008/11/the_new_economi.php

108. For a good discussion of Capex vs. Opex see "Capex vs. Opex: Most People Miss the Point About Cloud Economics," *CIO*, 13 March 2009. http://www.cio.com/article/484429/Capex_vs._Opex_Most_People_Miss_the_Point_About_Cloud_Economics

NOTES

109. "The Google-ization of Bechtel," *Network World*, 29 October 2008. http://www.networkworld.com/news/2008/102908-bechtel.html

110. Arthur, *The Nature of Technology,* p. 152.

111. "Don't focus too much on costs, cloud computing is about business agility," Capgemini, Capping IT Off blog, 24 April 2009. http://www.capgemini.com/technology-blog/2009/04/dont_focus_too_much_on_costs_c.php

112. Microsoft Case Studies: Eduify, July 2009, http://www.microsoft.com/casestudies/Case_Study_Detail.aspx?CaseStudyID=4000004936

113. "Cloud Computing: Pros and Cons," CIO.com, 18 May 2009. http://www.cio.com/article/492880/Cloud_Computing_Pros_and_Cons

114. "Cloud Computing Turns Virtual Teams Into a Competitive Advantage," *AJAXWorld Magazine*, 14 December 2008. http://ca.sys-con.com/node/774718?page=0%2C0

115. About the Nebula Platform, http://nebula.nasa.gov/about/

116. "Second Life at BT," 2008. http://globalservices.bt.com/static/assets/insights_and_ideas/innovation/pdf/Second_Life_at_BT_21CN.pdf

117. Ibid.

118. Ibid.

119. Erickson, Susan Spence, Michael Rhodes, David Banks, James Rutherford, Edwin Simpson, Guillaume Belrose and Russell Perry, "Content-Centered Collaboration Spaces in the Cloud," HP Laboratories white paper, 2009, pp. 3-4. http://connect.docuter.com/documents/11195422234992e7b0e83f11234364336.pdf

120. "Yahoo Cloud Serving," Surendra Reddy, Cloud Computing Conference & Expo, 3 November 2009. http://www.slideshare.net/ydn/walking-through-cloud-serving-at-yahoo

121. Lynda Gratton, *Hot Spots: Why Some Teams, Workplaces and Organizations Buzz with Energy — and Others Don't* (San Francisco: Berrett-Koehler Publishers, February 2007).

NOTES

122. "Cloud rEvolution: Laying the Foundation," CSC Leading Edge Forum, Volume 1, *Cloud rEvolution* series, September 2009, p. 10. http://assets1.csc.com/lef/downloads/LEF_2009CloudRev_Vol1_Foundations.pdf

123. Window to My Environment, http://www.epa.gov/enviro/html/em/

124. "Google map tracks deadly Australia bushfires," CNET, 8 February 2009. http://news.cnet.com/webware/?keyword=Google+Maps+mashup

125. "The New, Faster Face of Innovation," *The Wall Street Journal*, 17 August 2009. http://online.wsj.com/article/SB10001424052970204830304574130820184260340.html

126. Fail fast is a technique that allows many ideas to be tried out quickly so that those that prove to be unpromising can be discarded before large amounts of time and money have been wasted.

127. "OMB's Kundra sees innovation in the cloud," Federal News Radio 1500 AM, 10 March 2009. http://www.federalnewsradio.com/?nid=35&sid=1620108

128. "Cloud Computing and the Promise of On-Demand Business Innovation," IntelligentEnterprise, July 2009. http://intelligent-enterprise.informationweek.com/showArticle.jhtml?articleID=218500039

129. www.cordys.com

130. "Rightscale Brings Business Intelligence To The Clouds," CloudAve blog, 12 August 2009. http://www.cloudave.com/link/rightscale-brings-business-intelligence-to-the-clouds

131. "The Complete List of 2009 BI Predictions?," Timo Elliott's BI Questions Blog, 8 January 2009. http://timoelliott.com/blog/2009/01/the_complete_list_of_2009_bi_p.html

132. "SAS to build $70 million cloud computing facility," Dashboard Insight, 19 March 2009. http://www.dashboardinsight.com/news/news-posts/sas-to-build-70-million-cloud-computing-facility.aspx

133. Crane Pumps & Systems example from: Crane Pumps & Systems case study, LogiXML, http://www.logixml.com/resources/caseStudies/crane.pdf

134. Ibid.

NOTES

135. Ibid.

136. "Google Uses Web Searches to Track Flu's Spread," *The New York Times,* 12 November 2008. http://www.nytimes.com/2008/11/12/technology/internet/12flu.html?_r=2

137. Examples from: "Market Research Using the Google Playground," *Small Business Trends,* 31 August 2008. http://smallbiztrends.com/2008/08/market-research-using-the-google-playground.html

138. Ibid.

139. "Creating HIPAA-Compliant Medical Data Applications with Amazon Web Services," white paper, April 2009. http://awsmedia.s3.amazonaws.com/AWS_HIPAA_Whitepaper_Final.pdf

140. AWS Case Studies, http://aws.amazon.com/solutions/case-studies/ Search "HIPAA."

141. Example from: "Is That A Cloud On Healthcare's Horizon?," Plug Into The Cloud blog, *InformationWeek,* 16 June 2009. http://www.informationweek.com/cloud-computing/blog/archives/2009/06/is_that_a_cloud.html

142. "Amitive is First to Deliver SCM in the Cloud," press release, 27 May 2009. http://www.amitive.com/press_releases/2009/press_release_20090527.html

143. Ibid.

144. "A Cloud ecosystem for Inter Enterprise Visibility," Supply Chain Management blog, HP, 24 August 2009. http://www.communities.hp.com/online/blogs/manufacturing-distribution/archive/2009/08/24/a-cloud-ecosystem-for-inter-enterprise-visibility.aspx

145. William H. Davidow and Michael S. Malone, *The Virtual Corporation: Structuring and Revitalizing the Corporation for the 21st Century* (New York: HarperBusiness, 1992).

146. "Cloud rEvolution: Laying the Foundation," CSC Leading Edge Forum, Volume 1, *Cloud rEvolution* series, September 2009, p. 13. http://assets1.csc.com/lef/downloads/LEF_2009CloudRev_Vol1_Foundations.pdf.

ACKNOWLEDGMENTS

Rick Muñoz, Yale Esrock and Doug Neal conducted the research for the *Cloud rEvolution* report series. Working on *Cloud rEvolution* has deepened their appreciation for the innovation, efficiency and untapped potential of cloud computing for the enterprise.

Rick Muñoz (left) is a senior technology architect at CSC and a 2009 LEF Associate. He specializes in emerging information technology platforms and methods, including agile solution delivery using dynamic virtual environments. Rick has delivered technology strategies and IT solutions for many Fortune 500 companies. A member of CSC's Global Business Solutions and Services group, Rick now focuses on developing cloud computing services for clients across multiple industries. rmunoz@csc.com

Yale Esrock (center) is a business process architect in CSC's North American Public Sector and a 2009 LEF Associate. Yale has held key roles in the Program Management Offices of large military and civil government transformation programs, and was a key contributor to the incorporation of Service Oriented Architecture concepts in CSC's Catalyst℠ methodology. His interest in cloud is on meeting business objectives, while mitigating risk, through the creative application of cloud concepts. yesrock@csc.com

As Research Fellow in the LEF Executive Programme, Doug Neal (right) is responsible for research on "Innovating through Technology." Doug began researching enterprise cloud computing under the guise of IT consumerization. He led cloud computing study tours in Silicon Valley in 2008 and 2009 and consults with enterprises on cloud strategy. Doug's research interests also include green IT, collaborative technologies and Web 2.0. dneal@csc.com

The LEF thanks the many others who contributed to the *Cloud rEvolution* report series.

Jeff Allen, *Cisco*
Jeff Barr, *Amazon*
W. Brian Arthur, *Santa Fe Institute*
Justin Barney, *3Leaf Systems*
Randy Bias, *Stratospheric*
Brian Boruff, *CSC*
Lisa Braun, *CSC*
Jeff Budge, *CSC*
Simon Crosby, *Citrix*
Cees de Groot, *Marktplaats*
Scott Dowell, *CSC*
Mike Dyer, *CSC*
Martin English, *CSC*
Michael Ernesto, *CSC*
Jim Fenner, *CSC*
Chris Fleck, *Citrix*
Glenn Gravatt, *CSC*
Mike Groner, *Appistry*
Phil Grove, *CSC*
Daniel Gubber, *CSC*
Nigel Healy, *CSC*
Randy Hill, *CSC*
Christofer Hoff, *Cisco*
Gabe Kazarian, *CSC*
Ron Knode, *CSC*
Bob Lozano, *Appistry*
Steve Maher, *IBM*
Mark Masterson, *CSC*
Byron Miller, *CSC*
Daniel Mintz, *CSC*
Jim Moran, *ETS*
Peter Nickolov, *3Tera*
Erika Mir Olimpiew, *CSC*
Purnima Padmanabhan, *MokaFive*
Nicholas Payne, *CSC*
David Pickup, *CSC*
Dave Powers, *Eli Lilly*
Tony Puerto, *CSC*
Bob Quinn, *3Leaf Systems*
Billy Rollin, *CSC*
Robert Rosenwald, *CSC*
Alit Bar Sadeh, *GigaSpaces*
Bob Slook, *CSC*
Larry Smarr, *California Institute for Telecommunications and Information Technology (Calit2)*
Tomas Soderstrom, *NASA Jet Propulsion Laboratory*
Michael Stonebraker, *Vertica*
John Taylor, *ETS*
Simon Wardley, *Canonical*
John Willis, *Cloud Cafe*

www.ingramcontent.com/pod-product-compliance
Lightning Source LLC
Chambersburg PA
CBHW041417050326
40689CB00002B/550
9780578051161